The Unshakable Ledger

The Unshakable Ledger

Designing a Life of Enduring Wealth

Luca Moreau

Mindful Pages

Published in 2025

ISBN: 9789371775007 (PB)
ISBN: 9789371774338 (eBook)

Published by

Mindful Pages
Imprint of Alpha Editions LLC
312 W. 2nd St #1834
Casper, WY 82601, USA

This book was developed using advanced writing tools to support the drafting and ideation process. All content has been thoughtfully curated, refined, and reviewed to ensure quality and relevance.

Content

Introduction
Beyond the Balance Sheet

For years, personal finance guidance has come packaged in tidy fragments—catchy slogans and bullet-point formulas masquerading as wisdom. Save more. Spend less. Invest early. Diversify. Create passive income. Leave a legacy. On the surface, each of these maxims carries a grain of truth. But string them together without any real cohesion, and they amount to little more than a flimsy patchwork—more reactive than strategic, more appearance than intention.

This book opens with a single, pressing question: What if wealth isn't a checklist to be ticked off, but a design system to be built?

Mainstream financial advice tends to assume that wealth creation is a matter of mechanically applying a pre-set list of rules—often drafted by others, for circumstances that may not reflect your own. Rarely does it pause to ask: who is the person behind the plan? It overlooks your psychological patterns, your emotional backstory with money, your cultural influences, your responsibilities, and your unique aspirations. Worse still, it reduces wealth to a static destination—tracked in spreadsheets and asset allocations—when in truth, it ought to be seen as a dynamic, evolving structure, shaped by the ebb and flow of life itself.

This book offers a different path: Wealth Stacking.

The term is not metaphorical. Wealth Stacking is a structured, systems-based framework grounded in practical reality. It proposes that genuine wealth must be constructed across four interrelated layers: the Emergency Layer, the Investment Layer, the Income Layer, and the Legacy Layer. These aren't silos. They are interactive, living systems—each responsive to the others, each influencing the whole. One cannot be meaningfully developed in isolation. Building any one layer well requires an awareness of how it will adapt and evolve in the context of the rest.

And yet—even a solid structure will crumble without a strong foundation. Beneath every financial decision lies a hidden lattice of mental models, assumptions, emotional habits, and cultural scripts that shape how we relate to money. Ignore these, and even the most sophisticated strategy will falter. On paper, your wealth may grow—but its substance, integrity, or lasting impact may quietly decay.

This book, therefore, does not deal in prescriptions. It presents a philosophy of design. It does not claim to possess the perfect allocation model, the optimal budget ratio, or the definitive roadmap to passive income. Instead, it aims to reshape how you *think*. It asks you to become not just a manager of your money, but the conscious architect of your financial life.

And that shift matters. Not just because the economic terrain has changed—but because you have. Traditional financial planning took root in a world built on predictability: steady employment, employer-backed pensions, rigid social roles, and shared, largely unquestioned, life goals. That world is behind us. What remains is a landscape marked by volatility and complexity, where safety must be self-made, where finances are intertwined with identity and emotion, and where meaning is not handed down—but crafted.

Today, the average individual is bombarded with more financial decisions in a month than their grandparents might have faced in a year. The modern ecosystem—full of investing apps, gig economy options, asset varieties, and monetisable passions—offers freedom, but also fatigue. We are drowning in information; what we lack is discernment. The critical question is no longer what to learn—but what to ignore, what to pursue, and what to leave behind.

That is where this book steps in. It is not a rulebook, but a compass. It speaks to the financially overloaded, the quietly driven, the introspective, and the seekers. It is written for those who suspect that beneath the polished charts and financial hacks lies something deeper—those who are less interested in chasing money than in understanding their relationship with it.

This is not only about how much you earn or save. It's about whether the system you are crafting can bend when life bends—whether it reflects not just your needs, but your evolving identity.

Each chapter explores one vital aspect of this overarching system.

We begin with the Emergency Layer—not because it's sexy (it isn't), but because it's indispensable. It is the emotional and financial ground upon which every risk stands. Most people see emergency funds as little more than insurance against catastrophe. This book offers a reframing: they are tools of autonomy, granting you composure, options, and control during moments of upheaval.

Next is the Investment Layer. Often reduced to numbers, graphs, and guesswork about markets, investing here is treated as something far more personal: a mirror of your beliefs. What do you think about time, risk, sufficiency, and stewardship? How do your values show up in your investment choices? How do you steady yourself when the markets wobble—or when everyone else appears to be winning faster than you? This section won't promise quick riches. What it will do is help you build and hold wealth—with resilience, with clarity, and with conviction.

From there, we move to the Income Layer—your everyday engine. In a world drunk on side hustles and "hustle culture," this book offers a cooler lens. Income is not just something to chase, but something to *shape*. Not mere extraction, but meaningful contribution. Here, you'll learn how to cultivate income streams that don't just withstand stress, but evolve because of it. And perhaps most importantly, you'll be invited to re-examine your relationship with work. Is your labour about survival, social signalling, or a deeper form of service?

Then comes the Legacy Layer—the most overlooked, and often misunderstood. In popular imagination, legacy is about inheritance, estate planning, and end-of-life arrangements. But in truth, it starts now. Legacy is a living, ongoing act. It's the stories your children absorb, the assumptions your community replicates, the values reinforced by your financial decisions. Legacy is not the final chapter—it is the undertone running through every financial act you make.

Threaded throughout these layers are inquiries into the invisible yet powerful forces that steer our financial behaviour. Why do we compare ourselves so compulsively? Why is money still such a charged topic, even with those closest to us? What childhood patterns still echo in our adult choices? Why do some people seem to build with ease, while others unravel what they create? These aren't side issues—they are central. Because if your internal world is in disarray, your external wealth won't hold.

The final chapters are a shift from reflection to application. You'll be invited to conduct a Financial Design Audit—an honest assessment of your systems, assumptions, and blind spots. You'll learn to distinguish between ego-driven goals and design-driven choices. You'll encounter simple, repeatable practices—rituals, really—that transform financial planning into a kind of intentional living. And you'll consider what it truly means to pursue a sovereign financial life—not one rooted in isolation, but in conscious, integrated autonomy.

This isn't a book for those looking for quick fixes. It's for those willing to engage deeply, act intentionally, and navigate the long arc. It treats you like the thoughtful adult you are—capable of nuance, of course correction, of reimagining. And in exchange, it offers not just a sturdier financial future, but a more meaningful present. A life where money reflects—not defines—your values.

You are not a metric. You are not a score. You are not your net worth. You are a complex, evolving system—shaped by memory, by choice, by culture and will. This book hands you a blueprint. But only you can draw the lines.

Welcome to Wealth Stacking. Welcome to a way of thinking—and building—that begins not with cash, but with clarity.

Chapter 1
The Architecture of Enduring Wealth

Most modern financial advice presents itself like a set of tidy instructions—as though building wealth were no more complex than following a recipe. First, build an emergency fund. Then, invest. Maximise your income. Finally, consider your legacy. It's neat, sequential, and curiously mechanical. Do this, then that. Tick each box. Stay disciplined. And if you've executed each step to perfection, the promise is clear: you'll arrive. At what, exactly, is often less obvious.

Yet despite its orderly surface, this approach leaves many feeling unmoored—financially bewildered, emotionally drained, and spiritually disengaged. It gives the comforting illusion of progress, but quietly evades a more profound truth: wealth is not a checklist. It is a living system—one that shifts, expands, contracts, and pulses with the full messiness of real life.

To begin thinking in systems is to reject the illusion of separation. That emergency fund? It's not merely a figure tucked away in a savings account. It influences your appetite for risk, your readiness to invest, your psychological stability when life throws curveballs. Income, similarly, is far more than just a number on a payslip—it's a reflection of your identity, your energy, your values, your compromises. Investments, too, aren't floating in some vacuum; they are entangled with your temperament, your worldview, your inherited beliefs about time and trust. And as for legacy—well, that doesn't sit passively at the end. It ripples backwards, informing every decision you make, whether you recognise it or not.

Wealth, then, is not a pile to be stacked. It is an ecosystem—designed, maintained, inhabited. It has structure, yes, but also breath. Its strength lies not in the individual elements, but in the vitality of their relationships.

This chapter offers the framework that will underpin the entire book: a four-layered architecture for cultivating wealth that is not only enduring, but aligned. The Emergency Layer. The Investment Layer. The Income Layer. The Legacy Layer. Each has its own principles, demands, and measurements. Yet none can truly function in isolation. Their power is relational—they support, constrain, and shape one another. When coordinated thoughtfully, they generate not just financial stability, but clarity, direction, and resilience.

Take a moment to imagine someone with a large investment portfolio but no steady income and no emergency fund. On paper, they appear affluent. But the foundation is brittle. A market correction could upend their cash flow, erode their confidence, and force them into rash decisions—liquidating at the worst time, perhaps, or incurring debt to stay afloat. On the other hand, someone earning well and sitting on a healthy cash buffer, but with no investment strategy or long-term vision, risks stagnating—forever circling the present, never compounding momentum into something enduring. The structure lacks height. It doesn't breathe.

So, the first aim of this chapter is to shift your lens—from a jigsaw puzzle of discrete pieces to a design rooted in intentionality. To move away from the metaphors of ladders and silos, and toward the mindset of an architect—thinking in systems, with attention to both strength and symmetry.

But no architect begins without understanding the materials. And the first material—perhaps the most overlooked—is context.

Too often, financial advice pretends at universality. It proclaims ideal savings rates, ideal asset allocations, ideal paths to "freedom." These declarations soothe. But they also deceive. They ignore the truth that money is never abstract. It is always personal. Your past, your cultural backdrop, your psychological wiring, your health, your obligations—all of it plays into what wealth means for you, and what it requires of you.

Picture two people earning the same salary. One was raised in a household where money was stable, and risk felt manageable. The other grew up with financial precarity, and carries a latent fear of collapse. A shared investment plan will not feel the same to both of them. One may see opportunity; the other may feel dread. Their nervous systems, their mental scripts, even their sense of possibility—entirely different. And so, the architecture of wealth must reflect that variance. It must be responsive, not prescriptive.

This is why the humble ledger must be reclaimed. Not only as a record of debits and credits, but as a narrative artefact. Traditionally, a ledger logs the transactional—what came in, what went out. But in the design of enduring wealth, it becomes something more—a mirror, a journal, a space for reflection. It records not just the choices, but the trade-offs. Not just the spending, but the reasoning behind it. Over time, patterns emerge: fear-based decisions, repeated delays, values ignored or honoured. The ledger becomes a psychological tool, not merely a financial one.

To keep a living ledger is not to micromanage. It's to remain in conscious relationship with your money—and, by extension, with your evolving self.

Enter design thinking—a model typically found in innovation and engineering, but surprisingly well-suited to wealth-building. Unlike traditional financial models, which seek optimisation and predictability, design thinking begins with empathy. Who is this structure for? What does this person genuinely need? It prefers iteration to certainty, flexibility to dogma, human relevance over mathematical elegance.

To apply design principles to your finances is to accept that permanence is a fiction. Your circumstances will shift. The world will shift. What once worked may soon not. And so, your system must be able to adapt. It must be modular, revisable, alive. It should contain within it the capacity for feedback, reflection, and reconfiguration.

Let's ground this in lived reality. Imagine a freelance consultant whose income arrives in bursts. The temptation might be to focus on growing revenue. But a wiser move, in this case, might be to build a stronger Emergency Layer—six months of expenses, staggered across cash and low-volatility holdings. This not only buys them time, but also peace. With that psychological buffer in place, they're freer to invest long-term, to take bolder steps, even to contribute meaningfully to others—mentoring, volunteering, building something that echoes.

Or take a salaried worker who's steadily employed but finds the work spiritually numbing. They begin to treat their skill set not as a job title, but as a portfolio—something that can be reconfigured, developed, and redistributed. Over time, they build alternative income paths: perhaps teaching, creating, advising. The financial returns may start small, but the inner realignment is profound. The system evolves.

These stories are not blueprints. They are demonstrations—proof that real people, working within their own realities, can design financial lives that support both survival and selfhood.

And that, ultimately, is what makes the generic financial plan so insidious. It promises security. But when we inevitably fail to follow it—because it never fit us in the first place—we blame ourselves. We assume the error lies within. It doesn't. The template was never made for *you*. It was made for an abstract "average" that exists nowhere but in data models.

This book, and this chapter in particular, offers an invitation: to step out of that mould, and begin again—not from scratch, but from self.

Each of the four layers—emergency, investment, income, and legacy—will be explored not as sterile categories, but as human systems. They each carry their own emotional weight, their own vulnerabilities and tensions. But when interwoven with care, they can hold your ambitions, your limits, your contradictions—and still endure.

By the end of this chapter, you will no longer see wealth as a destination, or even as a sum. You will see it as a process—a reflective, responsive act of design. It won't promise you perfection. But it will offer something better: a structure that breathes, flexes, and lasts.

You are not being handed a map. You are being given a blueprint. It is incomplete by design. The terrain is yours. The materials, yours. The vision—yours alone. There are no shortcuts here, no formulas that fit all. But if you are willing to think carefully, act deliberately, and reflect often, what you construct can stand—through change, through time, through life.

The architecture of enduring wealth begins now.

Wealth as a System, Not a Stack

If you were to ask a room of financially literate individuals what wealth consists of, most would respond with a list: savings, investments, property, perhaps a pension or some passive income. The underlying model is unmistakably modular. Each element is treated as a silo—a goal to be reached, a box to be ticked. This is the logic of stacking: accumulate pieces, higher and higher, in pursuit of financial stability or freedom. Yet what happens when the stack is built on brittle assumptions? When one piece falls, how many others follow? And more importantly—what if the entire paradigm is wrong?

Wealth, properly understood, is not a stack but a system. A living, interacting whole. It is shaped as much by mindset and emotion as by spreadsheets and market performance. It is not simply how much you own, but how well the different parts of your financial life relate to each other—and to you. This is not semantics. It is a fundamental reorientation, with profound consequences for how we think about security, growth, freedom, and responsibility.

The logic of stacking comes from industrial models: segment, optimise, maximise. It lends itself to checklists and blueprints. But human lives do not function on blueprints. They function on feedback loops, constraints, aspirations, and unpredictable shocks. Systems thinking, long applied in biology, ecology, and organisational science, has gained traction in economics in recent decades—but it remains conspicuously absent in personal finance literature. The silence is telling. When we fail to treat wealth as a system, we not only create fragile financial structures—we perpetuate incoherence between what we build and what we need.

Consider this: someone diligently saves three to six months of living expenses in an emergency fund. They invest 15% of their income into a diversified portfolio. They earn a steady salary. They have a will drafted. By conventional metrics, they are financially "healthy." And yet, many such individuals find themselves paralysed during economic downturns, unsure how to adjust. They may suffer from financial anxiety disproportionate to their circumstances. Their spending may not align with their professed values. Or they may neglect meaningful goals—like supporting ageing parents, starting a business, or making a social impact—because those weren't on the checklist. The architecture is present, but the foundation is hollow. What's missing is integration.

Integration begins with understanding the nature of systems. A system is defined not by the sum of its parts, but by the quality of the interactions between those parts. In personal finance, this means recognising that your emergency fund is not just cash—it is a psychological safety net that shapes your risk appetite. That your investments are not merely vehicles for growth, but expressions of belief: about the future, about patience, about control. That income is not a simple inflow, but a reflection of skill, effort, time, and often, identity. That legacy is not an afterthought, but an ongoing narrative that begins in the present.

Each of these dimensions is a node in a living network. They speak to each other. A crisis in one can destabilise others. Strength in one can create leverage elsewhere. The person who understands this—*and designs accordingly*—builds resilience not by stacking more, but by connecting better.

Let's ground this in a practical example. Take two individuals, identical in net worth, but differing in design. The first has savings, a property, and some index funds. They work in a single-income household, have no clear long-term financial vision, and view legacy planning as something to consider "later." The second has a slightly smaller net worth but has actively aligned their financial decisions with their psychological comfort zones, ethical beliefs, and family dynamics. Their emergency fund is structured across levels of access; their investments reflect their risk tolerance and timelines; their income is diversified to reduce dependency. They've begun informal legacy planning—not as a legal task, but as an active set of values discussed with their children and embedded into everyday life.

Which of the two is wealthier?

The answer depends on how we define wealth. If we define it solely in monetary terms, the first individual has a slight edge. But if we define wealth as capacity—for adaptability, alignment, and impact—the second person is operating in a different paradigm altogether. Their system is not only functioning, but *alive.*

Understanding wealth as a system also invites us to grapple with the less tangible forces that shape our financial lives. The mental models we carry—often inherited from family, culture, or past trauma—function like invisible code. Some believe money must be hoarded; others believe it's meant to be spent. Some view wealth as independence; others as stewardship. These views are rarely examined, but they profoundly affect how each part of the system behaves. Emotional reactivity, for example, can distort investment decisions. Fear can prevent skill development, thus limiting income growth. Guilt can undermine the enjoyment of money or prevent generational transmission. The psychological is not adjacent to finance—it *is* finance.

Likewise, ethics plays a central, often unacknowledged role. What do you consider a worthy use of money? Are you comfortable profiting from industries that contradict your values? Do you consider taxation a civic duty or a burden? These questions are not rhetorical. They shape decisions about where to invest, what kind of work to do, how to give, and how to think about legacy. Ethics is not a footnote to financial planning—it is embedded in every decision, whether consciously or not. And when ethical dissonance is ignored, systems fracture. One part of your financial life pulls against another. You earn well but feel unfulfilled. You give generously but resent it. You invest successfully but feel uneasy about the outcomes. These tensions, left unaddressed, erode the internal coherence that sustainable wealth demands.

Systems thinking, then, is not a luxury—it is a necessity. It helps us see the financial self as a complex organism rather than a linear machine. It teaches us to look for interdependencies, feedback loops, and unintended consequences. It asks us not just what works, but *what fits*. A highly leveraged property investment may look good on a spreadsheet, but if it keeps you up at night, it's undermining your system. A portfolio full of ESG-compliant funds might signal virtue, but if it limits your returns below your required rate for long-term security, it too becomes a liability. There is no universal blueprint—only well-designed systems tailored to real, complex lives.

From a historical perspective, the idea of wealth as a system is not new. In many indigenous cultures, wealth was understood as relational—not in terms of assets, but in terms of connections: to the land, to the tribe, to future generations. Stewardship, reciprocity, and harmony were guiding principles. Colonial and industrial economic models shifted the emphasis towards individual accumulation, measurement, and control. The financial models we inherit today—while efficient—are built on these foundations. But they are increasingly out of sync with the lived realities of those navigating a fragmented, fast-changing world.

The future of personal finance will not be built on better budgeting apps or higher returns alone. It will be built on coherence. The ability to align what you have with who you are. To design financial systems that reflect the full spectrum of human complexity—cognitive, emotional, ethical, and practical. This requires not just information, but *insight.* Not just metrics, but *meaning.*

And meaning does not emerge from numbers. It emerges from reflection. This is why the act of maintaining a ledger must be reimagined. Not just as a record of transactions, but as a tool of awareness. What you spend on, what you earn, what you invest in—these are not just financial acts. They are values, enacted. When you review your financial history, you are reviewing your life. The ledger becomes a mirror. It shows you not just where your money went, but who you were when you spent it.

Seeing wealth as a system is, at its core, a practice in self-honesty. It requires discipline, yes—but also compassion. It recognises that financial behaviour is rarely about logic alone. People are not inefficient because they lack information. They are inefficient because they are human: emotional, social, aspirational. A coherent system accepts this and builds accordingly.

Ultimately, this redefinition of wealth is not just about effectiveness. It's about agency. When you stop treating financial components as isolated chores, and start seeing them as elements in an interconnected system, you regain control. You become not a passive consumer of advice, but an active architect of your financial life. And that shift—from manager to designer—may be the most valuable investment you ever make.

The Four Layers Explained

There is a fundamental flaw in the way most people approach personal finance: they attempt to solve permanent problems with piecemeal tactics. They set up an emergency fund, dabble in investing, search for income upgrades, or draft a will—each as a separate project. But these are not standalone missions. They are layers within a single, interdependent structure. When treated as isolated silos, they produce confusion, imbalance, and fragility. But when understood as an integrated architecture—built with intention, logic, and flow—they become a coherent system capable of withstanding pressure, adapting to change, and compounding impact over time. This architecture rests on four foundational layers: emergency, investing, income, and legacy.

The purpose of introducing these four layers is not to create new terminology. It is to provide a language and framework for designing financial lives that are not only technically sound but *existentially aligned.* These layers are not categories in a budgeting app. They are structural components—each with distinct roles, constraints, and psychological demands. And crucially, they do not function linearly. They operate in sequence *and* synergy, meaning the strength of each depends not just on its design, but on its relationship to the others.

Begin with the Emergency Layer. Not because it is the most exciting, but because it is the most essential. It is the bedrock of financial design. Without it, no other layer can function effectively under stress. The emergency layer is often misunderstood as a buffer for catastrophe—illness, job loss, disaster. In truth, it is a stabiliser of agency. A well-structured emergency layer allows for decision-making from a place of clarity rather than panic. It grants the time to respond, not react. It prevents short-term problems from metastasising into long-term damage. But more subtly, it affects the entire system upstream. A fragile emergency layer increases risk aversion, undermines confidence in investing, and makes income choices feel desperate. A strong one, by contrast, creates the conditions for intelligent risk-taking, strategic patience, and long-range thinking.

Yet no emergency buffer—however robust—can grow wealth. That role belongs to the Investment Layer. Investing is what transitions money from static security to dynamic productivity. But this layer is not merely about asset selection. It is about orientation to time. It requires a shift from immediate gratification to deferred value, from control to uncertainty, from activity to discipline. The Investment Layer interacts constantly with the Emergency Layer. If your emergency reserves are weak, you may be tempted to liquidate investments prematurely. If your investments are too volatile, they may erode the psychological safety that your emergency layer is meant to provide. This is why sequence matters. You cannot invest wisely if you are one surprise away from financial destabilisation.

Still, even the most elegantly designed investment portfolio is irrelevant without cash flow. This brings us to the Income Layer—the engine of daily life. Income is often treated as fixed, but it is anything but. It is shaped by skill, effort, negotiation, leverage, and systemic forces like labour markets and technological change. Yet income is also not purely economic. It is expressive. It reflects what we are willing to give in exchange for money—our time, energy, attention, and sometimes, our values. Many financial plans falter because they fail to address the qualitative side of income: is the way you earn money *sustainable*? Is it *aligned* with who you are? Does it grow with you—or trap you?

The synergy between income and the other layers is profound. Stable, aligned income reduces reliance on emergency funds. It creates surplus for investment. It allows space for legacy-building activities—whether financial or relational. But income without strategy becomes consumption. And income without identity becomes alienation. The goal is not just to earn more, but to earn *well*—to treat income as a layer that supports and is supported by the rest of the system.

The final layer—Legacy—is the least understood and most neglected. Often postponed to old age or estate planning, legacy is in fact a *living* layer. It shapes what you prioritise now, what you teach your children, what you build in your community, and what norms you transmit. Legacy is not only what you leave behind—it is what you *normalise* in the present. If your wealth design ignores this layer, you risk building a system that functions mechanically but lacks meaning. If you earn and invest successfully but leave no ethical framework, your success may end with you. Worse, it may burden those who inherit it. Legacy gives context to the rest of the system. It introduces timescales longer than one life. It brings moral gravity to financial decisions that might otherwise be purely technical.

The interaction between legacy and the other layers is often underappreciated. Consider a person who wants to leave a financial gift to future generations. Without a stable income, that gift may never materialise. Without investments, it may be eroded by inflation. Without an emergency layer, the gift may have to be liquidated during personal crises. Conversely, someone who has cultivated all three foundational layers can use the legacy layer not only for transmission but *transformation*—investing in causes, mentoring others, endowing opportunities, or encoding values into trusts or family constitutions. The legacy layer is not a destination. It is a horizon—a direction that pulls the entire system forward.

Crucially, these layers are not static. They expand, contract, and evolve. Early in life, the emergency layer may dominate as stability is established. Mid-career, the income and investment layers may take precedence. Later, the focus may shift towards legacy. But the point is not to treat these as chronological milestones. They are concurrent layers—alive at all times, requiring continuous attention, calibration, and intentionality. The system is adaptive.

This approach also accommodates diversity. Different lives will require different layer configurations. A single parent with volatile income needs a more fortified emergency layer. A high-earning professional may underweight legacy planning, assuming time is abundant. A first-generation wealth builder may need to overinvest in income diversification to overcome systemic disadvantages. The architecture adjusts to 'circumstance—but it must be built consciously. The illusion of permanence is dangerous. So is the temptation to focus on one layer to the exclusion of others. Many people become obsessed with investing, neglecting liquidity. Others hoard cash, paralysed by fear. Still others focus solely on earning, mistaking income for security. But any system that overweights one layer at the expense of others becomes fragile. True resilience comes from balance—not in static allocation, but in systemic integrity.

From a behavioural science perspective, this framework also provides cognitive clarity. Human beings struggle with abstraction. We are prone to tunnel vision, loss aversion, and present bias. We often optimise locally—maximising income while ignoring risk, or investing aggressively without a buffer. The four-layer model helps to structure attention. It makes abstract trade-offs visible. Should I add to my emergency fund or top up my investment account? Should I pursue a side income or strengthen the stability of my main job? Should I spend on lifestyle upgrades or invest in a legacy-building experience? These are not spreadsheet questions. They are design questions—requiring reflection, prioritisation, and self-awareness.

This is why thinking in layers is more than a framework—it is a practice. A way of seeing and re-seeing the whole. Each financial decision can be mapped to one or more layers. Each layer can be assessed not just in terms of quantity, but quality: is it coherent, resilient, aligned? The goal is not to reach perfection in each layer, but to maintain functional harmony between them. Like any good architecture, the beauty lies not in the individual parts, but in their integration.

Designing your wealth system around these four layers does not guarantee riches. But it does provide a foundation for making decisions that are intelligent, contextual, and sustainable. It helps reduce noise, expose blind spots, and align effort with purpose. It transforms financial planning from a reactive task into a generative discipline—one that supports not just stability or growth, but depth, coherence, and longevity.

Each of these layers will be examined in detail in the chapters ahead. But what matters now is the shift in perspective: to stop thinking of wealth as a sequence of disconnected moves, and start seeing it as a deliberately constructed ecosystem. No layer exists in a vacuum. Every layer affects—and is affected by—the others. The health of the system is not determined by how tall the stack is, but by how well the layers support each other under pressure, in uncertainty, and across generations. Designing for that reality is the difference between a financial life that merely functions, and one that endures.

The Myth of the One-Size-Fits-All Plan

Walk into any major bookstore, browse the personal finance section of a streaming platform, or scroll through social media financial influencers, and a clear pattern emerges. Advice is dispensed in crisp, confidence-soaked absolutes: "Always invest 15% of your income." "Buy, don't rent." "Index funds outperform active investing." "Six months of expenses in your emergency fund, minimum." The language is seductive, the formulas simple, the tone authoritative. But beneath this surface of certainty lies a troubling truth: much of modern financial advice is built on generalisations that ignore the complex, contradictory, and highly personal nature of real human lives.

The allure of universal plans is understandable. In a chaotic world filled with economic uncertainty, cognitive overload, and decision fatigue, a tidy rulebook provides relief. It offers the illusion of control, the comfort of predictability, and the reassurance of shared practice. But that comfort comes at a cost. When financial guidance detaches itself from context—psychological, cultural, generational, or situational—it risks doing more harm than good. What appears sound on paper often collapses under the weight of lived experience.

Consider the widely recommended "rule" of saving 20% of your income. For a dual-income household with stable jobs, no dependents, and modest living expenses, this may be both feasible and wise. But for a single parent managing variable income, supporting extended family, and living in a high-cost city, that same rule may induce shame, stress, or self-blame. The issue is not merely feasibility. It's the implicit message: *if you can't meet this benchmark, you're failing.* Financial prescriptions, when presented as universal truths, rarely leave space for nuance. They substitute formula for philosophy, and as a result, they can deepen inequality by reinforcing narratives that overlook structural disadvantage.

Psychology provides a deeper layer of critique. Research in behavioural economics has long demonstrated that financial decision-making is not governed solely by rational calculation. Cognitive biases, emotional associations, and subconscious scripts exert powerful influence. Two people with identical incomes and expenses can behave in radically different ways depending on how they interpret risk, time, scarcity, and control. A trauma-informed perspective adds further texture. Those who have experienced financial instability—whether through personal crisis, generational poverty, or sociopolitical disruption—may carry hyper-vigilance around money. They might hoard cash despite low returns, resist investing despite opportunity, or avoid budgeting altogether due to deep-seated avoidance patterns. In such cases, applying conventional advice can be not only ineffective but psychologically destabilising.

Culture too plays a defining role. Western financial planning literature, for instance, often assumes individual autonomy, stable employment, and a nuclear family structure. It tends to emphasise personal responsibility, long-term planning, and market participation. Yet in many cultures, financial decisions are intergenerational, collective, and relational. Money may be seen less as a tool for personal freedom and more as a resource for familial duty or communal obligation. Advice that instructs someone to "prioritise retirement over supporting relatives" may be technically sound from an actuarial perspective, but ethically and emotionally incoherent for someone raised with different norms. What is considered a liability in one context may be an honour in another.

Generational context is equally crucial. A millennial navigating their thirties in a post-2008, post-pandemic economy faces a radically different landscape from a baby boomer who bought a home in the 1980s and benefited from decades of wage growth, union security, and rising asset prices. Yet much of today's advice is retrofitted from a playbook written for previous generations. Take the emphasis on homeownership as the cornerstone of wealth-building. While historically valid in markets with low prices and stable employment, that model collapses in cities where home prices outpace incomes by orders of magnitude, or where gig work undermines mortgage eligibility. In such environments, owning a home may not be the smart move—it may be the financial trap.

Even risk tolerance, a central concept in investment planning, is rarely treated with the sophistication it demands. Risk is often quantified using questionnaires that produce neat scores: conservative, moderate, aggressive. But these designations often fail to capture the emotional, situational, and temporal factors that shape a person's true comfort with uncertainty. A young professional might appear risk-tolerant on paper, but buckle during their first market downturn. A retiree might appear risk-averse, yet take bold moves to support a struggling child. Context changes everything. A plan that ignores this dynamism is not a plan—it's a template, rigid and brittle.

This is not an argument against structure. Structure is essential. Without frameworks, financial life becomes reactive, chaotic, and vulnerable to both external shocks and internal impulses. But the right structure is one that adapts to individual reality. It is rooted in self-knowledge, not just spreadsheets. It asks not only, *What should I do with my money?*, but also, *What matters to me? What am I solving for? What are the trade-offs I can live with?* Good planning does not impose answers. It helps elicit the right questions.

The practical implication is clear: no two people should have identical financial plans. Even among those with similar incomes and goals, the underlying architecture must reflect difference—of temperament, history, values, and constraints. A person with entrepreneurial instincts may build around volatility, designing for cash flow agility and reinvestment opportunities. Someone who values predictability may prioritise conservative growth, strong buffers, and automation. These are not right or wrong approaches. They are responses to the underlying complexity of real life.

This reframing also calls for a new role for the financial planner, mentor, or advisor. Rather than dispensing standardised advice, their work becomes more akin to that of a systems designer or reflective guide—someone who listens deeply, maps context, surfaces assumptions, and co-creates strategies that are both functional and meaningful. This is a fundamentally human task. It cannot be fully automated or mass-produced. And it requires a shift in ethos—from efficiency to empathy, from optimisation to alignment.

A striking example comes from the financial lives of immigrants. A recent study by the Migration Policy Institute found that immigrant families are more likely to engage in informal savings networks, such as rotating credit associations, than formal investment vehicles. From a mainstream finance lens, this behaviour may seem suboptimal. But when examined through the lens of trust, access, and community norms, it reveals a logic of its own—one shaped by exclusion from institutions, cultural continuity, and resilience in the face of systemic barriers. To design effective plans for such individuals, one must first *see* this logic, not simply overwrite it with external benchmarks.

There is also a broader ethical dimension to consider. The dominance of one-size-fits-all advice reflects a deeper ideology—one that assumes financial behaviour can be decontextualised, rationalised, and standardised. This mindset not only erases individuality, but it often erases injustice. By focusing solely on personal decision-making, it overlooks structural inequities in housing, education, healthcare, and employment. It blames the financially struggling for their choices, rather than interrogating the systems that constrain them. A more honest model of financial planning acknowledges both agency and structure. It empowers the individual without pretending that context is irrelevant.

All of this points to a necessary evolution in how we approach personal finance—not as a science of certainty, but as a discipline of design. Like architecture, financial planning should respond to its environment. It should be grounded in principles, but flexible in application. It should be informed by evidence, but filtered through lived reality. It should adapt over time, as lives change and insight deepens. Above all, it should honour complexity—not flatten it.

The myth of the one-size-fits-all plan is not just flawed; it is fundamentally inhumane. It ignores that people are not spreadsheets. They are textured, evolving beings with contradictions, obligations, and aspirations. They deserve more than templates. They deserve systems that make sense—*to them.* Systems that support not just the accumulation of wealth, but the expression of purpose.

To move beyond this myth is not to abandon structure—it is to rebuild it, intelligently and empathetically. And in doing so, we create space for something more powerful than standardisation: *coherence*. A financial life that works not just on paper, but in practice. Not just for the average person, but for *this* person, in *this* life, with *these* trade-offs, at *this* moment in time. Anything less is not advice. It is abstraction, masquerading as wisdom.

The Ledger as a Mirror

We are often told to track our finances—to keep a budget, monitor expenses, review bank statements, and periodically assess our net worth. These acts are framed as rational, even mechanical: document income, subtract outgoings, observe the trend line. But what if these financial records—these ledgers—could tell us more than how much we've earned or spent? What if they could reveal who we are becoming? The ledger, properly understood, is not simply a financial document. It is a behavioural artefact, a mirror reflecting values, anxieties, trade-offs, priorities, and aspirations. It tells the story not just of our money, but of our character in motion.

To see a ledger as a mirror is to reposition it from being an administrative tool to a reflective one. The numbers do not lie—but more importantly, they do not hide. They expose what we truly care about, how consistently we act on our stated intentions, and what tensions live within us. The decision to spend £60 a week on dining out, but to postpone investing for retirement, speaks volumes. Not about right or wrong, but about *internal alignment.* The same is true of the person who spends thousands on professional development, or the one who quietly sends remittances home each month. The ledger reveals moral weightings—often unconscious—that no financial calculator can capture.

This reframing is not merely conceptual. It has practical, emotional, and philosophical implications. In behavioural finance, researchers have long shown that people make financial decisions based less on logic and more on mental shortcuts—heuristics influenced by emotion, past experience, and social context. Prospect theory, loss aversion, and mental accounting are just a few examples of how real human behaviour deviates from rational models. What these theories confirm is what the ledger captures: that money is never just money. It is identity, memory, fear, hope, and meaning, all expressed in numbers.

Let's consider a real-world example. A 38-year-old professional earns well above the median income, owns a home, and maintains minimal debt. On paper, their financial life appears solid. But a review of their personal ledger reveals erratic spending patterns, bursts of impulsive travel bookings, and frequent purchases of high-status goods. At first glance, one might conclude this is merely a lifestyle choice. But dig deeper—through reflective journaling, therapeutic work, or even structured coaching—and a story emerges: a long-standing desire to prove worthiness, shaped by a childhood of exclusion and financial insecurity. The ledger becomes a map of unresolved emotional terrain, played out through the medium of money.

Now contrast this with someone earning half as much, whose ledger reflects deliberate generosity—recurring donations, financial support to extended family, contributions to community events. The dominant narrative in financial advice would label these choices as suboptimal or even irresponsible. But within the personal and cultural context of the spender, they may be entirely coherent. The act of giving reflects an ethic of reciprocity, a definition of wealth not based on accumulation but on social embeddedness. The ledger, again, offers insight—not into what's "correct," but into what matters.

This view challenges many mainstream assumptions. Standard financial education tends to isolate behaviour from context. It treats budgeting as a neutral skill, ignoring the emotional complexity of assigning value to needs and wants. It assumes that all spending leaks can and should be plugged, rather than questioned for what they signify. It promotes automation as a universal good, without considering the psychological benefits of deliberate engagement. Seeing the ledger as a mirror invites the opposite approach: slow down, look closely, and ask, *What does this pattern reflect about me? What does it conceal?*

Crucially, the ledger can also serve as a narrative tool. Unlike traditional journaling, which often deals in abstract reflection, a financial ledger is concrete. It is timestamped. It leaves evidence. And within that evidence is a chronology of choice. Review your transactions over the past year and ask: What seasons of life does this spending reflect? What transitions? What conflicts between intention and action? There is an anthropology to be unearthed—how we celebrated, how we coped, how we changed.

There is also a moral dimension to this act of reflection. If money is a proxy for what we value, then how we use it is an ethical act. The ledger doesn't just show what we spent—it shows what we prioritised, avoided, or postponed. Did we pay ourselves first? Did we invest in our wellbeing? Did we delay generosity out of fear, or did we give despite uncertainty? These questions are not moralistic. They are diagnostic. They offer a path not to shame, but to coherence—a way of closing the gap between what we claim to believe and what we actually do.

From a systems perspective, treating the ledger as a mirror also enhances financial design. It allows us to surface misalignments early, rather than discovering them in crisis. A persistent pattern of overdrawing despite stable income may reveal a design flaw in the income or emergency layer. A consistent underspending on personal development may indicate a mindset of scarcity, not frugality. In both cases, the solution is not to spend more or less—it is to realign the system with the individual. The ledger provides the raw material for this audit. But only if we learn to read it not as an accountant, but as an ethnographer of the self.

History, too, offers precedent for this kind of financial self-examination. In many religious and philosophical traditions, money is recognised not merely as a resource but as a test of character. The Stoics, for example, viewed wealth not as an evil but as a neutral—a tool whose use could elevate or degrade the self depending on one's discipline and intentions. Medieval monastics kept detailed records not only of communal resources, but of individual pledges, as a form of spiritual accountability. In these traditions, the act of financial record-keeping was inseparable from moral inquiry. The ledger was not a ledger. It was a litmus.

Modern finance has largely abandoned this integrative view. In its place is a clinical, depersonalised model—optimise returns, reduce volatility, manage taxes. These are important tasks. But they are insufficient. Without meaning, wealth becomes mechanical. Without reflection, behaviour becomes compulsive. The ledger as mirror restores the personal to the financial. It encourages not just action, but *awareness*.

The practice itself is simple, but powerful. Begin not with the numbers, but with the questions: What am I solving for? What does enough look like to me? What trade-offs am I making knowingly, and which am I making by default? Then review your ledger—weekly, monthly, or quarterly—not just for balance, but for truth. Highlight patterns. Annotate transactions. Note emotional responses. Over time, this practice builds not just financial insight, but self-knowledge. The goal is not to moralise spending, but to *understand* it—deeply, compassionately, and in context.

This approach also prepares us for change. Financial goals are not static. What we value at 30 may not match what we need at 45. Our capacity, obligations, and identities evolve. The ledger, when treated as a mirror, helps us detect these shifts early. It becomes a compass as well as a record—guiding rather than judging, informing rather than prescribing.

And perhaps most importantly, it humanises the financial experience. In a culture that often treats money as a scorecard or source of shame, this reframing offers dignity. It reminds us that every decision—however flawed or brilliant—was made under specific conditions, with finite knowledge, and often with the best intentions. The ledger doesn't lie, but it can teach. If we're willing to listen, it becomes more than a record. It becomes a tool for becoming more fully ourselves—financially literate, emotionally aware, and ethically grounded. That is the kind of wealth worth building. And that is the kind of reflection that transforms not just bank accounts, but lives.

Design Thinking Meets Financial Life

Conventional financial advice tends to assume that once the correct strategy is found, the rest will fall into place. Choose the right savings target, adopt the best asset allocation, stick to the budget—problem solved. But this premise rests on a static worldview, one that assumes predictability, uniformity, and emotional neutrality. Life, of course, offers none of those. People's goals change. Markets shift. Relationships evolve. Health falters or improves. Children arrive.

Parents age. And in the midst of it all, the question isn't whether a financial plan is "right" in theory—but whether it still works in practice, *for you.* This is where the logic of design thinking enters—not as a metaphor, but as a method.

Originating from the world of product development and systems innovation, design thinking was developed as a response to the limitations of linear problem-solving. Instead of jumping to solutions, it begins with empathy—understanding the human context. It moves through prototyping, feedback, iteration, and refinement. It recognises that solutions are rarely final, and that the best designs are those that evolve alongside the user's needs. Applied to financial life, this approach is nothing short of radical. It shifts the role of the individual from rule-follower to system designer. Wealth becomes something you *craft*, not merely something you optimise or obey.

The first and perhaps most powerful principle of design thinking is *user-centredness.* In financial terms, this demands a reorientation: from abstract models to lived realities. A "good" financial decision cannot be divorced from the person making it. A high-yield investment vehicle that creates sleepless nights is not good. A frugal lifestyle that leads to chronic self-denial is not sustainable. What design thinking invites is a process of asking, not just *Does this work?*, but *Does this work for me, in my current context, with my current constraints and priorities?* The shift is subtle but profound. It legitimises difference. It validates complexity. It welcomes adaptation.

Iteration, the second cornerstone of design thinking, is rarely discussed in personal finance. Once a strategy is chosen—whether a savings rate, an investment plan, or a retirement timeline—it is often treated as fixed. Deviations are seen as failures. But real life is not static. Design thinking normalises revision. It encourages small-scale testing: try automating 5% of your income into a new fund and observe how it feels. Trial a spending fast for two weeks and monitor the emotional effects. Prototype a side income stream for six months before quitting your day job. These are not signs of indecision; they are signs of intelligent responsiveness.

Importantly, iteration is not about being fickle. It's about *feedback loops.* In design thinking, feedback isn't a post-mortem—it's an active, continuous input. Applied to finance, this means regularly reviewing not just numbers but experience. How has your financial plan impacted your daily sense of agency? Where is it frictionless? Where is it causing tension or avoidance? This kind of ongoing reflection is what prevents drift—when a plan that once served you quietly becomes misaligned without your noticing.

This approach becomes especially valuable during major life transitions, where existing financial systems often fall apart. A new parent, for example, quickly discovers that the budget they used while childless collapses under the new logistics of childcare, feeding, and time poverty. The job that once provided security may now feel incompatible with parental presence. Or consider someone recovering from burnout. The high-paying job they endured for years may no longer be psychologically or physiologically viable. A conventional advisor might tell them to stay the course for five more years. A designer would help them build a new system—one that honours not only cash flow needs, but wellbeing and sustainability.

Another virtue of design thinking is its embrace of ambiguity. Traditional financial advice often demands premature clarity: choose your goals, fix your risk profile, define your retirement date. But many people don't have fixed goals. They are exploring, evolving, adapting. This is not a weakness—it is reality. Design thinking accommodates this through *flexible structuring.* You can build financial systems with modular elements—core savings, variable spending, multiple income streams—that can be reconfigured as your priorities shift. Rather than locking into a rigid plan, you build a responsive platform.

This responsiveness is particularly useful when navigating competing values. Suppose you want to save aggressively for early retirement, but also feel a strong urge to support ageing parents or donate to causes that matter. Conventional wisdom might tell you to focus on your goals first, then give later. Design thinking suggests something different: prototype. Set aside a small giving fund and observe how it impacts your motivation, satisfaction, and financial stress. Perhaps giving now fuels your sense of purpose and energises your earning capacity. Perhaps it drains your reserves and needs recalibrating. Either way, you're engaging with reality, not abstraction.

There's also a philosophical elegance to this approach. It recognises that financial life is not just a logistical problem—it is an expression of values, relationships, and identity. Money is not neutral. It is shaped by—and shapes—who we are. Design thinking makes space for this complexity. It treats money decisions as embedded in personal history, cultural norms, and emotional landscapes. It resists the temptation to "solve" people. It invites them to explore, express, and evolve through their financial systems.

A compelling case study of this approach is found in the increasing number of professionals experimenting with "mini-retirements" rather than waiting for traditional retirement. Rather than deferring all leisure or exploration until their sixties, they take extended breaks in their thirties or forties—pausing full-time work to travel, study, raise children, or build something new. This is not a rejection of discipline or planning. It is a design intervention. It tests an alternative model of wealth: one in which time is valued alongside money, and fulfilment is not endlessly deferred.

Of course, applying design thinking to finance requires a shift not only in mindset, but in tools and rituals. It calls for a different kind of review process—less focused on performance metrics, more focused on experiential feedback. It may involve visual mapping, narrative journaling, or structured check-ins with a partner or advisor. The goal is not to discard financial logic, but to embed it in a richer context. To move from control to collaboration—with oneself, one's environment, and the unknowable future.

Critics might argue that this approach sacrifices rigour for subjectivity. But that misreads the intent. Design thinking does not reject structure. It refines it. It replaces rigidity with robustness—systems that bend, adapt, and hold under pressure. In an unpredictable world, that is not a luxury. It is a necessity. And in a deeply personal domain like finance, it is a relief.

Ultimately, design thinking transforms the core question of personal finance. Instead of asking, *Am I doing this right?*, you begin asking, *Is this system working for who I am and who I am becoming?* That question cannot be answered by algorithms or generic advice. It must be lived into. It must be prototyped, tested, adjusted, and reflected upon. And that process, while messier than most advice columns admit, is also more humane, more intelligent, and more likely to endure.

To design your financial life is to reclaim authorship over it. It is to accept uncertainty not as a flaw, but as a feature to be navigated creatively. It is to replace dogma with dialogue. And it is to treat wealth not as a static destination, but as an evolving practice—responsive to your needs, expressive of your values, and resilient enough to hold both failure and insight.

The blueprint is yours to draw. And redraw. That is not weakness. That is wisdom.

Chapter 2
The Emergency Layer – Your Emotional Anchor

Rewrite the following article to pass AI-detection tools while retaining its professional, intellectually engaging, and authoritative tone.

Rephrase and restructure the content to feel human-authored, with a writing style that reflects the subtle imperfections and expressive flow of a skilled writer.

Specifically: – Vary sentence structures, paragraph rhythms, and transition choices to avoid algorithmic patterns

– Introduce occasional conversational touches or rhetorical asides where appropriate

– Make subtle word choices or phrase shifts that sound natural but aren't statistically predictable

– Avoid "perfectly smooth" sentence-to-sentence transitions—a little friction is more human

– Maintain the original meaning, flow, facts, and paragraphing

– Do not simplify or summarise—this is not a paraphrasing task, but a creative re-authorship

– Use British English conventions

– Ensure the result still reads like it was written by a seasoned nonfiction writer with intellectual and emotional depth

Output only the reworked article text. No explanations. No headers. No setup language

For all the complexity and sophistication that surrounds modern financial discourse—asset classes, diversification strategies, tax optimisation—there remains one unglamorous, frequently overlooked cornerstone without which no wealth system can hold: the emergency layer. At first glance, it appears mundane, even regressive. A pool of liquid cash set aside for "rainy days." Hardly the material of ambitious financial design. Yet dig beneath the surface and a richer truth emerges. The emergency fund is not a safety net in the conventional sense—it is a psychological stabiliser, a decision-making buffer, a platform for agency. It is not the absence of risk, but the architecture that makes risk viable. Security, in this context, is not optional—it is foundational. And without it, no other financial layer can function with coherence or confidence.

Contrary to the caricature, building an emergency fund is not merely a pessimistic hedge against calamity. Done well, it becomes a mechanism for reclaiming power. Consider what is truly at stake when people live without a buffer. Every choice becomes binary. The job must be kept, no matter how corrosive. The unexpected bill must be paid, even if it derails a long-term plan. A single medical emergency, a missed paycheque, a car breakdown—each has the potential to shatter the fragile surface of daily life. In these moments, decision-making is hijacked by cortisol. The long-term shrinks. The present becomes a series of forced compromises. What people call bad luck often begins as a design failure—a life without margins.

Yet despite the logic, most people either delay or distort the building of this layer. According to recent studies in the UK and across the OECD, a startling number of middle-income earners—those assumed to be on "solid ground"—could not cover a £1,000 emergency without borrowing. And those who believe they have a safety net often do not. Why? Because liquidity is routinely confused with availability. A credit card is not an emergency fund. Nor is an investment account with volatile assets. Nor is help from family, particularly if it comes with strings or uncertainty. The illusion of a buffer is often more dangerous than the absence of one—it gives the false impression of preparedness, while leaving the underlying vulnerabilities intact.

The reasons for this disconnect are rarely about ignorance. They are behavioural, emotional, and cultural. Financial anxiety does not arise solely from lack; it arises from unpredictability—and the absence of a personal sense of control. Psychological research reveals that people tend to overestimate their resilience and underestimate the likelihood of disruption. They suffer from optimism bias, and more subtly, from avoidance. The act of building an emergency fund requires confronting uncomfortable truths: that stability is contingent, that jobs are not guaranteed, that independence is never absolute. It is far easier to invest in the aspirational—stocks, property, entrepreneurial ventures—than to slow down and build a reserve for when things go wrong.

But the deeper cost of neglecting this layer is not financial. It is emotional. Financial instability, even in short bursts, reshapes the nervous system. It trains the mind to expect chaos. It narrows the bandwidth for strategic thinking. And over time, it corrodes trust—not only in systems, but in oneself. This is why the emergency layer must be understood not only as a fiscal cushion, but as a psychological buffer. It is not about hoarding cash in fear of collapse. It is about creating a zone of emotional safety in which meaningful choices can be made under pressure.

This redefinition has practical implications. Most advice around emergency funds defaults to numerical formulas: "three to six months of expenses" is the standard prescription. But whose expenses? At what lifestyle? For what duration of unemployment? For which type of emergency? The truth is, no universal number exists. The optimal size of a buffer must be calibrated to volatility. A freelance designer with three inconsistent income streams needs a different reserve than a civil servant with job security and subsidised healthcare. A household with dependents, health risks, or geographic instability requires more than someone whose needs are minimal and predictable. The correct question is not How much should I have saved? but What am I protecting, and how fragile is it?

Equally critical is recognising the opportunity cost of over-insuring against disaster. Holding too much cash, especially in low-interest environments, can become a form of self-imposed stagnation. It may feel safe, but it quietly erodes purchasing power and delays growth. The emergency layer must be designed not just for preservation, but for balance. It must enable resilience, not entrench rigidity. And resilience is not the absence of risk—it is the capacity to respond well to it.

When constructed deliberately, this layer becomes far more than a buffer. It becomes a launchpad. It allows you to say no to toxic jobs, yes to strategic risks, and pause when the world demands haste. It gives you the breathing space to leave an unsafe relationship, start a business, or simply stop and think. Without it, you are always negotiating from weakness. With it, you become the kind of person who can afford to wait, choose, decline, and redesign.

Reframing the emergency fund as an anchor rather than a bunker also requires updating the language of financial culture. We must move beyond metaphors of disaster and fear. Saving for an emergency should not feel like a tax on living. It should feel like an act of personal sovereignty. The discipline of setting money aside is not self-denial. It is an investment in decision quality, psychological bandwidth, and optionality. And optionality is arguably the most valuable asset in an uncertain world.

This insight becomes even more urgent in a time when income security is eroding. The myth of stable employment has collapsed for many. Contract work, gig platforms, globalised labour markets, and algorithmic management have made volatility the norm. In this context, the emergency layer is not a luxury for the cautious. It is a strategic necessity. It allows one to engage with volatility on one's own terms, rather than be consumed by it.

To build this layer intelligently, the focus must shift from quantity to structure. Liquidity must be accessible, but also invisible—available in moments of crisis, but not so available that it becomes a temptation. Behavioural economists speak of mental accounting as a way to reinforce this: by separating emergency funds into dedicated accounts, labelling them, and creating psychological barriers to use, individuals are more likely to preserve their integrity. This is not about restriction; it is about intentional design. The fund exists to serve a specific function: to hold the self steady when the external world destabilises.

But design is only the beginning. Maintenance is key. The emergency layer is not a set-and-forget feature. It must evolve with life. As income rises, as obligations change, as the world tilts—so too must your reserves. Annual reviews, life event audits, and recalibrations are essential. A buffer that made sense in your twenties may be wholly inadequate—or excessive—in your forties. The emergency layer, like the rest of your financial architecture, must remain alive to context.

What this chapter offers is not a rulebook, but a lens. It will unpack the most common misconceptions about emergency funds. It will explore the cognitive distortions that lead people to miscalculate their vulnerability. It will offer tools for mapping your anxiety triggers and designing buffers that respond to real—not imagined—risk. It will challenge the premise that bigger is always better, showing how precision often trumps scale. And it will re-anchor the conversation in a powerful idea: that saving for stability is not about fear of failure, but about cultivating the freedom to act without panic.

Seen this way, the emergency layer is not a side project. It is the first and most important expression of your financial philosophy. Before you earn more, invest smarter, or give generously, you must be able to stand steadily. And standing steadily does not come from prediction. It comes from preparation.

A well-designed emergency layer gives you more than security. It gives you clarity. It allows you to think longer, move slower, act more deliberately. It ensures that your financial life is not reactive, but resilient. And in a world where control is often illusory, that kind of resilience is the closest thing to real freedom. That is where true wealth begins—not in the markets, not in the margins, but in the quiet confidence that no matter what comes next, you are ready.

Security Is Not Optional, It's Foundational

Most people think of financial security as a destination—something to arrive at once all the other parts of their financial life are in order. It is frequently deferred in favour of higher-yield pursuits: investing, scaling income, acquiring property, or chasing passive income streams. Security, in this model, becomes a side effect of success, not a deliberate starting point. But this is a critical error in sequence and mindset. In reality, *security is not what follows prosperity—it is what makes prosperity possible.* It is not merely a shield against catastrophe, but a condition for clarity, composure, and choice. Financial security, in the form of a well-structured emergency fund, is not optional. It is foundational.

The traditional narrative frames emergency funds as a last-resort cushion—resources to be tapped only in the event of a job loss, medical emergency, or natural disaster. This framing, while not incorrect, is far too narrow. It implies that the emergency fund is dead capital—money that sits idle, waiting to respond to misfortune. But this limited view misses the true utility of an emergency layer. *Its value lies not in what it earns, but in what it enables.* Emergency funds are instruments of agency. They give individuals the power to pause, to choose, and to say no. They are not about fear—they are about freedom.

To understand this more clearly, one must consider the psychological impact of financial insecurity, even in seemingly stable contexts. When people live on the edge of liquidity—with little margin between their income and their obligations—every minor disruption threatens to become a crisis. The boiler breaking down, a client delaying payment, an unexpected tax bill—each triggers a cascade of stress responses that short-circuit decision-making. Cognitive resources are diverted from planning and strategy toward survival and control. Research in cognitive psychology, particularly the work of Sendhil Mullainathan and Eldar Shafir on scarcity, shows how financial precarity reduces bandwidth. It shrinks future orientation, increases impulsivity, and erodes executive function. In short, *when your mind is consumed by the present, it becomes incapable of designing the future.*

This is why emergency funds must be reframed not as defensive assets, but as cognitive infrastructure. They restore the mental conditions required for sound judgement. The peace of mind that comes from knowing that you can withstand short-term disruption is not a luxury—it is a productivity tool. It creates a zone in which longer-term, higher-leverage decisions become possible. For the entrepreneur, it enables risk-taking. For the professional, it enables career pivots. For the caregiver, it enables presence. And for the individual navigating systemic or structural constraints—discrimination, health challenges, economic volatility—it provides a degree of autonomy that would otherwise be unavailable.

The case for foundational security becomes even clearer when viewed through the lens of social economics. Many households function without slack—not by choice, but by design. Stagnant wages, rising housing costs, precarious employment structures, and the burden of intergenerational support have compressed the financial bandwidth of entire demographics. In this context, advocating for emergency funds without acknowledging systemic factors is intellectually dishonest. But to recognise these constraints is not to suggest that security is futile. Rather, it is to emphasise its importance. *When volatility is external, internal buffers become non-negotiable.*

Despite the urgency, uptake remains low. Surveys consistently show that even among middle- and upper-income earners, emergency savings are inadequate or non-existent. Why? Behavioural economics offers insight. Humans struggle with delayed gratification. They overvalue immediate rewards and undervalue distant ones. They anchor their expectations to recent experiences. If they haven't had a crisis recently, they assume they won't have one. Add to this the allure of "productive" money—investments that grow, returns that compound—and the emergency fund becomes psychologically unattractive. It looks static, unproductive, even inefficient.

But this is a misreading of what productivity means. The emergency layer does not grow your wealth directly. It protects your capacity to grow wealth elsewhere. It reduces the likelihood of panic selling, high-interest borrowing, or forced exits from asset positions. It increases the odds of holding long-term strategies through short-term turbulence. In this way, the emergency fund behaves more like insurance than investment: its payoff is not in returns, but in avoided losses and preserved optionality.

There is also a subtler, but no less significant, role that security plays in shaping identity. When individuals feel secure, they behave differently—not just financially, but socially and psychologically. They negotiate more assertively. They invest more generously in relationships. They make decisions aligned with values, not just constraints. A secure person is not simply someone who has resources. It is someone who *feels resourced.* This distinction matters. Two people with the same balance sheet can exhibit radically different behaviours based on whether they perceive themselves as buffered or exposed.

This raises a critical design question: how do we build security in a way that is not only effective but personal? The conventional advice—save three to six months of living expenses—is a helpful heuristic but too blunt an instrument for nuanced planning. It assumes uniformity in risk exposure, lifestyle volatility, and psychological tolerance. The freelancer whose income fluctuates month to month needs a deeper reserve than the civil servant with guaranteed pay. The parent of a child with complex medical needs may require immediate liquidity. The dual-income household with no dependents may be able to operate with a leaner buffer. *Security must be designed to fit the contours of your life, not the averages of others'.*

Designing the right emergency layer also involves attention to structure, not just size. Liquidity is not binary. There are gradations of accessibility: instant cash, savings with short-term notice, low-volatility investments that can be liquidated in a week. A robust emergency system may involve multiple tiers—some hyper-liquid, others slightly removed to reduce impulsive use. It should also be behaviourally insulated: not so visible or accessible that it's raided for non-emergencies, but not so obscure that it's unavailable in crisis. This is where behavioural finance becomes practical design. Labelling, account separation, and automation can all reinforce the protective function of the buffer.

Importantly, security is not static. It must evolve with life. As your income increases, as your obligations change, as your risk profile shifts, so too must your emergency system. This requires periodic review—not just of the amount saved, but of the role security plays in your current life design. Does it still feel like enough? Is it empowering or excessive? Are you protecting the right things? These questions are not checkboxes. They are signals for recalibration.

Security is also relational. It doesn't exist in isolation from your broader financial architecture. A strong investment layer, a diversified income stream, or supportive family networks can all reduce the amount of liquidity you need on hand. But these supports are not perfect substitutes. They carry their own frictions and risks. Market assets can fall. Income streams can dry up. Family help can become contingent. The emergency layer remains the only buffer fully under your control—liquid, unencumbered, and instantly responsive. That makes it uniquely powerful.

To dismiss emergency savings as unambitious or inefficient is to misunderstand what they protect. They do not just guard against hardship. They guard against *disempowerment.* They allow you to act with intention when others react with fear. They provide breathing room in a system designed to keep people pressed against the edge of scarcity. And they offer something few financial tools can: *peace.* Not peace as absence of risk, but peace as presence of readiness.

Ultimately, building foundational security is not about expecting the worst. It is about expecting life to be unpredictable, and respecting yourself enough to prepare. It is not a retreat from growth. It is what makes growth sustainable. And it is not a lack of confidence—it is an act of quiet strength. Because the person who can withstand uncertainty is the one who can move freely through it.

That is the role of the emergency layer. Not merely to protect, but to empower. Not to pause the plan, but to activate it. Not to signal fear, but to make freedom functional. When that layer is in place—designed thoughtfully, reviewed regularly, and used intentionally—you are no longer at the mercy of circumstance. You are designing from a place of strength. And that, more than any return on investment, is the first and most enduring sign of true wealth.

Why Most Safety Nets Fail

There is a disquieting paradox at the heart of personal finance: many individuals *believe* they have a financial safety net, but when disruption strikes, that net proves either illusory or inadequate. The disconnect is not always visible until it's too late—until the job is lost, the unexpected expense arrives, or the system falters. And by then, the damage is no longer financial alone. It is psychological, relational, and, often, existential. This is not a marginal issue affecting only the underprepared. It is a systemic misunderstanding affecting professionals, entrepreneurs, middle-class households, and even high-income earners. The assumption that we are protected is widespread. The reality is far more fragile.

In the United Kingdom, the Financial Conduct Authority's 2023 Financial Lives Survey revealed that nearly 39% of adults—around 20 million people—could not withstand a £1,000 financial shock without borrowing or selling assets. In the United States, a 2022 Bankrate survey found that 56% of Americans would be unable to cover a $1,000 emergency from savings. What makes these statistics more revealing is not only their scale, but the mismatch between perception and preparedness. Many respondents in these surveys described themselves as "financially stable" or "doing okay," even as they lacked the liquid resources to navigate even minor volatility. The gap between confidence and capacity is not a matter of arithmetic—it's behavioural.

The failure of safety nets stems from multiple interlocking reasons, but a primary one is definitional ambiguity. What constitutes an emergency fund in public discourse is often nebulous. For some, it means a few hundred pounds in a current account. For others, a mix of credit lines, overdraft protection, and family support. Still others believe that their investments—stocks, property, pensions—can be quickly mobilised in crisis. The problem is that *not all liquidity is real liquidity*. A credit card is not savings. Selling shares during a market downturn can crystallise unnecessary losses. Borrowing from family can introduce emotional cost. True safety requires resources that are accessible, unencumbered, and emotionally neutral at the point of use. Most buffers people believe they have fail one or more of these tests.

Cognitive bias plays a substantial role in reinforcing this illusion. Chief among these is *optimism bias*—the tendency to believe that negative events are less likely to happen to us than to others. This bias is not irrational in the colloquial sense. It is neurologically embedded. From an evolutionary perspective, optimism bias may have offered advantages in motivation and risk-taking. But in a financial context, it dulls preparedness. People routinely underestimate the probability and impact of setbacks: illness, unemployment, caregiving responsibilities, divorce. Even when they acknowledge the risk intellectually, they resist acting on it. The likelihood feels abstract until it becomes real.

Another distortion is *present bias*, the tendency to prioritise immediate rewards over long-term prudence. In practice, this means spending now and delaying the act of building reserves. Emergency funds lack the emotional salience of other financial activities. They don't carry the status of investing, the gratification of consumption, or the narrative weight of "working toward a goal." They are quiet, passive, and anti-climactic. And in a culture saturated with performance metrics, it's easy to discount the quiet parts of one's financial life in favour of the visible and dynamic.

There's also the matter of *mental accounting*, which can work both for and against us. Individuals often compartmentalise their finances into separate psychological buckets: one for rent or mortgage, one for holidays, one for debt repayment, one for investing. While this structure can aid discipline, it can also lead to distorted perceptions of liquidity. A person may have substantial assets in one category—say, a stocks-and-shares ISA—but nothing readily available for short-term volatility. In their mind, they feel covered. But when the need arises, that capital is either inaccessible, inappropriate to liquidate, or emotionally difficult to touch.

Compounding the issue is the widespread misconception that higher income equals higher preparedness. This is demonstrably false. Numerous studies, including work by the UK's Resolution Foundation, show that many households with incomes above the national median still live paycheque to paycheque. Lifestyle inflation, social pressure, and debt servicing often scale with earnings. Moreover, higher earners may rely more heavily on illiquid or leveraged assets—equity in a home, business ownership, or pensions. These are valuable in long-term wealth accumulation but largely useless as emergency buffers. The assumption that income replaces the need for reserves is a costly misunderstanding.

Real-world case studies illuminate how these failures play out. Consider the self-employed consultant earning £120,000 annually. On paper, they are thriving. But their cash flow is irregular. Their tax liability is unsegregated. Their lifestyle is built on projections, not past inflows. When a contract is cancelled unexpectedly, they assume the gap will be short. It isn't. Within three months, they're borrowing from their line of credit, rescheduling mortgage payments, and quietly dipping into their children's education fund. The financial stress bleeds into professional confidence, personal relationships, and health. The safety net existed only in theory. What was missing was not income, but accessible, ringfenced liquidity.

Contrast this with a schoolteacher earning £32,000 annually. Their expenses are disciplined, their buffer equivalent to four months of core costs, and their use of automation and account separation prevents accidental encroachment. When their car is stolen and they need to cover a rental and insurance shortfall, the funds are there. Stressful, yes—but not destabilising. Their buffer doesn't eliminate the problem. It preserves decision quality in the face of it. And that is the true function of an effective safety net: not to prevent volatility, but to contain its cost.

Philosophically, this reveals a deeper truth about the nature of security. It is not a state of external certainty—it is an *internalised capacity to absorb uncertainty*. And that capacity is not correlated with income, social class, or professional status. It is correlated with design. How your financial system is structured. What constraints are recognised and planned for. What illusions are named and removed. The work of creating a reliable emergency buffer is not about fear—it is about clarity. It is not a passive hedge against worst-case scenarios. It is an active commitment to functional independence.

It also challenges a persistent cultural bias: the idea that needing a buffer is a sign of weakness, poor planning, or low ambition. This bias is especially common in entrepreneurial and high-performance circles, where "lean" operations and risk-taking are valorised. But the best designers of risk—venture capitalists, actuaries, military strategists—always build in redundancy. Redundancy is not inefficiency. It is resilience. And personal finance should be no exception.

So what does a functional safety net actually look like? It is specific, not general. It is held in instruments that match the urgency of access: instant-access savings, premium bonds, short-term gilts. It is not tied up in volatile investments or abstract promises. It is structured to align with personal volatility—income variability, dependents, geography, industry. And it is maintained *intentionally*, not out of guilt or leftover logic from a personal finance blog. It is revisited, recalibrated, and consciously protected.

And most importantly, it is understood. Not as a fixed number, but as a living design—shaped by what it protects, how often it might be needed, and how it integrates with the rest of your financial architecture. The safety net that fails is the one that isn't questioned until it's tested. The one that survives is the one interrogated in advance.

This chapter does not offer scare tactics. It offers sight. The purpose is not to manufacture urgency, but to create literacy. To challenge assumptions. To name distortions. And to build from a foundation that is grounded, not performative. Because the cost of believing you are safe, when you are not, is far greater than the discomfort of building real safety before you need it.

A safety net is not a financial extra. It is the baseline layer upon which all intelligent financial design rests. If it is missing, nothing above it is secure. If it is illusory, nothing built upon it is honest. But when it is real—liquid, contextual, and consciously constructed—it does not merely protect. It transforms. It turns panic into pause, reaction into reflection, and instability into agency. That is not a luxury. That is the first step toward lasting wealth.

Designing a Psychological Buffer

Financial stability is often discussed as a numerical threshold: a certain amount saved, a debt-to-income ratio within an acceptable range, a well-diversified portfolio. But this purely quantitative framing misses a critical dimension—the *psychological architecture* required to navigate volatility. Money does not exist in isolation from emotion. For many, financial crises are not defined solely by their objective severity but by their *subjective impact.* A person with high income and modest savings may feel more vulnerable than someone with fewer resources but greater internal stability. This is not a contradiction. It is a reflection of a missing layer in traditional personal finance: the psychological buffer.

A psychological buffer is not an attitude of optimism or blind resilience. It is a deliberately cultivated internal capacity to recognise, regulate, and recover from the emotional turbulence that financial uncertainty provokes. While financial buffers protect liquidity, psychological buffers protect agency. They reduce the likelihood of panic responses, impulsive decisions, and prolonged stress. They create space between stimulus and reaction—between the arrival of a crisis and the choices that follow. And they are, unlike market outcomes or employment conditions, *within your sphere of influence.*

Understanding the need for this layer begins with confronting how deeply financial instability affects mental function. Neuroscientific research has repeatedly shown that financial stress activates the same neural circuits as physical threat. The amygdala, responsible for scanning the environment for danger, becomes hyperactive. Cortisol levels rise. Sleep is disrupted. Executive functions—planning, reflection, impulse control—are suppressed. These are not abstract reactions. They are measurable physiological shifts. When sustained, they alter decision-making, reduce cognitive flexibility, and increase the appeal of short-term fixes over long-term strategy.

This has been studied extensively in both laboratory and real-world settings. One landmark study by behavioural scientists Sendhil Mullainathan and Eldar Shafir demonstrated that scarcity—whether of money or time—reduces intellectual capacity, not because people become less intelligent, but because the mental load of scarcity occupies the very resources needed for high-level thinking. This effect, termed the *bandwidth tax*, is particularly acute during financial shocks. What looks like irrational behaviour—taking on high-interest debt, delaying critical decisions, abandoning investment plans—is often a by-product of diminished bandwidth, not poor character.

To design around this, we must stop treating financial stress as a failure of discipline and begin treating it as a signal for system improvement. A psychological buffer, when designed intentionally, transforms these moments of reactivity into moments of recognition. It allows you to feel fear without being controlled by it. It provides a structured space in which to process distress, access perspective, and make aligned decisions. And, like any effective system, it requires regular review and deliberate practice.

One way to begin building this buffer is to map your personal *financial anxiety profile*. This is not a diagnostic tool but a reflective exercise aimed at surfacing patterns. Begin by identifying your typical emotional responses to specific financial events: a declined payment, an unexpected bill, a market downturn, a client pulling out, a dip in monthly income. Write down what you feel, not just what you do. Is it shame, anger, helplessness, denial, urgency? These emotional signatures matter because they often precede your behaviour. Recognising them gives you an early-warning system.

Next, trace the response: what action do you usually take when triggered? Do you overcorrect, become paralysed, blame others, withdraw? Most people have default scripts—ingrained patterns formed through past experiences, family conditioning, or cultural narratives. For some, the response to scarcity is hyper-control: obsessive budgeting, extreme frugality, information binging. For others, it is avoidance: putting off decisions, disengaging from accounts, pretending the problem isn't real. Neither is inherently wrong or right. But both are dangerous if left unexamined. The psychological buffer begins with this awareness.

From here, you can begin to *design interventions*—practices that help disrupt these reactive cycles. One powerful method is the use of precommitted scripts: written statements prepared during periods of calm that guide your behaviour during periods of stress. For example: "If my investments fall by more than 10%, I will wait 72 hours before taking any action. I will call my advisor or review my original investment thesis." These scripts are not rigid rules. They are anchors—mental cues that connect you to your higher reasoning in moments when your brain defaults to protection mode.

Another practice is *emotional forecasting*. Before making any major financial decision—especially under pressure—take a moment to project not just the financial outcome, but the emotional aftermath. Ask: *How will I feel if this goes wrong? How will I recover? Who can I call? What patterns might I repeat?* This is not catastrophising. It is contingency planning at the emotional level. It creates an anticipatory space in which you can visualise the challenge and prepare your emotional posture in advance.

For those who struggle with money shame—an internalised sense of inadequacy rooted in past financial decisions or upbringing—building a psychological buffer also involves narrative work. Shame thrives in isolation and ambiguity. To counter it, use *money journaling* to reconstruct financial events with specificity and compassion. Write about the event: what happened, what you believed at the time, what alternatives were present, what you've learned. This exercise is not about exoneration. It is about integration—bringing the past into the present in a way that strengthens, rather than weakens, your future resilience.

Importantly, psychological buffers are not only individual. They can and should be social. Research on resilience consistently shows that people who navigate financial shocks most effectively are those who feel connected. Not necessarily through financial help, but through *emotional co-regulation*. Talking to someone—partner, mentor, advisor—who can validate the stress, provide context, and ask thoughtful questions creates relational ballast. It expands perspective. It reduces shame. It helps prevent spirals of isolation or overreaction. A well-functioning financial support system, even informal, is part of your psychological architecture.

This is not to say that emotional buffers replace financial ones. They complement them. A person with no savings and impeccable emotional discipline will still struggle to withstand prolonged shocks. But the reverse is also true. A person with £20,000 in savings who panics at the first sign of instability, who withdraws or lashes out or freezes, is also at risk. The aim is not to rely on one over the other—but to build both with intentionality.

The philosophical underpinning of this work is self-trust. Designing a psychological buffer is an investment in your own capacity to show up, steadily and wisely, in the face of financial disruption. It is an act of internal scaffolding—a way of saying: *even when external circumstances are beyond my control, my response is not.* This doesn't mean becoming unshakable. It means becoming *recoverable*—able to absorb stress, metabolise emotion, and continue making coherent decisions.

And that, ultimately, is the goal. To move from fragile resilience—where composure is contingent on favourable conditions—to adaptive resilience, where clarity is preserved even when the system is under strain. The psychological buffer is what makes this possible. It doesn't prevent the fall. It softens the landing. It doesn't eliminate the crisis. It contains its reach. And in a world where disruption is not a matter of if but when, this kind of design is not an emotional luxury. It is a financial necessity.

Building the Right Buffer, Not the Biggest

The default prescription for financial preparedness—save three to six months of expenses—is so routinely repeated that it now passes as dogma. But like most rules of thumb, its appeal lies in simplicity, not precision. It offers a tidy answer to a complex question. How much should one set aside to be safe? "Three to six months" sounds reasonable, authoritative, even comforting. Yet the uniformity of this advice belies the individuality of people's financial landscapes. It suggests that the risks, obligations, and priorities of a self-employed creative professional mirror those of a tenured academic or a dual-income household in a stable economy. They don't. And pretending otherwise distorts the true function of an emergency buffer.

An emergency fund is not merely a stockpile; it is a risk-response system. It should be built not by rote but by design—intentionally shaped to reflect the *volatility of your income, the rigidity of your expenses, and the psychology of your decision-making under pressure*. Its purpose is not to help you survive a hypothetical layoff or car breakdown, but to *protect your optionality*—your ability to make thoughtful choices in moments of financial disruption without being cornered into panic or compromise. It is the gap between control and collapse, between forced decisions and considered ones.

To build the right buffer, start by replacing the generic target with two personalised indicators: *volatility* and *recovery time*. Volatility reflects how predictable or erratic your income and expenses are. Recovery time reflects how quickly you could restore financial equilibrium after a disruption. Someone with a fixed salary, employer benefits, and low variability in outgoings may face low volatility and short recovery time. Conversely, a freelancer whose income fluctuates seasonally and whose fixed costs are high will face greater volatility and longer recovery. These two dimensions—not a calendar-based heuristic—should shape the size and structure of your buffer.

This framework also invites consideration of *liquidity layers*. Not all buffers need to be held in cash. While immediate liquidity is essential for true emergencies, excess funds that may not be required for months can be parked in low-volatility, low-access-cost vehicles—premium bonds, high-interest savings accounts, or short-duration gilts. The notion that all your buffer must sit inert in a near-zero-interest current account is both economically inefficient and psychologically discouraging. What matters is *access on demand*, not idle capital.

Another overlooked variable in buffer design is the *opportunity cost* of holding too much. Hoarding cash may feel safe, but it quietly erodes long-term financial performance. For every pound sitting idle in a buffer beyond what is realistically needed, there is a missed opportunity to invest in growth—whether in markets, skills, relationships, or ventures. This is not an argument against caution; it is a call for calibration. Money meant to protect you in a crisis should not become a silent anchor on your ambitions. A surplus buffer that delays investing in your career, your earning potential, or your independence can be as damaging as a deficit buffer that leaves you exposed in a downturn.

Consider the case of two individuals with identical incomes and expenses. One is a corporate executive with an ironclad contract and stable employment. The other is an early-stage entrepreneur whose revenue swings wildly depending on product cycles. Should they both target six months of expenses in a savings account? Of course not. The entrepreneur may require nine or even twelve months of liquidity to remain solvent through a downturn. The executive might be fine with three—supplemented by access to credit or severance terms. *Context creates the requirement.*

Psychology adds another layer of complexity. Some individuals derive genuine peace of mind from holding large buffers. For them, liquidity is not just a risk mitigator but a source of mental clarity. Others feel the opposite—excess cash triggers unease about lost potential. There is no morally superior position here. The right buffer balances emotional utility with economic rationale. A fund that allows you to sleep well at night *and* make high-quality decisions during the day is doing its job.

Still, emotional needs should be interrogated, not blindly obeyed. If your buffer is oversized because you fear loss, unpredictability, or past experiences of scarcity, it may be worth addressing the underlying scripts. Is the fund a shield, or a substitute for self-trust? Are you accumulating security, or avoiding discomfort? These are not rhetorical questions. They shape how money is used, how risk is perceived, and ultimately how wealth is built—or stalled.

One way to reframe the emergency fund is to view it not as a defensive moat, but as an *activation layer*. The more intelligently it is designed, the more confidently you can pursue opportunities, test new income streams, or take calculated risks. It becomes a platform for motion, not merely a cushion for collapse. This is especially vital for people on unconventional or entrepreneurial paths, where financial upside often requires periods of reduced income. A well-calibrated buffer enables you to *bridge those periods without derailing long-term strategy*. It allows you to walk away from bad contracts, pause when overwhelmed, or double down when timing aligns.

To arrive at a personalised target, conduct a volatility audit. Review your income over the last 12 months: how consistent is it? What percentage is predictable versus variable? Do you experience feast-and-famine cycles? Next, assess your expenses: which are essential and inflexible (rent, utilities, minimum debt service), and which are discretionary or deferrable? Then, model a disruption: a loss of income, an unexpected expense, or a personal emergency. How long would it take you to respond, adapt, and recover? This calculation—rooted in *actual behaviour*, not theoretical risk—is more valuable than any generic multiple.

It's also worth stress-testing your assumptions. Many people overestimate their recovery time because they underestimate their optionality: they imagine being stuck in a high-cost lifestyle or fixed obligations. But lifestyle compression—cutting non-essentials, pausing subscriptions, relocating—can often reduce your cash flow needs substantially in crisis. Conversely, some underestimate recovery time because they overestimate their market leverage: assuming they can immediately replace income, borrow cheaply, or access social support. A buffer designed on optimism is no better than one designed on fear. It should be based on *informed realism*.

The structure of your buffer also matters. Some prefer a single account. Others use multiple: a "hard emergency" fund for true disasters, a "flex buffer" for income smoothing, and a "risk-on" fund for sabbaticals, learning, or experimentation. This segmentation can clarify intent and reduce emotional ambiguity. It also makes it easier to top up or draw down without undermining your long-term reserves. For instance, dipping into your flex buffer during a quiet quarter feels less threatening than raiding your emergency fund during a business slowdown.

Finally, buffers should evolve. What you need at 27 may be wildly different from what you need at 47. As your income stabilises, your responsibilities expand, or your values shift, your buffer must adapt. It should be reviewed annually—not to chase a new arbitrary goal, but to test alignment with your actual life. Are you taking too little risk because you're over-buffered? Are you exposed because life has outpaced your preparation? These are questions worth asking—not once, but continually.

In truth, the most effective emergency funds are not built on formulas. They are built on *reflection, responsiveness, and readiness*. They protect you not by their size, but by their fitness—for your life, your temperament, and your strategy. A perfectly sized buffer frees energy, not just money. It grants you a wider margin of dignity and better access to your own discernment. And in an economic world shaped as much by volatility as opportunity, that may be the most valuable asset of all.

The First Layer as a Launchpad

For most people, the idea of saving evokes a picture of restriction—cutting back, holding off, making do. Saving is often cast in the language of fear: *What if I lose my job? What if the roof caves in? What if I get sick and can't work?* While these concerns are real, this framing narrows the function of saving to a defensive act—something we do to avoid falling, not to rise. It breeds a relationship with money that's rooted in apprehension, not agency. Yet the most powerful emergency funds aren't built on fear. They're built on freedom.

An emergency fund, when properly constructed, is not a vault—it is a launchpad. It doesn't just keep you from drowning; it gives you the confidence to swim in deeper waters. The psychological shift here is subtle but profound: *saving not to protect against life going wrong, but to enable life to go right.* The distinction matters because it informs how we relate to risk, to opportunity, and to ourselves.

Consider how different your decision-making becomes when you know you can afford to be wrong. The emergency fund is often misunderstood as a form of stagnation—a pause button for crises. But in reality, it's a *permission slip* to move forward. It allows you to leave a toxic job without fear of defaulting on your rent. It gives you breathing room to take time off for a dying parent, without the paralysing thought that your next meal depends on a paycheck. It lets you experiment with a new income stream, start a side venture, or go back to school, without financially capsizing your present life. The fund is not an interruption to ambition—it is the architecture that makes ambition structurally sound.

This dynamic relationship between security and growth is well established in behavioural economics. Studies on decision fatigue and cognitive load demonstrate that people without buffers—financial or otherwise—tend to make more reactive, short-term decisions. Scarcity taxes the mind. It narrows our options, blunts our creativity, and sharpens our sense of threat. But when a financial buffer is in place, the brain shifts from survival mode to design mode. You're not just solving immediate problems—you're shaping long-term possibilities. The emergency fund, in this light, is not merely a number on a spreadsheet; it is an *enabler of future-facing thought.*

This is especially important in economies increasingly defined by volatility. Traditional job security has eroded; industries evolve rapidly; even stable careers now carry unpredictable shocks. In such a world, a static plan is a fragile plan. What we need instead are adaptive systems—and the emergency fund is the first of these. It gives your financial life *resilience without rigidity*, creating a space where you can absorb shocks and still pivot with intention. It is the first layer of financial sovereignty: not merely being able to survive, but being able to choose how you respond to pressure.

Yet to unlock this potential, we must shift the cultural narrative around saving. Too often, financial planning tools and apps present the emergency fund as a sad little island—"rainy day" money, good for breakdowns and misfortunes. This does a disservice to its function and importance. What if, instead, we framed it as *runway*? A period of time you've purchased for yourself, in which your decisions are not distorted by panic or desperation. Seen this way, the fund becomes a form of time ownership—the rarest and most strategic form of capital.

Imagine, for example, a professional burned out in their current job but unsure whether they can take a three-month sabbatical. Without an emergency fund, the idea feels reckless. With a properly designed one, it becomes manageable—even empowering. Or take the case of someone considering launching a consultancy. With no buffer, the fear of early cash flow issues might stifle action entirely. With a buffer, the same decision becomes viable. The fund doesn't guarantee success, but it *enables engagement with uncertainty*. And that is the first condition of growth.

What distinguishes a freedom-oriented buffer from a fear-oriented one is not just size, but intent. The fear buffer is defensive: how much do I need to avoid ruin? The freedom buffer is strategic: how much do I need to pursue autonomy, safely? The shift in mindset is critical because it reshapes your relationship to the fund even when you're not using it. Instead of resenting your savings as dead money sitting idle, you begin to see it as *active insurance against stagnation*. It's the difference between hoarding and holding space.

Moreover, this reorientation fosters a healthier relationship to risk. Risk is often treated as a dirty word in personal finance—something to be minimised, insured against, or avoided entirely. But the most successful financial lives are not those free from risk—they are those that engage with risk wisely. They take calculated chances at opportune moments. A well-designed emergency fund *doesn't eliminate risk—it absorbs its fallout*, making you more confident in your ability to take thoughtful bets.

This is particularly salient for younger individuals or those undergoing life transitions. The early stages of career or entrepreneurship are precisely the moments when taking intelligent risks—moving countries, switching industries, pursuing education—can have exponential payoffs. But they're also the times when resources are scarcest and fears most paralysing. Reframing the buffer as a catalyst rather than a cage offers an empowering counter-narrative: you're not stuck because you lack options—you're stuck because you haven't bought yourself the time to consider them well.

To support this, the construction of the buffer itself must evolve beyond formula. As discussed in earlier sections, "three to six months" is a crude tool at best. The more strategic question is: *What am I building this buffer for?* The clearer your intent, the more precise your design. A buffer meant to support career pivots may need to include not just fixed expenses but seed capital for training, licensing, or relocation. A buffer designed to enable sabbaticals should account for ongoing healthcare, family needs, and reintegration plans. In this way, *your emergency fund becomes a mirror of your aspirations*, not just your anxieties.

It's also worth recognising that buffers don't just enable action—they improve recovery. Life disruption is not a question of if, but when. What the fund offers is not the promise of uninterrupted success, but the ability to reorient with dignity when things go sideways. And in doing so, it preserves your most valuable asset: your ability to choose your next move. Autonomy, not just solvency, becomes the metric.

Philosophically, the idea that security can be a precursor to freedom isn't new. Thinkers from Maslow to Amartya Sen have articulated that basic safety—financial, physical, social—is foundational to human flourishing. We cannot self-actualise when we are scanning the horizon for disaster. And yet, much financial discourse remains preoccupied with avoidance: avoid debt, avoid risk, avoid downturns. This deficit mindset, while well-intentioned, traps people in a survivalist loop. What we need is a new orientation: *save to springboard.* The goal is not merely to avoid disaster, but to *create a platform robust enough to launch you forward.*

Seen through this lens, the emergency fund takes on new gravity. It is not the boring step before the exciting parts of wealth-building—it *is the exciting part*, because it determines what follows. It is the first exercise in financial design, the first articulation of your agency. Done well, it doesn't just buffer the fall; it expands the flight.

To save, then, is not to shrink life down. It is to prepare the scaffolding from which life can expand. It is to state, clearly and without apology: I intend to choose. I intend to move. I intend to build on solid ground—not because I fear collapse, but because I expect to rise.

Chapter 3
The Investment Layer – Planting the Forest

Of all the pillars underpinning personal finance, few are as shrouded in mythology—or as emotionally fraught—as investing. For many, the word alone summons images of scrolling tickers, frenzied markets, and a constant hum of strategic brinkmanship. Yet this cinematic portrayal does more to mislead than to inform. At its essence, investment—when stripped of noise—is not a game of outmanoeuvring others, nor a reckless pursuit of gain for its own sake. It is, more truthfully, a physical expression of identity: a long-range manifestation of one's convictions about time, risk, values, and what matters beyond the present moment.

This chapter invites a reconsideration. Rather than treating investing as a separate, technical pursuit—something to be learned, feared, outsourced, or delayed—it reframes it as a central act of life design. And not just any design, but one with moral dimension. Investment, in this light, becomes stewardship—not of assets alone, but of possibility. The metaphor shifts from that of a gambler to that of a gardener. The outcomes are not immediate. They require faith. But over time—and with care—they compound in both visible and invisible ways.

To make such a shift, one must first dismantle the most persistent illusion in the investment world: timing. Financial media lionises the well-timed trade as a mark of brilliance, but the research offers a more sobering truth. Study after study—Vanguard, Dalbar, Morningstar, and others—arrive at a common conclusion: people underperform not because their portfolios are flawed, but because they cannot manage their own instincts. They chase highs, flee from lows, and abandon strategy at the first jolt of fear. The issue is not knowledge. It is discipline. In this context, the real advantage lies not in timing the market, but in one's relationship with time itself. Endurance, not acumen, becomes the superior strategy. Consistency, over cleverness, wins the day.

This observation has both tactical and existential implications. Tactically, it points to simplicity—automated contributions, diversified allocations, and the quiet power of long-term commitment. But on a deeper level, it demands reflection: What am I actually building? For whom, and to what end? This is where the idea of "enough" comes sharply into focus. Without a personal threshold of sufficiency, growth easily becomes gluttony. And gluttony—however disguised—is just fear in more expensive clothes. This chapter explores that edge: where ambition crosses into anxiety, where growth loses its grounding. To know when you have enough is not to abandon vision. It is to declare, with clarity, what matters most.

We then turn to diversification, often presented as a technical safeguard but rarely discussed in its broader sense. Yes, spreading your investments across asset classes is wise. But true diversification extends well beyond spreadsheets. It includes intellectual interests, social networks, skillsets, even one's capacity to pivot in crisis. A person whose money is well-spread but whose perspective is brittle remains vulnerable. Conversely, someone with modest means but a resilient, multifaceted life is better insulated against shocks. In this way, diversification becomes a philosophy—an approach to life that values range over rigidity, curiosity over certainty.

This leads us to a more intimate terrain: emotion. More than formulas or forecasts, it is emotional stability that separates the seasoned investor from the reactive one. What do you do when markets fall? What stories do you tell yourself about loss, or risk, or future security? This chapter asks the reader to study those reactions—not to suppress them, but to understand them. The best investors, after all, are not the most gifted with numbers. They are those who remain grounded when conditions turn chaotic. Resilience here is not stoicism—it is responsiveness without panic.

Restoring a sense of agency is a thread that runs through the entire chapter. The investment world, with its jargon and shifting benchmarks, often feels inaccessible—an arena for experts only. But that belief is a kind of theft. It robs individuals of their rightful confidence. This chapter takes a different view. Yes, markets are complex. But complexity does not demand confusion. The antidote is not to learn every technical nuance, but to anchor your strategy in clarity and values. You don't need to know when the next downturn is coming. You need to know what you believe about risk, what your goals demand of you, and what you're willing to withstand in the meantime.

To aid this process, the chapter introduces a suite of reflective exercises—not as gimmicks, but as tools for aligning intent with action. These include prompts for identifying emotional blind spots, visualising future needs, and mapping out a system that can hold steady when the external world falters. The aim is not perfection. It is coherence. Investment must fit within the broader structure of one's financial life—not as an appendage, but as a layer that builds upon stability and prepares for contribution.

That structure is no accident. Previous chapters outlined wealth as a system: layered, interdependent, and alive to circumstance. Investment belongs as the second tier for a reason. It draws its strength from the stability of the emergency layer beneath it, but extends further—it imagines a future and then begins to shape it. A well-constructed investment plan resembles a designed landscape—perhaps a forest, with varying timelines for growth, different species of returns, and an ecosystem that changes over time. Some trees are for shelter. Some for fruit. Some for beauty. All matter.

Eventually, as this architecture matures, a more generative question arises: what now? What is this growth for? Without a meaningful destination, accumulation becomes inert. But growth with intent—with a view toward contribution, legacy, or creative reinvestment—becomes something far richer. It becomes a means by which investment transcends the personal and steps into the communal or generational. This is where finance begins to resemble philosophy.

So what does this chapter offer? Not a formula, but a reorientation. Not rules, but a set of invitations—to reflect, to design, to build with patience. Investing, rightly approached, is not a sideline activity or a competition for those with sharp elbows and sharper data. It is a long act of tending. If your wealth is to outlive the markets, it must be rooted in something deeper than yield curves or earnings forecasts. It must grow from who you are, what you value, and the kind of future you believe is worth investing in.

That is the soil from which enduring wealth grows. Not the speculation of the moment, but the clarity of intent. Not the drama of timing, but the quiet rhythm of time. And from that rhythm, something lasting can be built—something that doesn't just perform, but means something.

Investing as Identity, Not Just Activity

Ask someone to describe their investment approach, and they're likely to answer with portfolio allocations, fund choices, or risk tolerances. They might recite what percentage they keep in equities versus bonds, or explain their preference for index funds over active management. These answers, while valid, are insufficient. They reflect *what* someone does, not *who* they are. This subchapter begins with a simple but disruptive premise: investing is not just a technical task or a financial strategy—it is an identity-defining act. What we choose to invest in, how we behave in moments of uncertainty, and how we define success in financial terms ultimately reveals more about our beliefs and values than any balance sheet could.

This reframing matters. Too often, investing is reduced to a game of optimisation. We are told to "beat the market," "maximise returns," and "ride the trends." But those imperatives originate from a culture of external comparison, not inner clarity. The average investor, bombarded with noise and volatility, becomes reactive—fluctuating not only with markets but with moods. Investing then becomes a performance, staged for validation, driven by fear of missing out or anxiety over underperformance. It is precisely this detachment from self-authorship that leads to poor outcomes—not just financially, but psychologically. When we separate investing from identity, we invite misalignment, confusion, and self-sabotage.

Investing with identity, by contrast, demands introspection. It compels us to ask: *What matters most to me? What future am I trying to build? How does this financial decision reflect the person I am becoming?* These are not rhetorical questions. They are design constraints, and like all good constraints, they clarify. A person who sees wealth not as a scoreboard but as a tool for autonomy will invest differently than one who sees it as a measure of superiority. One might optimise for flexibility and low-maintenance vehicles; the other might chase high-yield opportunities at the expense of long-term calm. Neither is inherently right or wrong—but the consequences of that philosophical difference will compound, both financially and emotionally.

Consider the rise of environmental, social, and governance (ESG) investing. While this category has attracted both legitimate criticism and opportunistic marketing, its popularity signals something deeper: people want their money to express something. They no longer accept that profit must come at the expense of principle. Nor should they. Investing with identity means treating each allocation as a moral and strategic statement—not in a performative or puritanical sense, but in a self-consistent one. If your day-to-day choices reflect one set of values, and your portfolio another, you are—quite literally—financing your own dissonance.

This coherence between money and meaning also influences behaviour in volatile times. Research in behavioural finance has shown that value-aligned investors are less likely to panic sell during downturns. Their portfolios are not just composed of assets; they are composed of convictions. Because they understand *why* they hold what they hold, they are better able to withstand what Daniel Kahneman called the "noise" of short-term irrationality. They invest not to predict what markets will do, but to support what they themselves stand for. In a landscape of algorithmic trades and high-frequency speculation, this approach is not naïve—it is anchoring.

We see this dynamic most clearly during crises. During the 2008 financial crash, or the COVID-19-induced market plunge in 2020, millions of investors fled equities at the worst possible moment, locking in losses and forfeiting recoveries. But those who had a clear personal philosophy—whether that meant holding dividend-paying stocks to fund retirement, maintaining ESG commitments, or staying the course on a 30-year plan—exhibited greater resilience. Identity, in this case, acted as ballast. It transformed conviction from an abstract virtue into a practical advantage.

The implications extend beyond traditional asset classes. Think of entrepreneurship as an investment. Or higher education. Or taking a sabbatical to reorient your life. Each of these decisions is a form of capital allocation, one that reflects not just market logic but personal vision. The question is no longer "what's the return?" but "what return matters *to me*?" When investing is seen through this broader lens, a richer calculus emerges—one that factors in time, energy, values, relationships, and potential future states. It's not just about buying low and selling high; it's about building coherence between your money and your life.

This reframing also reshapes the meaning of risk. In traditional finance, risk is volatility—the standard deviation of returns. But in identity-based investing, risk is misalignment. The costliest mistake is not a temporary market loss, but a life misinvested: years spent climbing a ladder leaning against the wrong wall. An identity-driven investor, therefore, measures risk in terms of opportunity cost against one's purpose. They understand that failing to invest in areas that matter deeply—to them, not to pundits—is a form of long-term impoverishment.

To embody this shift, readers must abandon the fantasy of objectivity. There is no such thing as a purely rational investor, nor should there be. Emotions, values, and intuitions are not distractions from financial intelligence—they are its foundation. What is needed is not the suppression of subjectivity but the integration of it. This means developing an investment thesis that is not only financially sound but personally meaningful. That thesis must be revisited regularly, not just in times of crisis, but as a discipline of self-awareness. Investment strategy, then, becomes a reflection of identity over time, not a frozen snapshot.

One practical exercise introduced later in this chapter involves creating a "financial belief map"—a tool for articulating how you think about growth, security, ownership, and obligation. By surfacing these often-unspoken assumptions, you can begin to notice patterns, gaps, and contradictions. Do you say you value long-term thinking but obsess over short-term market moves? Do you claim to prioritise security but keep taking uncalculated risks? These misalignments, if left unexamined, are not just intellectually dishonest—they are financially dangerous. Clarifying your beliefs allows your investment behaviour to emerge from your values, rather than from ambient anxiety or external comparison.

Identity-based investing is also inherently intergenerational. When we think beyond our own lifespans, we are forced to clarify what kind of legacy we want to leave—not just in assets, but in examples. How we talk about money with our children, how we model patience, integrity, and stewardship—these are investments, too. The returns may not be liquid, but they are enduring. And perhaps more importantly, they are contagious. Values, once embodied and shared, tend to replicate.

Ultimately, reframing investing as identity is not about moralising your portfolio or adding performative virtue to your financial decisions. It is about integrating your strategy with your sense of self. Because if money is a proxy for energy and attention—and it is—then investing is nothing less than the art of allocating your future. The question, then, is not *what should I buy?* but *who am I becoming through what I hold?*

That question doesn't just change how you invest. It changes how you live.

Time, Not Timing

If financial markets are theatres of risk, then market timing is the illusionist act that continues to seduce both novice and seasoned investors. The appeal is instinctive: the idea that, with the right data, intuition, or algorithm, one might enter the market at its lowest and exit at its highest. The mathematics of this fantasy are tantalising. A few timely trades, the story goes, could eclipse years of disciplined investing. And yet, this mindset is both statistically flawed and psychologically corrosive. The data, spanning decades and across geographies, makes one point unmistakably clear: *time in the market* consistently outperforms *timing the market.* The distinction is not semantic—it is foundational.

To understand why timing fails, we must begin with a behavioural truth. Humans are pattern-seeking creatures operating in systems driven by randomness. This mismatch creates fertile ground for cognitive errors. One of the most pervasive is hindsight bias—the belief, after the fact, that past events were more predictable than they actually were. In investing, hindsight masquerades as foresight. The mind edits its own memory to confirm the illusion of skill, reinforcing the temptation to time the next move. However, historical market data repeatedly shows that missing just a few of the market's best days can irreversibly damage long-term returns.

A landmark study by J.P. Morgan Asset Management illustrates this vividly. Between 2003 and 2022, an investor who remained fully invested in the S&P 500 would have earned an annualised return of roughly 9.8%. But missing the market's ten best days—just ten days over twenty years—would slash that return to 5.6%. Miss the best twenty days and the return drops to 2.6%. The pattern is unambiguous: the cost of missing key upswings vastly outweighs the benefit of avoiding downturns. And when do those best days usually occur? Often within weeks of the worst ones—when fear is highest, liquidity is lowest, and timing feels least attractive.

This is not merely a matter of statistical quirk but of behavioural design. Market recoveries are not smooth. They are jagged, compressed, and emotionally inaccessible to the average investor. As Daniel Kahneman and Amos Tversky's prospect theory explains, the pain of losses weighs more heavily than the pleasure of gains. This asymmetry leads investors to sell at the bottom and re-enter cautiously, if at all, ensuring they miss the very gains they seek. Timing, then, is not only hard—it is *anti-instinctual.* It demands perfect execution of two decisions: when to exit and when to re-enter. Both require a precision that even professional fund managers routinely fail to achieve.

The alternative is deceptively simple: consistent, long-term participation. Time in the market is not passive; it is a form of active patience. It reflects a commitment to process over prediction, discipline over drama. And crucially, it is the only reliable way to harness the exponential power of compounding. Albert Einstein reputedly called compounding the eighth wonder of the world—not because it was complex, but because it rewarded consistency in a world obsessed with intensity.

Consider this example. Investor A begins contributing £500 per month at age 25 and stops at 35, letting the money compound untouched. Investor B waits until age 35 to start, contributing the same £500 monthly until age 65. Despite contributing more than three times as much, Investor B often ends up with less—because they gave up the early, most powerful years of compounding. Time, not timing, is the multiplier. And this remains true across market regimes: booms, busts, inflationary shocks, and geopolitical turbulence.

Yet acknowledging this is not enough. Understanding the mathematics of compounding is different from internalising it. The real challenge lies in emotional resilience. Staying invested through downturns demands a psychological buffer that most people have not built. Market corrections are not abstract; they trigger stress, self-doubt, and social comparison. The temptation to act—any action—intensifies. This is where behavioural finance merges with emotional intelligence. The most successful long-term investors are not those with the highest IQs or the fastest trading platforms; they are those who can sit still while others panic. Patience, in this context, is not inertia—it is mastery.

This calls for systems, not just slogans. One such system is automated, rules-based investing. By setting predetermined investment schedules—monthly contributions into diversified portfolios—investors remove timing from the equation. They dollar-cost average across market cycles, buying more when prices are low and less when prices are high. This not only smooths volatility but also inoculates against impulsive decisions. Behavioural economists refer to this as a "commitment device"—a tool to protect long-term goals from short-term emotions.

Still, automation alone is not sufficient. Investors must also construct narratives that justify consistency. This is where personal finance intersects with identity, as explored in the preceding subchapter. When investing is tied to purpose—whether that's financial independence, legacy-building, or funding meaningful work—staying the course becomes an act of alignment, not discipline. One invests not because the market will rise tomorrow, but because the alternative is fragmentation: a life of reaction rather than design.

Even professional investors struggle with timing. A 2016 study by Morningstar found that the average investor's return in mutual funds was consistently lower than the funds' published returns—a gap driven largely by mistimed buying and selling. This "behaviour gap," as advisor Carl Richards famously termed it, is not a niche problem. It is the central cost of the timing illusion. And it reflects a deeper truth: markets may be volatile, but humans are even more so. The only antidote is to build a process that transcends the human tendency to confuse motion with progress.

From a philosophical standpoint, the obsession with timing reflects an underlying discomfort with uncertainty. We crave control. We believe that with enough data or insight, we might outmanoeuvre randomness. But markets, like life, are not predictable. They are probabilistic. Embracing time over timing is a way of making peace with this truth. It is an act of intellectual humility—and in many ways, of maturity. It says: I cannot know what the market will do next. But I do know what I value. I know how I want to live. And I trust that, over time, aligned action compounds.

This shift also liberates investors from the tyranny of financial media. The constant stream of predictions, alerts, and expert forecasts is designed not to inform, but to stimulate. Its business model is attention, not insight. Timing the market keeps you hooked. Trusting time frees you to focus on what matters more: your habits, your decisions, your goals. In the end, investing is not about being right more often—it is about being aligned more often, and letting time do the heavy lifting.

That lifting is powerful, but it is also patient. As Charlie Munger once remarked, "The big money is not in the buying and selling—but in the waiting." Time doesn't just reward capital. It refines character. It filters noise. And it reveals whether we are building our lives around prediction, or around principle. Investors who understand this don't just outperform. They outlast.

"The Philosophy of Enough":

One of the most radical questions a modern investor can ask is also one of the simplest: *What is enough?* Not as a rhetorical musing or an economic abstraction, but as a deliberate, numerate, value-based decision. The very act of posing the question disturbs a culture built around open-ended accumulation. In a system where more is reflexively equated with better—more income, more returns, more assets—the idea of drawing a line and stepping back demands both courage and clarity. Yet without that boundary, even the most successful investment strategy can become a treadmill—perpetual motion without psychological arrival.

The philosophy of enough does not call for asceticism. It does not celebrate poverty or deny ambition. Rather, it interrogates the premise that financial success is synonymous with *limitless* expansion. It proposes that optimal investing is not merely technical; it is existential. To invest without a conception of enough is to mistake growth for fulfilment. To define enough is to reconnect investing with purpose—aligning risk, return, and behaviour around a destination, rather than a race.

This idea has deep roots in philosophical and economic history. The Stoics, from Epictetus to Seneca, cautioned that without internal limits, external gains would never suffice. More recently, thinkers like John Stuart Mill and E.F. Schumacher challenged the assumption that human welfare is a function of continuous economic growth. Schumacher's *Small is Beautiful* explicitly argued that "the aim ought to be to obtain the maximum of well-being with the minimum of consumption." This was not a call to austerity but a defence of proportionality—a plea to elevate sufficiency over accumulation for its own sake.

Psychologically, the need for enough is supported by the diminishing marginal utility of wealth. Behavioural economists such as Daniel Kahneman and Angus Deaton have shown that above a certain income threshold (often cited around $75,000 to $100,000 in Western contexts), additional money ceases to increase day-to-day emotional well-being. Beyond that, wealth may still increase life evaluation—how satisfied one feels when reflecting on life as a whole—but it does not linearly improve emotional experience. More money may bring options, but it does not necessarily bring peace.

And yet, in financial culture, the conversation rarely stops to ask: *For what?* The dominant narratives urge savers to become investors, investors to become entrepreneurs, and entrepreneurs to become owners of multiple assets and scalable systems. In this worldview, the horizon constantly shifts forward. Retirement projections inflate. Passive income becomes an end unto itself. The language of freedom is used to disguise obsession. The danger is not merely overwork, but a creeping detachment from values—the slow erosion of contentment by the logic of escalation.

This is why defining enough must begin with introspection, not benchmarks. It is not merely a spreadsheet calculation—though numbers are essential—but a reflection of what matters. For some, enough might mean being able to take a sabbatical every five years to recalibrate. For others, it could mean providing full education for their children, owning a modest home outright, or having the freedom to walk away from toxic work. The financial contentment of a single parent with low volatility preferences will look radically different from that of a 25-year-old digital nomad with a high risk appetite. *Enough is not a number—it is a narrative.*

Here, minimalism enters the conversation—not as an aesthetic trend, but as a philosophical tool. The minimalist investor asks: What am I optimising for? What costs—emotional, relational, ethical—am I incurring in pursuit of marginal financial gains? Rather than simply seeking maximum returns, the minimalist approach privileges clarity, intentionality, and resilience. It rejects the false binary between growth and stagnation. By focusing on *enough*, minimalism offers a third path: sustainable prosperity that doesn't compromise one's health, relationships, or ethics in the process.

Importantly, defining enough protects against one of the most dangerous financial behaviours: *moving the goalposts*. Many investors find themselves wealthier today than they were a decade ago, and yet no closer to satisfaction. Why? Because their expectations inflated in parallel. What was once aspirational becomes baseline. This phenomenon, known as the "hedonic treadmill," erodes contentment as quickly as wealth is built. Without a firm sense of enough, no achievement satisfies. Every milestone becomes prelude to another.

To counter this drift, practical strategies must complement philosophical insight. One powerful technique is reverse financial planning: starting not with how much one can earn, but with what one wishes to experience, give, and preserve. From there, one works backward to calculate the true capital required. Another approach is the "stoplight" method of portfolio design: assigning clear boundaries between needs (green), wants (yellow), and luxuries (red). Investments are then aligned accordingly—ensuring the basics are secure before allocating risk toward discretionary ambitions.

This mindset also shifts how risk is perceived. For someone without a defined threshold of enough, risk is often tolerated in pursuit of more. But for someone with clear boundaries, risk becomes a variable to *manage*, not *maximise*. The question becomes: *What is the minimum risk required to meet my values-aligned goals?* This reframing leads to more conservative, intentional portfolios—not out of fear, but because they are fit for purpose. Optimisation yields to sufficiency. Scarcity anxiety gives way to strategic contentment.

There is also an intergenerational dimension to enough. Parents who fail to articulate or model it often pass down not wealth, but worry—a belief that safety lies in perpetual striving. Children inherit a scarcity mindset even amid abundance. Conversely, those who live out enough model a more secure kind of prosperity—one that teaches self-trust, stewardship, and gratitude. Defining enough, then, is not only a personal act. It is pedagogical. It shapes the stories our families and communities inherit.

None of this is static. Enough is not a fixed point. It evolves with life stage, family structure, health status, and global conditions. But this dynamism is not a flaw—it is a feature. Just as portfolios must be rebalanced, so too must definitions of sufficiency. What matters is not the precision of the target but the *discipline of asking the question*—and the courage to adjust when the answer changes. Those who revisit their vision of enough every few years tend to invest more intentionally, spend more wisely, and worry less overall. They do not chase markets. They calibrate lives.

In the end, the philosophy of enough is not about limitation. It is about liberation. It is the recognition that the goal of investing is not to outperform others, but to *fund a life well-lived.* It shifts the locus of success from external comparisons to internal coherence. It allows the investor to say, with clarity and without apology: *I have enough, I do enough, I am enough.* This is not the end of ambition. It is its ethical refinement. And it is perhaps the most important decision any investor can make.

"Diversification as a Life Practice":

In investment circles, the principle of diversification is a given. No credible advisor would endorse placing one's entire capital in a single stock, sector, or geography. The logic is mathematically sound: spreading risk reduces exposure to volatility and cushions the impact of underperformance in any one area. But beyond spreadsheets and asset classes, diversification holds far broader implications—ones that stretch into how we learn, work, relate, and live. Financial diversification is not just a technique; it is a worldview. It mirrors, and can inform, a philosophy of life stability through plurality.

The tragedy of specialisation, particularly in high-performance environments, is that it often breeds fragility. A surgeon with no hobbies. A tech founder whose identity is bound entirely to a venture's valuation. A trader whose confidence is shackled to market performance. In each case, life is optimised for efficiency at the cost of resilience. When one pillar falters, the entire structure strains. This mirrors an undiversified portfolio—high yield in good times, catastrophic downside when tides turn. The lesson: *concentration may build faster, but diversification survives longer.*

Consider the behavioural finance insight that investors who anchor their wealth to single stocks—often their employer's shares—demonstrate higher stress and lower satisfaction than those with diversified holdings, even when the concentrated portfolio outperforms in the short term. The discomfort lies not only in volatility, but in the psychological overexposure: one's fate becomes singular. The same can be said of relationships. A person who relies solely on a romantic partner for emotional support is not unlike an investor who bets everything on a single asset. When that relationship wobbles, so too does their emotional stability. Diversification, here, is not dilution; it's design.

The modern individual navigates multiple portfolios, even if they don't realise it. There is the financial portfolio, yes—but also the relational, intellectual, creative, and spiritual portfolios. All demand deposits and generate returns. Diversifying them doesn't mean scattering one's focus. It means ensuring that life's meaning and momentum are not overly reliant on any one domain. A well-diversified life, like a portfolio, blends risk profiles: stable sources of identity (family, core values), growth assets (career, enterprise), speculative ventures (artistic projects, new geographies), and passive yields (friendships, traditions). The composition will differ by temperament, age, and context—but the logic holds.

Educational researcher and author David Epstein, in his book *Range*, challenged the popular belief that deep specialisation is the surest path to success. His argument, backed by cross-disciplinary studies, suggests that generalists—those who cultivate breadth—are often more adaptable, creative, and fulfilled. This has striking parallels with investing. A generalist investor, diversified across asset classes, themes, and time horizons, may not match the extreme highs of niche bets—but they are vastly better positioned for long-term sustainability. Similarly, individuals who cultivate curiosity across fields are more resilient to disruption and burnout.

Diversification also speaks to cognitive humility. It accepts that we don't know the future. We cannot predict which market will boom, which job will become obsolete, which relationship will deepen or decline. To bet singularly is, in effect, to claim omniscience.

Diversification is an ethical posture as much as a strategic one: it acknowledges uncertainty without paralysis. This humility is what underpins the most effective asset allocation models—and it is equally vital in life design.

Take career trajectories. A narrowly defined professional identity—"I'm a lawyer" or "I'm a consultant"—may serve for a time, but offers little flexibility when external shifts occur. By contrast, those who see themselves as problem-solvers, communicators, or systems thinkers retain optionality. Just as investors diversify across industries to hedge sector-specific shocks, professionals who cultivate diverse competencies maintain adaptability across domains. An engineer who writes, a teacher who codes, a marketer who understands behavioural psychology—these are diversified human portfolios. They weather storms better not by luck, but by preparation.

In personal development, diversification shows up in how we structure learning. Single-source thinking—anchoring to one ideology, one school of thought, one discipline—may feel efficient, but often produces brittleness. Intellectual diversity, by contrast, makes ideas more robust. The polymathic tradition, from Leonardo da Vinci to Benjamin Franklin, was rooted in this principle: cross-pollination fertilises insight. In investing terms, this is akin to the "uncorrelated assets" principle. Two equally risky assets that move independently provide more stability together than two similar ones. The same is true of beliefs and skills.

And yet, diversification is not without tension. Critics argue that diversification can dilute excellence or lead to scattered focus. But this misunderstands its purpose. True diversification is not the pursuit of everything—it's the cultivation of *complementarity*. It's about curating, not hoarding. The key lies in synergy: identifying elements of life or investment that support each other without overlapping unnecessarily. In portfolio construction, this might mean balancing equities with bonds, or domestic with international exposure. In life, it might mean combining high-stakes ambition with low-stakes creative hobbies; demanding intellectual pursuits with restorative social rituals.

Interestingly, empirical data suggests that investors who diversify not just by asset type but by *purpose* often display greater long-term satisfaction. That is, those who allocate some capital toward causes they care about, or vehicles that align with their values, report higher financial contentment—even when returns are modest. The same holds true for time allocation. People who diversify their calendar to include service, solitude, challenge, and connection tend to report higher well-being than those who maximise only one domain. This reveals that *balance is not a constraint—it is a capability*.

Diversification also acts as a hedge against identity foreclosure. When one defines themselves too narrowly—by title, role, or financial status—they risk existential whiplash when circumstances change. Retirement, job loss, divorce, illness—these are not only logistical disruptions but identity ruptures. Diversified identities absorb shocks better. A retiree who is also a mentor, reader, community member, and learner will face the loss of work with less disorientation than one whose entire sense of self was tied to a job title. In this sense, diversification is not only smart planning; it is psychological self-preservation.

Even social capital benefits from this principle. In network theory, diverse connections—not merely close ties—are the greatest source of opportunity. Sociologist Mark Granovetter's "strength of weak ties" theory shows that acquaintances, not close friends, are more likely to provide novel information or career leads. This suggests that social diversification—engaging with people across professions, ideologies, and backgrounds—yields higher life returns than staying within familiar tribes. The investor who seeks uncorrelated returns should also seek uncorrelated conversations.

Ultimately, the discipline of diversification trains us to think in systems. It prompts us to ask: What am I exposed to? Where am I overconcentrated? What shocks can I absorb? These questions, while often applied to portfolios, are equally applicable to parenting, citizenship, and selfhood. A diversified life, like a resilient investment strategy, is not built in haste. It requires intention, review, and periodic rebalancing. But the outcome is profoundly worthwhile: a self that is not only successful but sustainable—capable of adapting without fracturing, of thriving without fixating.

To live and invest well, then, is to diversify not by default, but by design. It is to assemble a life composed not of fragile bets but of mutually reinforcing elements. The goal is not to do everything. It is to ensure that no single failure defines you—and no single success contains you. This is not merely an investment philosophy. It is a blueprint for modern existence.

Resilience Over Returns:

It's not difficult to find someone boasting about a stellar year in the markets. Double-digit returns, winning stock picks, a savvy exit just before a downturn—these stories populate financial media and cocktail conversations with equal frequency. But far less celebrated, though infinitely more consequential, is the investor who endured—who watched their portfolio fall 35% and didn't flinch, didn't sell, didn't abandon their plan. *Resilience rarely makes headlines, yet it is the foundation of enduring wealth.*

Financial resilience is not simply about staying solvent through volatility. It's about maintaining clarity, conviction, and composure when the world around you panics. That resilience is not innate—it is learned, reinforced, and deliberately cultivated. And it proves far more predictive of financial success than any attempt to chase alpha, time markets, or game complex models.

At its core, the obsession with maximising returns often conceals a deeper fear: that we are behind. That we must catch up. That we must outperform, or we are somehow failing. This psychology, when left unexamined, becomes a trap. Investors stretch for yield, over-leverage, or abandon principles under pressure. They confuse complexity with competence and risk-taking with courage. And when markets inevitably punish hubris, they retreat in shame rather than reflection. *Resilience demands a different mindset altogether—one rooted in process over performance, principles over prediction.*

Behavioural finance offers compelling evidence that emotional self-regulation, more than knowledge or technical skill, is the defining trait of long-term investors. The Dalbar studies, which track investor behaviour over time, consistently show that the average investor underperforms the funds they invest in—not because the funds are flawed, but because they enter and exit at the wrong times, driven by emotion rather than logic. Fear and greed erode returns more efficiently than management fees ever could.

This reality reframes the question: What should we optimise for—returns or behaviour? The answer becomes clearer when we examine the role of downturns. Markets do not grow in straight lines. They breathe—expanding and contracting, cycling through exuberance and despair. During these contractions, two groups emerge: those who recalibrate and those who recoil. The first group—resilient investors—see corrections not as threats to be avoided, but as expected features of the terrain. They've rehearsed this scenario emotionally and structurally. Their portfolios are diversified. Their cash reserves are intact. More importantly, their *narrative* is intact. They know who they are and why they invest.

Consider the difference in outcomes during the 2008 financial crisis. While many panicked and sold into historic lows, a smaller subset—those who had cultivated behavioural resilience—rebalanced, reinvested, and emerged stronger. The same was true in 2020. The pandemic-triggered sell-off saw global equities plunge more than 30% in a matter of weeks. But the investors who had the psychological bandwidth to hold their nerve, or even to lean in, participated in one of the fastest recoveries in market history. *Resilience is not about optimism. It's about discipline under duress.*

That discipline can be cultivated through what psychologists call "emotional inoculation." Just as vaccines train the immune system by introducing a small, manageable challenge, investors can train themselves to remain steady through controlled exposure to volatility—via simulations, journaling, or retrospective analysis of past crises. Reflecting on prior decisions, and how they were shaped by emotion or bias, is not indulgent—it's strategic. Memory, when examined critically, becomes a tutor. Which brings us to a practical tool: the financial resilience journal.

At the heart of this practice is self-inquiry. The goal is not simply to recall what happened, but to understand *how you responded*—and why. Below are several prompts that seasoned investors have used to build resilience through reflection:

What was the last time I felt real financial anxiety? What triggered it—was it external (market news, job loss) or internal (self-doubt, status comparison)?

During that period, what actions did I take? Did I sell, pause, distract myself, overconsume news?

What narrative was I telling myself at the time? Was it grounded, exaggerated, inherited?

Looking back, were those actions aligned with my long-term strategy—or were they reactive?

What would I do differently next time, not in theory, but in practice? What systems can I set up now to reduce future reactivity?

These reflections are not about perfecting past decisions—they are about strengthening future ones. Resilient investors do not avoid fear. They build scaffolding around it. They name it, track it, and work with it, rather than letting it dictate terms.

Resilience also calls into question the financial media's obsession with performance benchmarks. The S&P 500. The FTSE 100. Bitcoin. Private equity. Every quarter, a new yardstick emerges, and with it, the subtle implication that one is either winning or losing. But personal investing is not a leaderboard—it is a reflection of context, constraint, and character. *Resilient investors measure success not by outpacing others, but by staying aligned with their values under pressure.*

To make this personal: imagine two investors. One earns 6% annually, year after year, through a disciplined, boring, diversified portfolio. The other oscillates wildly—up 20%, down 30%, chasing trends and reacting to headlines. Ten years later, the first investor not only has more money, but far less stress. They've slept better, made fewer mistakes, and kept compounding intact. Resilience, it turns out, is the true generator of returns.

And yet, even the most seasoned investor is susceptible to internal saboteurs—comparison, impatience, regret. Here, philosophy becomes an ally. Stoic thinkers like Seneca and Epictetus remind us that the only true control we have is over our response. External shocks will come. The market will rise and fall. But the quality of our internal landscape—our ability to remain principled amidst noise—determines whether we act with wisdom or with impulse.

That insight reorients financial education itself. Too often, it is framed as the study of tools: stocks, funds, tax shelters. But a more mature education includes the study of temperament. Not just how to build a portfolio—but how to *be with it* during extremes. Not just what to do—but how to wait. The truly sophisticated investor is not the one who maximises returns. It is the one who can delay gratification, hold tension, and stay faithful to long arcs in a short-term world.

Of course, resilience is not an excuse for passivity. It is not stoicism in the face of obvious error. But it is the ability to discern between noise and signal, between discomfort and danger. Most of what feels urgent in markets is not important. And most of what is important requires patience. That paradox sits at the heart of investing. *To build wealth, one must learn to be bored by drama and fascinated by endurance.*

Resilience is also relational. Those who surround themselves with equally steady minds—partners, advisers, communities—are more likely to stay the course. Accountability matters. So does environment. A person who checks their portfolio five times a day, reads panic headlines, and consumes financial Twitter like a ticker tape will inevitably feel more volatility—not just externally, but emotionally. Resilience, then, is partially about curation: of information, relationships, and routines.

In practical terms, investors would do well to reallocate not just capital, but attention. Rather than spend hours backtesting strategies, spend time reviewing your psychological blind spots. Rather than obsess over returns, focus on systems that reduce overreaction. Build buffers, both financial and emotional. Set boundaries around screen time and market watching. And, above all, build a narrative that frames investing as a lifelong practice—not a series of winning trades.

When that mindset takes root, something shifts. The markets stop feeling like a test of intelligence or fortune. They become a mirror—revealing one's ability to stay present, humble, and steady in the face of uncertainty. That, ultimately, is the real return: *a self that can withstand volatility without losing vision.*

Chapter 4
The Income Layer – Your Daily Engine:

Income is often treated as the unshakeable foundation of personal finance—a fixed point from which every other decision unfurls. But that perception, tidy though it may seem, conceals a deeper reality: income is no static given. It's not simply a salary handed down like a law of nature. It is, rather, the product of design—shaped by deliberate choices, underpinned by convictions, and bounded or liberated by the stories we tell ourselves about value, effort, and exchange. In this light, income is authored more than earned. And like any worthy architecture, it ought to reflect not just what we do, but the direction in which we're evolving.

Modern economies tend to cast income as something extracted from work—drawn out like water from a dwindling well, with urgency and a hint of competition. This zero-sum script, baked into the psyche of hustle culture, suggests that if you don't move fast enough, someone else will get to the prize first. But such a view, rooted in scarcity, is not only psychologically exhausting; it's also increasingly outdated. When income is understood not as a slice of a finite pie but as the fruit of value creation, the conversation shifts. It becomes less about what one can take, more about what one can generate, refine, and expand through intentional, skillful design.

This shift—from extraction to creation—is not simply academic. It marks the divergence between exhaustion and sustainability. Extraction-based income often leans on leverage: position, asymmetrical knowledge, or the raw trade of time for money. It drains individuals while exposing them to volatility. Creation-driven income, by contrast, emerges from trust, resonance, and competency. It raises different questions: Where do my strengths solve meaningful problems? What value do I reliably produce? In what contexts does my contribution compound? These aren't rhetorical—they are diagnostic. And in a world that privileges adaptability over brute repetition, they are essential.

To begin constructing an income model fit for this era, one must unlearn the illusion of linearity—the notion that more hours must equal more income. It's a seductive fallacy, especially in a culture that equates effort with virtue. But doing more isn't the same as designing better. In reality, scattering oneself across too many low-leverage tasks creates fragility, not abundance. It exhausts focus, squanders strategic capacity, and ultimately limits growth. Multiplying income does not require multiplying stress. And certainly not hours.

This chapter unpacks income not as a single pipeline but as a layered, intentionally structured system. A system that blends active, semi-passive, and strategically chosen income flows into something resilient and adaptive. Consider a full-time professional who leads workshops—not for side income per se, but to hone public speaking, which amplifies their influence at work. Or a designer licensing assets—not as a hustle, but as market research for future ventures. These are not random side gigs. They're interconnected elements of a cohesive income strategy. It's synergy by design, not scattershot accumulation.

To construct such a system, one must treat skills as capital—investable, expandable, and worthy of thoughtful stewardship. It's not about amassing certificates or chasing every trend. It's about locating core competencies, identifying adjacent possibilities, and positioning those in markets where demand is credible and persistent. A data analyst who can tell stories visually becomes indispensable in strategy roles. A teacher with a flair for facilitation unlocks doors to consulting, public programming, or digital education. These aren't distractions from the "main job." They are levers—each one designed to multiply impact without fracturing identity.

There is, too, a particular quality that distinguishes enduring income systems: antifragility. The concept, coined by Nassim Nicholas Taleb, refers to things that grow stronger through stress. Translated to income, it suggests structures that not only withstand volatility but thrive because of it. Think royalties, licensing, subscription-based models, digital platforms. These require upfront investment—in content, reputation, or intellectual property—but they scale without a matching increase in effort. Once built, they're remarkably hard to disrupt. They are not get-rich schemes; they are stay-resilient frameworks.

This chapter also presses readers to reconsider their relationship with work itself. For many, work is either a burden—something endured to survive—or a badge, worn for status. But both views flatten what income, at its best, can symbolise. Ideally, income reflects alignment. It signals that what you offer is meaningful enough to be rewarded. To reach that point, however, one must evolve beyond the survival mindset. The operative question shifts from "What job can I find?" to "Where do I generate unique value—and how can that be sustainably recognised?"

That evolution is not an instant shift, but a process—a winding one, often non-linear. Economically, it involves a movement from wage-based markets to value-based networks. Philosophically, it's the difference between alienated labour and engaged contribution. And practically, it becomes the foundation of a daily rhythm that doesn't just cover expenses, but supports progress.

Throughout this chapter, you'll encounter a carefully selected mix of frameworks, prompts, and real-world examples. You'll learn to recognise fragile income patterns—those overly reliant on single points of failure—and replace them with models that are structurally sound. You'll analyse your skills as if reviewing a portfolio: not just in terms of breadth, but in terms of strategic fit and compounding potential. You'll confront the subtle emotional narratives—around self-worth, identity, status—that often operate beneath the surface of financial decisions. Most importantly, you'll come away with a clearer sense of how income can become elegant, scalable, and aligned with your values.

Ultimately, the real measure of income is not what lands in your account each month. It's whether that income reflects your purpose, respects your time, and supports your long-term direction. When those conditions are met, earning ceases to be an endless loop—it becomes a platform. Not just a response to necessity, but a source of agency, alignment, and optionality.

This isn't a rejection of employment or a romantic plea for everyone to become an entrepreneur. It is, rather, a redefinition of income's role in an intentional life. When we stop chasing income and begin constructing it—with rigour, clarity, and integrity—we reclaim more than earnings. We reclaim the narrative. The shift is not about squeezing out more revenue. It is about earning with design, with meaning, and with durability. And in a world where noise is abundant but clarity is rare, that shift may prove to be the most valuable form of wealth.

Earning vs. Extracting:

Ask someone how they earn their living, and they'll likely respond with a job title or a profession. Dig deeper—*how* do you earn?—and the answers begin to thin. The language we use around income is revealing. We "make money", we "bring home the bacon", we "get paid". These metaphors suggest acquisition, not contribution. But what if income isn't something we *get*, *take*, or *extract*—but something we *generate* through the continual creation of value?

This shift is more than linguistic. It's philosophical, economic, and deeply ethical. It challenges a dominant but flawed view of income as a transactional entitlement. In that view, you show up, you work, and you're compensated—regardless of impact, alignment, or usefulness. But in today's knowledge-based, increasingly automated economy, this framework is fast eroding. *The market no longer pays for effort; it pays for usefulness, relevance, and resonance.* It rewards value creation—not extraction.

Extraction, in economic terms, refers to deriving gain from a system without necessarily contributing to its productive capacity. Classic rent-seeking behaviour is a textbook example: charging fees or accruing income through ownership, gatekeeping, or friction without enhancing the underlying good or service. In the worst-case scenarios, extraction manifests as exploitative labour practices, monopolistic pricing, or short-term arbitrage strategies that erode trust and long-term sustainability.

Contrast this with the principle of *value creation.* Here, income is a by-product of improvement—of making something better, clearer, faster, more humane, more accessible. The best creators, professionals, and entrepreneurs earn not because they demand compensation, but because their output improves life for someone else. A designer creates clarity. A doctor restores function. A software engineer builds tools that multiply effectiveness. *Earning, in this frame, is ethical leverage—it flows from making others better off.*

This distinction is not new. Classical economics and modern business ethics have long wrestled with the tension between productive and extractive roles. Adam Smith, in *The Wealth of Nations*, celebrated the "invisible hand" only in the context of mutually beneficial exchange—not blind accumulation. More recently, economist Mariana Mazzucato has critiqued the way modern financial systems often conflate value *extraction* with value *creation*, especially in financial engineering, tech platform monopolies, and speculative markets. The result is distortion: those doing the most useful work are not always those rewarded most highly.

But the implications run deeper than economics. Psychologically, the difference between earning and extracting shapes how we see ourselves. When we believe we are *generating* income through meaningful contribution, the experience is often one of alignment, dignity, and flow. When we believe we are merely extracting income from a reluctant system, the result is alienation, entitlement, or anxiety—especially in downturns. *Your philosophy of earning becomes your experience of work.*

This is particularly visible in the growing divide between jobs that are merely procedural and those that are generative. The procedural job follows rules, ticks boxes, and processes tasks. Its output can be tracked, timed, and eventually replicated by a machine. It is, by nature, extractable. The generative role, by contrast, is context-aware, creative, and adaptive. It sees opportunities, not instructions.

It doesn't ask, "What do I do?" but "What needs doing?" That posture is un-automatable—and therefore valuable.

The modern income earner must increasingly think like a designer. What is the system in which I operate? Who benefits from my decisions? Where is the friction that I can remove, the clarity I can provide, the transformation I can enable? Income becomes not a fixed wage, but a moving signal—a form of feedback from the market indicating where your effort lands. *And the better you understand the shape of that impact, the more intelligently you can position yourself for future earning.*

This does not mean that all extraction is unethical or that all earning must be noble. Ownership, licensing, and investment can be forms of legitimate value creation when they fuel innovation, fund risk, or enable scale. But the key distinction lies in *whether your income reflects a net contribution to the ecosystem—or merely control over it.* An author who writes a book that changes minds and sells a million copies earns by contribution. A landlord who raises rent without improving housing quality earns by control. The system will reward both—but only one outcome strengthens the broader social fabric.

To explore this idea personally, consider a simple thought experiment: If your income were to *disappear tomorrow*, what would someone miss? Whose life is better because you show up, consistently, with your skills, your insight, your lens? If the answer is unclear, it may be a signal to re-anchor your income in contribution. *Resilience flows not from having a job, but from being useful in changing contexts.*

The economic landscape is tilting toward this mindset. The fastest-growing career paths—product strategy, UX research, data science, coaching, content design—share a common theme: *translation of complexity into utility.* These roles don't extract—they distil. They take ambiguity and return value. They require empathy, pattern recognition, and conceptual agility. And they reward those who can earn *by improving outcomes for others, not by inserting themselves as middlemen.*

On a societal level, this reframing also challenges our attitudes toward compensation. When we equate high income with high value, we obscure the difference between impact and advantage. A hedge fund manager might earn hundreds of times more than a teacher, but the ethical question is not *what the market will bear*, but *what contribution is being made?* Capitalism, untethered from ethics, creates these distortions. But individual earners can choose to re-align by anchoring their efforts in *usefulness*, not just visibility or prestige.

Practically, this means auditing our income sources for coherence. Are we being paid because we truly improve a process, experience, or result? Or are we positioned advantageously in a flawed system? Are we extracting compliance from others, or facilitating meaningful change? These are not soft philosophical musings—they are sharp strategic questions. *The future of income will be defined not just by intelligence or ambition, but by ethical architecture.*

One of the clearest ways to enact this philosophy is to define your own "value loop": what you care about, what you're good at, and who benefits when the two meet. In this loop, you continually learn, refine, and deliver value—not for applause, but for evolution. It makes you magnetic to collaborators and trustworthy to clients. It makes earning feel not like a struggle, but like alignment.

From this place, income becomes a renewable signal—a reflection of where your efforts resonate. It ceases to be a grind and becomes a *conversation with the world.* One in which the question is no longer "How much can I make?" but "Where can I serve best, and be rewarded justly for it?"

Ultimately, earning is not a transaction. It is a mirror. It reflects how we think about value, worth, agency, and contribution. To earn with integrity is not to hustle harder—it is to generate smarter. And in a world saturated with noise, the clearest value wins.

Multiplying, Not Splitting Attention:

The allure of the side hustle is everywhere—platforms praise it, influencers flaunt it, and cultural narratives increasingly romanticise the image of the tireless multi-tasker building five streams of income before breakfast. But behind the glamour lies a subtle erosion of cognitive clarity. Most side gigs, contrary to their promotional slogans, don't multiply income—they fracture attention. They don't amplify energy—they disperse it. And in doing so, they risk producing not wealth, but burnout. *Multiplying income through synergy is not the same as accumulating gigs through stress.*

To understand the distinction, we must revisit a first principle of economics: opportunity cost. Time, energy, and focus are not infinite. Every hour spent on one activity is an hour not spent sharpening another. If the new task fails to build upon existing skill, reputation, or infrastructure, it behaves more like a distraction than a supplement. This is the central failure of most hustle-culture prescriptions—they ask us to *divide* attention rather than *stack* leverage. And what gets divided, gets diluted.

True income layering does not mean indiscriminately stacking projects. It means building concentric circles of value—where each layer strengthens the core, rather than pulling against it. In this paradigm, income streams are not separate roads, but tributaries feeding a shared riverbed. A well-designed income layer multiplies returns without multiplying confusion. It is *synergistic, not additive.*

Take the example of a skilled software developer. The hustle trap says: spend evenings selling crafts on Etsy, or flipping retail arbitrage items online. The layered approach says: write a newsletter about clean code practices, license snippets of original tools, offer periodic high-ticket consulting for architecture reviews. Each of these streams deepens the developer's craft, sharpens visibility within the ecosystem, and broadens earning potential—all without stepping outside the domain of competence. *This is not multitasking; it is multi-scaling.*

Psychologically, this difference matters deeply. Research in behavioural science consistently shows that humans are cognitively miscalibrated for fragmentation. Task-switching, especially between unrelated domains, imposes a neurological tax. Studies from Stanford, MIT, and the University of London have demonstrated significant IQ drops and reduced working memory in individuals who attempt frequent context switching. What the mind gains in novelty, it loses in coherence. The result is a shallow engagement with many things, and mastery of none.

In contrast, layered income reinforces identity and mastery. When all efforts stem from a common locus of skill and purpose, the mind enters a state of flow more readily. Momentum compounds, not just in earnings but in expertise. There's less friction in moving from one project to another, because they share scaffolding: same audience, same knowledge base, same narrative arc. *Income becomes an ecosystem—not a zoo.*

But the illusion of diversification remains persistent. Many confuse diversification with dispersion. The idea that "more streams = more security" fails when the streams are leaky, inefficient, or antagonistic. A copywriter doing freelance, affiliate marketing, dropshipping, and ridesharing is not diversified—they are exhausted. Worse, they are building parallel ladders without ever climbing one. The work feels perpetual, but progress remains shallow.

Contrast this with a "synergistic triangle" model: a public speaker also offers executive coaching and sells a companion book. Each income stream feeds and legitimises the others. The coaching gives anecdotes for speeches. The book builds authority that commands higher speaking fees. The talks attract new coaching clients. This is not hustle—it is harmony. *It's not how many plates you're spinning, but whether they spin around the same axis.*

History offers instructive models. Leonardo da Vinci wasn't great at many things by switching between disciplines; he was great because each pursuit—art, anatomy, engineering—served a shared fascination with structure and beauty. Similarly, polymaths like Benjamin Franklin or Marie Curie advanced across domains by following the gravity of their core questions. Their work layered, it did not scatter.

In today's professional context, the best earners treat their time and focus like investors treat capital. They look not only at return, but *integration.* Does this opportunity compound or conflict with my other efforts? Does it drain bandwidth or build capability? Does it push my identity forward or blur it? Most side hustles fail this test because they were chosen reactively, not strategically—taken on to fill income gaps rather than to strengthen value loops.

To practically apply this, readers can conduct a "synergy audit." List all current income-generating activities. Ask: *Which of these build on my core skills? Which enhance my reputation within my field? Which can scale with relatively less effort over time?* Eliminate those that don't score on at least two of the three. Then focus on depth, not breadth. It's not glamorous advice, but it's profitable.

Technology, often touted as the enabler of multitasking, ironically offers the best argument for layered focus. The most successful digital creators—those earning through courses, memberships, podcasts, and speaking—rarely launch everything at once. They go deep, then wide. They teach a concept, refine it in coaching, write about it, then codify it into a product. At every step, *one idea gets turned inside out*, not thrown away for the next. The hustle culture rewards novelty; layered income rewards refinement.

There's also an ethical and emotional dimension to consider. Scattered hustling often leads to transactional thinking. Every task becomes a commodity. Every minute must be "monetised." This mindset is corrosive. It treats life like an invoice. Layered income, by contrast, encourages stewardship: build something once, well, and let it serve others—and you—over time. Royalties, licensing, premium content, and productised services are expressions of this ethos. They honour time as a non-renewable resource. *They allow wealth to be built with wisdom, not just willpower.*

A powerful example is the teacher who begins recording short tutorials, eventually curates them into a course, then offers limited mentorship. Not three different jobs—but three dimensions of the same value. Each leverages the others. And importantly, the teacher can stop hustling and start scaling. That is the path to both resilience and peace.

In economics, diminishing returns arise when more input yields proportionally less output. But in layered systems, the opposite can occur: *increasing returns to focus.* One hour of work may yield not one, but three outcomes—because the same idea shows up in a client call, a piece of content, and a long-term product. Time, instead of being spent, gets *invested.*

To move from hustle to harmony is not about ambition—it's about architecture. The best earners are not always the busiest; they are the most *integrated.* They treat income as an extension of focus, not a substitute for it. They build not more ladders, but stronger ones—and they climb.

This is the discipline of multiplying, not splitting. It is the posture of a professional, not a panicked opportunist. And it is the only path to income that is scalable, ethical, and sustainable across time.

Your Skill Portfolio:

Most people understand the value of financial portfolios—diverse, actively managed, strategically rebalanced to reflect evolving goals. Yet few apply that same logic to the one asset class that underwrites all long-term earning power: their skills. If income is the yield, then skills are the principal. But unlike stocks or real estate, the value of one's skill portfolio isn't passively determined by market trends. It's shaped by choice—by where, how, and how often one reinvests. *The modern economy does not reward certificates—it rewards compound capability.*

The language of "skillsets" has become so ubiquitous that we forget its metaphorical roots. Skills are not fixed traits but adaptive instruments. They carry risk, offer return, and require maintenance. And like any asset, they depreciate when ignored. What's misunderstood is that professional stagnation rarely feels like sudden collapse. It feels like slow erosion—competence becomes familiarity, then obsolescence. *Relevance is perishable.*

Consider the research from David Deming at Harvard, who showed that the skills commanding the greatest wage growth over the last two decades are not merely technical, but "soft-hard hybrids"—problem-solving, analytical communication, leadership in ambiguity. These are not learned once and deployed forever. They evolve. Just as financial assets require reallocation, high-performing individuals must periodically reassess whether their skill capital is still earning its keep in a changing market.

This reframes the personal development challenge entirely. The question is no longer "Do I know enough?" but "Is my skill portfolio properly diversified, resilient, and positioned for where the economy is going—not where it's been?"

Treating skills like assets begins with recognising their categories. Foundational skills are akin to bonds: stable, always useful—communication, basic digital literacy, discipline. Growth skills behave more like equities: higher volatility, higher return—AI fluency, data literacy, complex negotiation. And leverage skills are the equivalents of options: they don't just add value, they *amplify* other abilities—systems thinking, public speaking, platform design. A healthy portfolio contains a thoughtful spread, updated in response to career cycles and industry trends. What you needed to ascend may not sustain you at the summit.

Yet it's not just accumulation that matters—it's intentionality. The accumulation mindset leads to scattered upskilling: a webinar here, a certification there, driven by fear of falling behind. The strategic investor, by contrast, asks: *How does this new skill integrate with my existing stack? Does it reinforce my core value proposition? Does it open new revenue paths or deepen current ones?*

To illustrate this, take the example of a mid-career financial analyst who notices diminishing returns in traditional reporting tasks. She could chase another Excel credential. But a wiser move might be building visualisation fluency—learning how to tell stories with data. Or even better, developing the meta-skill of stakeholder education—translating complex financial models for non-technical decision-makers. The technical upgrade is helpful; the communicative upgrade is transformative. It turns her from functionary to strategist.

This distinction echoes Peter Drucker's insight that effectiveness is a habit, not a gift. Highly effective individuals don't just collect tools; they build toolkits around *outcomes*. The skill portfolio approach avoids the trap of skill hoarding. It says: if this tool doesn't increase impact, influence, or autonomy, it's not an asset—it's clutter.

But there's also a temporal aspect. All skill assets exist on a depreciation curve. Some devalue quickly (e.g., a coding language losing market adoption), others more slowly (e.g., interpersonal coaching). The key is continuous reinvestment—not in everything, but in the highest leverage areas. This doesn't mean constant learning for learning's sake. It means *cyclical reinvestment*: setting quarterly reviews to identify where obsolescence is creeping in, and where opportunity is emerging. Skill strategy, like portfolio strategy, is not about constant motion—it's about *deliberate rebalancing.*

To act on this, readers can adopt a quarterly skill audit. Map current skills by three filters: revenue contribution, relevance in your industry's future, and uniqueness in your peer group. Anything low across all three is a candidate for pruning. Anything high on two and rising on the third deserves reinvestment—via practice, mentorship, or monetisation.

Monetisation is often where the philosophy breaks down. Too many view skills as static credentials for employment, not dynamic engines for independent earning. Yet in the creator and freelancer economy, a skill unused is a cost. A lawyer who never teaches misses licensing revenue. A designer who doesn't document her process loses the chance to coach. *In the modern labour market, knowledge must be portable, projectable, and preferably productisable.*

The academic roots of this idea go back to Gary Becker's theory of "human capital," but contemporary thought has evolved the concept into something more agile: *personal capital.* This includes not just your knowledge, but your method of applying it, your ability to explain it, your capacity to adapt it to new contexts. It also includes relational and reputational capital—how others perceive the *depth* of your capability, not just the breadth.

Consider the case of an executive with deep operations experience in retail. Her technical skill lies in inventory systems, but her strategic skill—built over decades—is *change orchestration.* If she starts consulting or mentoring, her income won't stem from SKU knowledge—it will stem from pattern recognition and cultural fluency. These meta-skills are often latent until one asks: "What is the transferable layer beneath what I do?" Portfolio thinking demands this reflection. It turns invisible assets into visible value.

None of this diminishes the need for occasional brute-force learning. Sometimes a skill gap is urgent and tactical—learning a client's CRM system or a new compliance framework. But even here, the mindset should be additive: "Can I turn this learning curve into a competitive advantage? Can I create content, teach others, build IP around this?" If not, the time cost may not justify the marginal utility.

Importantly, building a skill portfolio isn't always additive. It is just as much about pruning. The "overgrown garden" problem afflicts many mid-career professionals: a cluttered CV, outdated competencies, mixed messaging. Every skill that dilutes your narrative weakens your positioning. Simplicity is not shallowness. *It is clarity of edge.* And clarity sells.

Finally, the healthiest skill portfolios are regenerative. They do not just accumulate knowledge—they cultivate *learning systems.* This means building habits that expose you to adjacent disciplines, that integrate new insights into old frameworks, and that generate feedback loops. A writer who regularly speaks, a speaker who podcasts, a podcaster who writes—all are using their skills to renew each other. This is not merely clever—it is antifragile.

As the economy accelerates in complexity, the half-life of skills continues to shrink. But that is not a reason for panic. It is a reason for precision. In finance, the best portfolios are those that know when to hold, when to fold, and when to double down. The same is true for your capabilities. *You are not a job title. You are a portfolio manager of your own potential.* And in the long run, nothing compounds like mastery.

Building Anti-Fragile Income Streams:

Income that breaks when life does is not income worth depending on. For decades, the dominant model of earning—selling time for money—has been upheld as both necessary and virtuous. Yet its fragility is now undeniable. A job loss, a health scare, a market downturn: each exposes how brittle linear income truly is. It stops the moment you do. What's needed instead is a shift—not just towards diversification, but towards income systems that *gain strength under stress.* These are not simply passive income streams. They are *anti-fragile*—designed to adapt, absorb volatility, and sometimes even expand under conditions that cause others to collapse.

The term "anti-fragile," popularised by Nassim Nicholas Taleb, refers to systems that don't just endure shocks—they *improve* because of them. Whereas a fragile object breaks, and a resilient one survives, an anti-fragile entity thrives on randomness, uncertainty, and disorder. Most income is structured in precisely the opposite way. Salaries cap upside and concentrate downside. Freelance labour scales poorly and offers no shelter from disruption. Yet royalty payments, licensing models, intellectual property, subscription ecosystems, and educational assets demonstrate an overlooked principle: *some income models are not only resistant to change—they are enhanced by it.*

Consider the musician whose streaming royalties spike when an old track goes viral on TikTok. Or the author whose book sales double during an economic downturn because it speaks directly to the moment. Or the coder whose open-source tool, once downloaded in obscurity, becomes the backbone of an entire software niche and starts attracting sponsorships, consultancy offers, and paid integrations. These are not anomalies. They are examples of leverage intelligently deployed—where effort, once invested, creates a structure that responds positively to attention, volatility, or network effects.

To build such systems, we must rethink the nature of value creation. Most people equate earning with effort. But anti-fragile income is predicated on *separation* between effort and earning. This is not a moral short-cut—it is a structural redesign. Royalties, for instance, are not magical windfalls. They are the result of up-front creative labour that produces a durable asset—an eBook, a design, a training module—that can be licensed repeatedly without the original creator's time being continually consumed. It is effort that compounds.

This model demands a longer time horizon, but it also provides psychological insulation. Consider a software engineer who spends weekends building a niche app and releases it on a subscription basis. The app earns little at first. But over time, bug fixes are automated, customer support is streamlined, and word-of-mouth drives user acquisition. After two years, it earns £3,000 a month—tax-efficient, recurring, and scalable. That income may not replace a full-time salary, but it fundamentally changes the engineer's relationship to risk. He no longer *needs* every contract to go right. He can say no. He can negotiate better. He can leave toxic environments. That *optionality* is the essence of anti-fragility.

Recurring revenue is a natural expression of this principle. Subscription businesses, membership platforms, licensing agreements, and recurring consulting retainers all shift the income curve from erratic peaks and troughs to smoother, more predictable flows. And crucially, these streams often *strengthen* during market chaos. When people feel unstable, they seek consistent value. The consultant offering ongoing guidance to a cohort of anxious small business owners during a recession is not exploitative—they are *protective infrastructure.* When value is sustained over time, revenue becomes resilient.

Teaching is perhaps the most undervalued anti-fragile model of all. Not just teaching in classrooms, but packaging expertise into formats that scale: courses, workshops, playbooks, frameworks. The power of teaching lies not only in reach but in reflexivity—the more one teaches, the more one learns, refines, improves. This creates a flywheel. Content becomes curriculum. Curriculum becomes IP. IP becomes licensing opportunity. Over time, the teacher's "product" evolves faster than competitors because it is constantly exposed to real-world feedback and use cases.

And while teaching appears labour-intensive, much of its burden can be frontloaded. Asynchronous courses, live cohorts that are later repurposed, white-label training that companies can buy and rebrand—these models turn insight into infrastructure. They are not just jobs; they are systems that outlast effort.

To clarify: building anti-fragile income is not about escaping work. It's about *elevating the strategic quality of work*. The question shifts from "What pays well now?" to "What continues to pay when I'm not present?" This requires identifying where your capabilities intersect with durable demand. For instance, a designer may focus on building a portfolio of templates, UI kits, or visual assets that serve startups—a market likely to grow and pivot, but not disappear. A writer may create playbooks for small business owners facing regulatory shifts—a persistent pain point. A researcher may build a proprietary database or insights product that others rely on monthly. These are not get-rich-quick schemes. They are *get-wiser-slowly* models—economically and cognitively more sustainable.

The best anti-fragile income models also acknowledge *distribution.* It is not enough to create valuable assets. They must circulate, be discoverable, and accrue network effects. A book that sells well is rarely the best-written—it's the best-positioned. A course that drives royalties is not necessarily the most original—it's the most *embedded.* That means investing in visibility: partnerships, publishing, audience building. It also means designing income so that each user or client makes the system stronger—not just wealthier. This is how Airbnb became anti-fragile. Each new host made the platform *better.* The same principle applies to solo creators.

From a philosophical perspective, anti-fragility is about rejecting the myth of permanence. Salaries feel secure but are context-dependent. A single employer, a single industry, a single economy—all can disappear. Anti-fragile income, by contrast, is layered, redundant, and stress-tested. It functions like a coral reef: decentralised, self-regenerating, and resilient to surface disruption. It also demands a new ethic: *you are not simply working for money—you are engineering income ecosystems.*

Importantly, these ecosystems thrive on imperfection. An anti-fragile stream is not one that is invulnerable—it is one that adapts when tested. If a licensing agreement collapses, it may expose a clearer contractual clause. If a client withdraws, it may prompt a platform-based offer. If attention dips, it may signal the need for iteration. Anti-fragile systems treat shocks not as threats but as *information*—data for design improvement.

For those beginning this process, a practical first step is mapping your current income not just by size, but by *fragility.* Ask: Which income sources stop if I get sick? Which require constant marketing?

Which have network effects? Which are scalable? Then ask: Which capabilities do I possess that could be repackaged into products, services, or experiences that scale without synchronous labour? This will surface your leverage points. From there, the goal is not to replace income, but to *de-risk dependency.*

No income system is truly future-proof. But some are future-sensitive. They adapt because they are *built on insight, not inertia.* And insight, once deployed well, is remarkably hard to unseat. If you can create value that renews itself—through knowledge, content, relationships, tools—you have done more than earn money. You have built a financial structure that mimics nature: adaptable, decentralised, and *alive under pressure.*

The measure of an income stream is not just its quantity. It is its *survivability.* And in a world that shifts with every algorithm, regulation, or geopolitical tremor, survivability is no longer a luxury. It is the *criterion.* Fragile income rewards short-term performance. Anti-fragile income rewards design. One is effort-heavy and future-blind. The other is thoughtful, asymmetric, and quietly unstoppable.

The Narrative of Work:

Most people don't choose their first narrative about work—it's inherited. It arrives quietly, often in childhood, embedded in the rhythms of home life, school expectations, and societal assumptions. It may sound like: "Work is what you have to do." Or: "Work is what earns your worth." Or: "Work is the cost of survival." These inherited scripts are rarely examined because they're reinforced by culture, policy, and media. But beneath the slogans—"rise and grind," "pay your dues," "follow your passion"—lies a more fundamental question: *what do you believe work is for?*

For centuries, the answer has been survival. The Industrial Revolution embedded a model in which humans were units of production, time was commodified, and income was inseparable from obedience. You exchanged labour for wages, hours for subsistence, identity for a job title. That model still shapes expectations today—even in an era supposedly transformed by remote work, freelancing, and entrepreneurship. The surface has changed. The story hasn't. Work, for most, remains a transaction wrapped in anxiety: perform, or perish.

This assumption has consequences. When work is treated solely as survival, it becomes a source of chronic stress and diminished agency. Burnout, presenteeism, quiet quitting—these are not character flaws. They are symptoms of a misaligned paradigm. In this paradigm, your value is externalised and conditional. You are only as worthy as your current output. This is not merely demoralising—it's dangerous. It restricts creativity, suppresses innovation, and severs people from the deeper satisfactions that work can offer: mastery, service, impact, coherence.

Re-authoring the narrative of work begins with a shift from extraction to *contribution*. In this frame, work is not what you do to "get" something. It is what you *offer*—to your clients, your community, your craft, your field. This shift does not romanticise labour. It refines it. Contribution-oriented work is not necessarily more glamorous or profitable. But it is more *intellectually sustainable* because it aligns effort with meaning. It allows individuals to see themselves not as passive recipients of income, but as active participants in shaping value.

Take the example of a teacher who reframes their role not as "delivering curriculum" but as "engineering transformation in young thinkers." Or a software engineer who sees their role not as "building features" but as "designing invisible infrastructure that helps millions live easier lives." These may sound semantic, but the implications are profound. One model reinforces task-based fatigue. The other embeds a sense of authorship and evolution. The task remains the same. The story shifts. And so does the quality of engagement.

The difference between labour and work is not effort—it's *ownership*. Labour is what is imposed. Work, when re-authored consciously, becomes a practice of integration. It integrates skills with values, time with purpose, effort with learning. It becomes a feedback system: the more one works, the more one refines one's sense of where their effort is most valuable. This is particularly essential in an economic landscape defined by volatility. The only truly defensible income is that which emerges from *alignment*, not compliance.

A useful test: would you do your work if it paid less—but offered more integrity? Would you do it if it earned nothing, but solved a real problem? These are not abstract questions. They help surface what your current narrative of work *protects*, and what it *prevents*. Many professionals, especially in high-paying sectors, report that they feel like they're "trapped in golden handcuffs." The pay is excellent. The meaning is absent. What keeps them there is not laziness, but narrative inertia. The story that "I can't afford to change" becomes a self-fulfilling prophecy, even as well-being erodes.

Re-authoring that story requires emotional and structural courage. Emotionally, it requires confronting inherited beliefs: that prestige matters more than impact; that busyness equals importance; that exhaustion signals virtue. Structurally, it requires gradually building income systems that are less dependent on singular employers and more reflective of one's distinctive contribution. This may take the form of teaching, consulting, building tools, writing, or investing in scalable skills. The goal is not to escape work—it is to escape *alienation from your own labour.*

Importantly, this re-authoring is not a solitary act. It is relational. The stories we tell about work are co-created. They are shaped by the stories we hear from others—colleagues, mentors, parents, peers. Cultural narratives, too, set the perimeter of what feels acceptable. This is why so many people feel tension between their inner aspirations and their outer obligations. They are operating within an outdated social script. Rewriting that script often starts with *conversation*—finding others who are also challenging inherited assumptions and designing their work life around contribution, not compensation alone.

The rise of portfolio careers, creator economies, and values-based entrepreneurship signals that this shift is already under way. Yet even these movements are not immune to distortion. The same hustle logic can infiltrate the most purpose-driven projects. Passion becomes commodified. Contribution becomes performance. "Doing what you love" becomes another arena for perfectionism. The solution is not to abandon ambition—but to interrogate it. What kind of ambition is truly yours? What kind of legacy are you unconsciously building through your current work habits?

Ethically, the narrative of work must also account for privilege and access. Not everyone can afford to reimagine their work life from scratch. Systemic inequalities constrain the options of many. But the point is not perfection—it is *progression*. Even a modest shift in mindset—from "I must do this to survive" to "I am using this to learn, to contribute, to evolve"—can restore agency. And that agency, over time, compounds. It leads to better decisions. It informs where you invest your skills. It shapes which opportunities you say yes to, and which systems you choose to exit.

Philosophically, work is one of the primary ways humans enact meaning in the world. To treat it merely as a transaction is to truncate its potential. Viktor Frankl, the Austrian psychiatrist and Holocaust survivor, wrote that meaning—not happiness—is the primary motivator of human behaviour. Work, in his view, was a potent source of meaning precisely because it requires struggle. But not all struggle is dignifying. The kind of work that yields meaning is work that connects us to something beyond ourselves: an idea, a cause, a lineage, a future.

That is what contribution-based income seeks to reflect. It's not a utopian dream. It is a practical framework for choosing and designing work that leaves both the self and the world incrementally better. And ironically, this kind of work is often more financially sustainable in the long term. Why? Because it creates trust. Because it leads to mastery. Because it generates outcomes that others value and return to. Reputation, in this model, is not branding—it's the compound interest of integrity.

To begin re-authoring your own work narrative, ask: *What does my work currently signal about my values?* Then ask: *What would I like it to signal?* These are not theoretical prompts. They are navigational tools. They help you bridge the space between income and identity. They help you separate productivity from presence. They help you turn work from a site of depletion into a platform for design.

Ultimately, the question is not whether you will work. It is *what your work will mean*. If it only ever means survival, then even success feels hollow. But if it begins to mean contribution—real, rigorous, resonant—then work becomes more than a task. It becomes a *statement*. And from that statement, everything else—strategy, income, resilience—flows more intelligently.

Chapter 5
The Legacy Layer – Wealth That Outlives You

Legacy. For many, the word drapes itself in the formality of estate planning and final testaments—dusty legal documents signed in sterile rooms by ageing hands. It carries the whiff of the afterlife, of something decided once the living is done. But let's be honest: that understanding is no longer fit for purpose. If anything, it delays the far more urgent and intimate question—what mark am I making now, whether consciously or not?

This chapter turns the concept on its head. Legacy isn't the punctuation at the end of life's sentence. It's what accumulates mid-paragraph, shaped by how we spend, give, speak, show up. Every financial decision, every act of care or neglect, every stance we take on fairness or generosity—we're already writing the story. The only question is whether we're doing so with our eyes open.

Inheritance, when reduced to money changing hands, often misses the point entirely. Yes, wealth that endures can create extraordinary good—but only when it carries context. Values, history, intention—these are the invisible threads that bind generations together or let them unravel. In the absence of those, wealth can just as easily become a source of friction, or worse, quiet decay. We've all heard the stories—inheritance that fractures siblings, businesses lost in confusion, fortunes squandered out of detachment. That isn't failure by ledger. It's a narrative collapse.

To get serious about legacy, we must first rethink ownership itself. Modern economic life tells us to gather—more capital, more property, more control. But "more" comes at a price. It demands maintenance, brings complexity, ties us down. Without a deeper framework—a sense of stewardship rather than dominion—wealth can erode the very freedom it was meant to enable.

Older traditions knew this instinctively. In many Indigenous and Eastern societies, wealth wasn't a static possession—it was a current, meant to flow. Elders didn't just guard resources; they passed down perspective. The "what" of wealth was always tied to the "why." Tools came with stories. Rights came with duties. And legacies were never just bank balances—they were philosophies in motion.

This chapter offers a call to return—not to romanticise the past, but to revive its wisdom through thoughtful modern practice. Legacy, after all, is a system. It includes material resources, yes—but also belief systems, assumptions, habits, and the emotional climate surrounding all of the above. The numbers are often the easy part. The harder work lies in tracing the hidden architecture beneath them.

Pause for a moment and consider: what were you taught about success? Was money a source of pride, anxiety, secrecy? Did your family model generosity, or frugality laced with fear? These may sound like reflective prompts, but they serve a structural purpose. If you're unaware of the legacy you've inherited emotionally, you'll likely re-create it—no matter your financial sophistication.

Many people approach legacy planning with spreadsheets and solicitors—tools, in other words. But tools without a philosophy are brittle. This chapter proposes a complementary approach: the Wealth Constitution. It's not a formality. It's a living document that expresses the principles guiding your financial decisions. Not what you own, but what you believe about that ownership. Not just where your money should go, but why.

Think of it less as a rulebook, more as a compass. One that can orient your heirs in a moment of disorientation. Because let's be frank—money often arrives at emotional junctures: death, conflict, transition. Clarity of intent, offered in your own voice, is a gift no spreadsheet can replace. It doesn't control the future, but it prepares it.

Of course, family legacy is only one strand. For many, the more resonant form of legacy lies elsewhere—in the causes championed, the communities uplifted, the knowledge shared. A scholarship fund. A mentoring programme. A neighbourhood transformed through quiet acts of leadership. These are the legacies that rarely make headlines but echo far longer. A child's education. A restored sense of dignity. These aren't accounted for in net worth statements—but perhaps they ought to be.

And then there's emotional capital—the most overlooked asset class of all. This isn't about therapy-speak or soft skills. It's about what your presence teaches. The calm you bring in a storm. The way you handle a mistake. The standards you hold yourself to when no one's keeping score. These are legacies in action, not abstraction. They leave imprints, not instructions.

Neglect this layer, and the best technical planning may still falter. Friction between siblings. Misaligned expectations. Charitable foundations that drift from their mission within a generation. But when emotional wisdom underpins structural decisions, the result is not just durability—but depth.

We'll spend the rest of this chapter exploring precisely how to design such a legacy. We'll look at stewardship not as a noble burden, but as a strategic orientation. You'll see how intergenerational planning isn't about locking wealth away—it's about liberating it responsibly. We'll discuss how to reckon with inherited money narratives that no longer serve, and how to construct new ones rooted in clarity and coherence.

You'll also confront what I call invisible legacy—the things you're passing down without realising it. A casual comment repeated by your children. A pattern of avoidance around conflict. A hundred small decisions that form a moral atmosphere. Legacy is never neutral. It accumulates whether we tend to it or not.

The most enduring legacies aren't the ones marked by grandeur. They're the ones that feel like an extension of the person behind them—coherent, intentional, alive. They don't just preserve the past; they equip the future. And they remind those who come after not only what was built, but what mattered.

If you've never thought of yourself as someone who "builds legacy," now is the time to reconsider. You already are. The question is: what kind are you building—and is it one you'd be proud to leave behind while still fully present to shape it?

"Legacy as Living Design"

It is a curious quirk of modern finance that legacy is most commonly discussed in legal offices and life insurance brochures—an afterthought, postscript, or estate plan drafted in the shadow of mortality. The assumption is nearly universal and almost entirely unexamined: that legacy is something you *leave*, not something you *live*. But this idea is not only narrow—it is costly. It reduces one of life's most significant responsibilities into a clerical matter. Worse still, it delays the act of meaning-making until the moment you are no longer here to participate in it.

To challenge that assumption is to shift the entire framework of wealth, time, and contribution. *Legacy is not the residue of life; it is a function of how life is lived.* It is not the artefact that remains once you're gone, but the architecture you build—deliberately or not—through decisions made while fully alive. This chapter insists on a more dynamic model: legacy as living design.

Living design does not mean turning your daily choices into grandiose gestures. It means recognising that every relationship you invest in, every standard you uphold, every injustice you confront or tolerate, and every opportunity you cultivate or ignore *already composes the scaffolding of your legacy*. Wealth, in this context, becomes only one medium among many. Financial assets matter. But they are rarely the most enduring or instructive part of what we leave behind.

To begin reframing legacy, we must first understand how it became synonymous with inheritance. In the industrial and post-industrial West, wealth accumulation became both an aspiration and a protective mechanism—guarding against scarcity, social displacement, or vulnerability. Legacy, in turn, was cast as a container for that protection: a vault for property, stocks, deeds, and succession. The tools were designed accordingly—wills, trusts, tax vehicles, and legal proxies. And while those structures serve essential purposes, they also flattened the deeper philosophical dimensions of legacy into mere mechanics.

Other civilisations tell a richer story. In ancient Egypt, the concept of *ma'at*—order, balance, truth—was not only spiritual but intergenerational. To live ethically was to transmit stability across time. In Confucian China, family honour extended beyond obedience; it was a form of cultural wealth, protected and passed through ritual and responsibility. Among the Igbo of Nigeria, the idea of *ndu* connotes life as a shared inheritance—each generation borrowing from the next. None of these systems treated legacy as static. Each required *active participation* in shaping continuity.

In contemporary practice, this means legacy must be re-centred in *intentional behaviour*, not merely end-of-life documentation. Consider the difference between writing a cheque for a grandchild's education and spending years mentoring them in how to think, decide, and carry forward shared values. One is a gift; the other is *a formation*. The same amount of money may be involved—but the *impact curve* is vastly different. The first assumes that resources alone can confer advantage. The second acknowledges that wisdom, context, and example are irreplaceable transmitters of resilience.

This distinction also reorients our view of timing. Traditional estate planning is retrospective. It assumes that legacy begins when productivity ends. Living design flips that premise. It asks: What are you modelling *now*? What systems of thought, attitude, or bias are you normalising? What opportunities are you expanding—or hoarding? Who benefits from your competence and who is excluded from it? These are legacy questions disguised as ordinary choices. Their accumulation is not hypothetical. It is happening in real time.

Indeed, some of the most powerful legacies are built not at retirement but in moments of pressure and transition. How a leader exits a company. How a parent responds to financial setback. How a person uses influence when there is no obvious gain. These decisions often leave deeper imprints than grand donations or memorial foundations. *Because they reveal not only what a person valued, but what they stood for when it mattered.* Living design recognises that integrity, transparency, and generosity—if practised consistently—become far more infectious than money alone.

Of course, this view of legacy requires more of us. It does not permit the deferral that traditional models implicitly encourage. It demands integration—between public and private self, between action and intention, between aspiration and architecture. It raises the stakes on how we use our platforms, however modest or vast. But it also offers something richer than a ledger of possessions: the possibility of continuity with coherence.

There is also a practical benefit to adopting this mindset early. By thinking of legacy as something to be lived, individuals gain clarity around priorities. They begin to see capital not as an end in itself, but as a *means of alignment.* The question becomes not "How do I maximise my estate?" but "How do I design a life and legacy that reflect the highest use of my abilities, values, and resources?" This shift tends to simplify decision-making. It removes the noise of comparison and centres on conviction.

In institutional contexts, we see this approach playing out in innovative ways. Universities now increasingly build "living legacies" with donors—programmes in which contributors actively mentor students, shape curriculum, or seed long-term initiatives rather than simply attach their name to a building. Social entrepreneurs build ecosystems around their ideas—not just products—and ensure those ecosystems survive their tenure. And in the family office world, a growing number of wealth holders are crafting governance documents that articulate not just fiscal wishes, but *philosophical mandates*: how wealth should be stewarded, what values it must respect, and what lines must not be crossed, regardless of future incentives.

Even at the household level, the principle is accessible. Teaching children the reasoning behind financial decisions. Inviting them into charitable choices. Documenting the "why" of wealth alongside the "what." These small acts of intentional transparency become inheritance in the truest sense—not just *what* you bequeath, but *how* it should be carried. They minimise ambiguity, reduce future conflict, and foster accountability across generations.

To be clear, living design does not guarantee a perfect legacy. People change, cultures evolve, and interpretation is not always within the originator's control. But what it *does* guarantee is that the legacy was crafted with intentionality, not inertia. That its arc was shaped by values, not accidents. And that its transmission included not just resources but reasoning.

For the thoughtful reader, then, the challenge is neither technical nor ceremonial. It is ethical. *What kind of future am I preparing others to inherit?* Not merely in assets, but in norms, expectations, and beliefs. Am I designing a legacy that liberates, that dignifies, that educates? Or am I deferring that responsibility behind layers of formality?

This chapter—and this book—encourages a shift away from the myth that legacy begins with the writing of a will. It begins with the writing of your life. Every decision is a brushstroke. The composition is not finalised when you die. It is finalised when you stop caring who it affects. To design your legacy while living is not to control it. It is to dignify it. It is to invite participation. And it is to offer the next generation not just a map, but a compass.

"From Ownership to Stewardship"

There is a silent pivot that separates those who merely possess wealth from those who are trusted by it. That pivot is stewardship. It begins when the question shifts from "What do I own?" to "What am I responsible for?" and it matures when ownership ceases to be the destination and becomes instead a medium for transmission, not accumulation. In an age dominated by asset portfolios, titles, and shareholder value, this distinction might appear semantic. It is not. It is philosophical—and it alters everything.

The dominant economic narrative of the past century has venerated ownership. From land and companies to intellectual property and financial products, the logic has been linear: acquire, control, grow. Ownership confers power, legal rights, and in many societies, identity. It is the cornerstone of capitalist participation. But this emphasis has often eclipsed a more enduring form of economic agency: the ethic of stewardship, in which the emphasis is not merely on what one holds but on *how one holds it*, for how long, and in whose interest.

Stewardship is neither a rejection of ownership nor an ascetic appeal to renounce wealth. It is a reconfiguration of the role the owner plays. A steward understands wealth as both opportunity and obligation. A steward acts not simply to enlarge the pie, but to ensure it nourishes beyond the self. *Where ownership says, "This is mine," stewardship asks, "What is this for?"*

This concept is hardly new. Long before the emergence of modern private property law, many civilisations embedded stewardship at the heart of their wealth systems. Among the Māori of Aotearoa (New Zealand), land was not owned in the Western sense; it was *whenua*, a living ancestor, to be cared for and passed on. In medieval Islamic waqf institutions, wealthy individuals endowed property for public benefit—schools, hospitals, mosques—not as charity, but as an ongoing fiduciary commitment. These assets were protected from sale or inheritance, precisely to reinforce their communal purpose. And in Andean cultures such as the Quechua, stewardship over crops, livestock, and water sources was collectively practised and spiritually grounded. Resources were not seen as commodities but as entrusted blessings.

Contrast this with the modern conception of the self-made entrepreneur who maximises profits, optimises taxes, and names a foundation in their twilight years. Despite the rhetoric of generosity, such gestures are often post-hoc and transactional. They are designed to preserve reputation, minimise estate leakage, or signal virtue. Stewardship, by contrast, begins upstream. It shapes the architecture of decisions long before the plaque goes on the wall.

One reason this transition remains rare is that stewardship demands a form of self-diminishment. It requires the ego to make room for continuity. In practical terms, it may mean foregoing a higher return to align with ethical sourcing, delaying gratification to prioritise intergenerational equity, or designing structures that reduce dependency on the founder. None of this is instinctual in a culture that rewards accumulation as the ultimate signal of intelligence or ambition. But it is indispensable for any legacy that aims to *last.*

Consider the case of Chuck Feeney, the billionaire co-founder of Duty Free Shoppers, who quietly gave away over 99% of his fortune during his lifetime, not in his will. His giving was anonymous, strategic, and front-loaded—guided by the belief that wealth should *do* something, not simply *be* something. His model, later dubbed "giving while living," not only altered philanthropy but introduced a radical idea: that wealth should be deployed when its creator is still accountable for its use.

This reorientation has implications far beyond charitable giving. In family businesses, for example, the absence of stewardship often leads to dynastic decay. The founding generation may be adept at creating wealth, but if their philosophy remains extractive—focused solely on capital accumulation—their successors frequently inherit assets without purpose. This vacuum of meaning leads to infighting, mismanagement, or apathy. Stewardship, however, cultivates a *narrative of continuity*. It embeds expectations, responsibilities, and values alongside spreadsheets. It clarifies that wealth is not just a windfall but a mandate.

One of the most powerful tools for this is transparent governance. Families and institutions that practise stewardship tend to document not just legal intent, but *philosophical position*. They write family constitutions, host intergenerational retreats, and discuss not just what the money will do, but *why it exists in the first place.* These activities are not performative—they are preventative. They protect against the entropy that arises when wealth loses its logic.

Crucially, stewardship also addresses the question of *limits*. A steward is more likely to ask, "When is enough?" than an owner fixated on perpetual scale. This ties back to the philosophy of *sufficiency*, which values balance over accumulation for its own sake. Stewardship, therefore, is not only about how assets are transmitted but about how desires are regulated. It challenges the delusion that more is inherently better and reorients decision-making toward *enduring value.*

This perspective finds echoes in behavioural economics as well. Studies in the psychology of wealth transmission have shown that recipients of uncontextualised inheritance—i.e. wealth passed down without guidance or preparation—often experience confusion, anxiety, or entitlement. By contrast, those who have been invited into stewardship-based practices—such as contributing to philanthropic decisions or participating in business governance—develop stronger financial literacy, emotional maturity, and social responsibility. *In this way, stewardship is not merely a financial philosophy—it is a pedagogical one.*

It also prompts a reevaluation of what counts as wealth. Under an ownership lens, wealth is that which is bankable, saleable, or leverageable. But from a stewardship perspective, wealth includes trust, story, ethics, and the systems that make dignity possible. A well-tended community garden, a mentorship culture, or an oral history archive may yield no ROI in conventional terms. Yet these are forms of capital that enrich lives across generations. They prevent the corrosion of meaning that afflicts families or societies that inherit money but not memory.

There is a growing movement among next-generation wealth holders to reclaim this broader view. They are increasingly asking: What structures perpetuate harm? What traditions need interrupting? What does it mean to transmit wealth without transmitting power imbalances, ecological damage, or exploitative business models? These are not sentimental questions. They are systemic ones. And they can only be answered through the framework of stewardship—not as a trend, but as a discipline.

In this light, the transition from ownership to stewardship is not a soft pivot. It is a moral upgrade. It reframes wealth not as an endpoint but as a passage. It forces us to ask not just how much is left behind, but *how it is left.* And perhaps more importantly, *how it continues to serve.*

The invitation, then, is to step beyond possession into purpose. To think not only about what is held, but what is enabled through the act of holding. To recognise that wealth is not simply a private affair, but a relational one—with time, with people, and with the future. The owner asks, "How can I protect this?" The steward asks, "How can I protect what *matters*?"

That question, when asked consistently, becomes a practice. And that practice, when sustained, becomes a legacy.

"Family Systems and Financial Narratives"

Wealth rarely travels alone. It is carried in stories—some spoken, many not. Families don't just pass on assets; they pass on beliefs, anxieties, roles, and rules about money that are deeply embedded in their relational systems. These narratives often shape financial behaviour more powerfully than any economic trend, tax code, or investment strategy. Before we ask what a family *owns*, we should ask what it *believes*—about scarcity, success, entitlement, shame, obligation, or risk. Because these beliefs tend not to originate in spreadsheets. They are forged in silence, reinforced through patterns, and transmitted through generations like a kind of psychic inheritance.

At the heart of this transmission is the family system: a dynamic, interdependent web of roles, relationships, loyalties, and emotional undercurrents. Drawing from systems theory and intergenerational psychology, we understand that no individual makes financial decisions in a vacuum. They make them within a structure that reflects accumulated experiences, cultural scripts, and often, unresolved trauma. A parent who grew up amid financial insecurity may overcompensate with rigid control. A child raised in affluence but emotional neglect may seek autonomy by rejecting the family enterprise altogether. These decisions may appear irrational from a purely economic lens—but they make perfect sense within the emotional architecture of the family.

This is where narrative becomes essential. Every family has a money story. For some, it's a story of survival—where wealth is precarious, constantly under threat, and must be protected at all costs. For others, it's a story of status—where money is a proxy for identity, achievement, or legitimacy. Still others live under a narrative of guilt, where having more than previous generations brings psychological discomfort, or even paralysis. These stories are rarely discussed openly. Yet they shape inheritance plans, spending habits, philanthropic choices, and even marital dynamics. *To understand a family's financial reality, we must first understand the script they are unconsciously following.*

One particularly influential—and often overlooked—element of these scripts is trauma. Financial trauma is not limited to those who grew up in poverty. It can stem from sudden loss, parental fights over money, betrayal in a business deal, or even the internalisation of culturally inherited narratives about money and morality. Trauma tends to create rigidity: compulsive saving, risk aversion, secret accounts, or cycles of boom and bust. It thrives in opacity. And unless surfaced and metabolised, it tends to repeat.

This is particularly salient in families with newly acquired wealth. First-generation wealth creators often carry the psychic residue of struggle. Their drive may be fuelled by deprivation, scarcity, or a desire to prove worth. But this success story, if unexamined, can calcify into an implicit expectation for the next generation: *You must deserve this. You must not waste it. You must replicate it.* These messages, though unspoken, can weigh heavily. Children may feel like they're auditioning for an inheritance they already possess. Or worse, they may reject the wealth altogether to escape its psychological freight.

Conversely, families with multigenerational wealth can fall into patterns of entitlement, co-dependence, or disengagement. Without a narrative of purpose, inherited wealth becomes inert—something to protect, flaunt, or escape from, but rarely something to engage with critically. In both scenarios, the issue is not the wealth itself but the absence of a coherent, shared story that gives it meaning.

To intervene in these patterns, families must first become narratively literate. This involves asking not just *what happened*, but *what was said about what happened.* For instance: When did your family first talk to you about money? What role did each parent play in financial decisions? Was wealth associated with joy, shame, power, or silence? Who was praised or blamed in conversations about money? Who was kept in the dark? These are not idle questions—they are diagnostic tools. They reveal the implicit scripts governing behaviour, and they open space for those scripts to be re-authored.

Psychologists like Murray Bowen and Virginia Satir have long emphasised the intergenerational transmission of emotional patterns. Applied to wealth, this suggests that without intentional disruption, families will replay the same financial dramas under new guises. A son who resents his father's control may one day exert that same control over his own children. A daughter who grows up feeling excluded from family decisions may unconsciously exclude her spouse from future financial planning. Patterns persist not because they are rational, but because they are familiar.

But familiarity need not dictate fate. Once brought into awareness, these patterns can be challenged. Consider a family that experiences a liquidity event—such as the sale of a business or the passing of a matriarch. Rather than rushing into tax minimisation or legal structuring, they pause to articulate their shared values. They reflect on their history, examine their emotional associations with wealth, and construct a new narrative together: one that names past pain, honours divergent perspectives, and sets clear intentions. *This is not therapy disguised as estate planning—it is the necessary foundation for healthy transmission.*

Culture adds another layer. Different cultures encode different meanings around money, family, and hierarchy. In collectivist societies, wealth is often communal and relational—distributed through kinship obligations rather than individual autonomy. In Western liberal democracies, financial success is frequently equated with independence and merit. Migrant families may inhabit both worlds simultaneously, creating internal tension. A second-generation professional may feel torn between Western norms of self-actualisation and ancestral expectations of family remittance. These tensions, if unaddressed, can lead to conflict, misunderstanding, and fractured legacies.

It's also worth acknowledging the gendered dimensions of family financial narratives. Many families, consciously or not, reproduce patriarchal patterns: men handle investments, women handle consumption; sons inherit businesses, daughters receive gifts. Even in highly educated households, these roles can persist under a veneer of modernity. Challenging them requires more than policy—it requires storytelling. It requires the deliberate inclusion of women's financial voices, experiences, and authority in both narrative and practice.

This is where wealth planning must evolve into *wealth meaning-making*. Financial advisors, trustees, and family office executives are increasingly recognising that the most successful families are not those with the most zeros, but those with the clearest narratives. They invest not just in assets, but in alignment. They host family meetings that prioritise listening. They build frameworks that honour individuality without eroding cohesion. They ask not just what each person wants, but what they fear, what they long for, and what they believe wealth is *for*.

Of course, this is uncomfortable terrain. Talking openly about money can trigger defensiveness, shame, or resentment. But avoiding the conversation only guarantees that the subtext remains unchallenged—and that the next generation inherits not just the capital, but the confusion. *Silence is not neutral; it is its own form of transmission.*

To move forward, families must be willing to unearth what has been buried. They must identify the scripts they've inherited and decide—consciously, collectively—whether those scripts still serve. This does not mean manufacturing consensus or forcing premature harmony. It means creating a container where multiple truths can coexist, and where new narratives can be co-authored.

Ultimately, family wealth is not just a financial construct. It is a psychological system shaped by memory, myth, and meaning. Until these elements are examined, no amount of legal sophistication will prevent relational entropy. But when they *are* examined—with rigour, empathy, and imagination—families gain not only the tools to preserve wealth, but the wisdom to wield it well.

"Writing Your Financial Ethos"

Most families have a will. Far fewer have a philosophy. The legal apparatus of wealth transfer—trusts, deeds, succession plans—may tell future generations *what* they receive and *when*, but rarely *why*. And yet it is the *why*—the personal reasoning, values, and long-term intentions—that most often determines whether wealth endures or unravels. The formal instruments of wealth preservation are necessary but not sufficient. What's missing in many family legacies is not structure, but *ethos*—a shared framework of meaning that binds generations together with clarity and purpose.

To write a financial ethos is not merely to document your preferences or jot down a few hopes. It is to articulate, with rigour and introspection, your foundational beliefs about money, value, responsibility, and continuity. It is to craft a guiding document—a *Wealth Constitution*—that doesn't dictate outcomes but shapes orientation. Done properly, it becomes a touchstone for generations, grounding financial decisions in shared intent rather than inherited ambiguity.

The notion may feel novel, but its antecedents are ancient. In tribal cultures, legacy was transmitted not only through possessions, but through oral codes, stories, and rituals that clarified the group's relationship to land, labour, reciprocity, and status. In Confucian tradition, familial ethics around wealth and duty were codified through proverbs and parables passed down for centuries. Even in Western religious traditions, financial life was often inseparable from moral instruction: tithing, stewardship, humility, and charity were embedded into the economic fabric of family life. These were not accidental customs. They were *intentional transmissions* of ethos.

In contrast, modern wealth is often dislocated from philosophical anchoring. The acceleration of financial complexity—global portfolios, digital assets, fluid family structures—has outpaced our cultural capacity to encode meaning. As a result, heirs inherit assets without inheriting context. And context is everything. Without it, wealth can be experienced not as a gift but as a burden: arbitrary, unearned, or emotionally charged. With it, even modest inheritance becomes a form of moral capital—something to interpret, steward, and extend with integrity.

This is where the Wealth Constitution becomes not just useful, but essential. It is not a contract. It is not a set of instructions. It is a codified philosophy—living, revisable, and deeply human. It addresses questions legal documents cannot: *What does this family believe about work? About sharing? About enough? About obligation, freedom, and risk?* Its purpose is not to constrain the future, but to illuminate it.

Constructing such a document demands more than sentiment. It demands *discernment.* Begin with critical self-inquiry: What has shaped your own financial worldview? What experiences—personal, familial, historical—have left a lasting imprint on your relationship with money? Who did you admire financially, and why? What behaviours in others have repelled you? These questions are not idle reflections. They are the raw material of your philosophy.

From there, you begin to distil values into statements. Not platitudes, but convictions. For example:

"We believe that money is a tool for long-term contribution, not short-term display."
"We honour risk when it is aligned with learning, innovation, or service—but not when driven by ego or impulse."
"We do not measure success by account size but by how well our resources support our values."

These are not slogans. They are internal compasses. And once clarified, they can anchor a wide range of decisions—from philanthropic giving to intergenerational gifting, from business succession to family governance.

A well-formed ethos also acknowledges *tension.* It does not pretend all values coexist peacefully. Most families wrestle with competing impulses: growth vs. security, independence vs. support, tradition vs. innovation. A strong Wealth Constitution does not resolve these tensions prematurely. It *names* them. It surfaces them openly, so that future generations can engage with them consciously, rather than inheriting unspoken conflict.

One powerful exercise for surfacing these nuances is to write a financial origin story. Not a list of accomplishments, but a narrative: how you first learned about money, how your family handled financial hardship or windfall, what shaped your beliefs about generosity, thrift, or risk. Storytelling, in this context, is not indulgent—it is foundational. Because financial behaviour is rarely shaped by data. It is shaped by story. And the clearer the story, the less likely the next generation is to distort or abandon it under pressure.

This ethos need not be individual. In fact, its power is multiplied when co-authored. Spouses, adult children, trusted advisors, or long-time collaborators can all contribute to the shaping of a family's Wealth Constitution. The process of co-writing fosters alignment, surfaces blind spots, and builds emotional ownership. It transforms the document from a statement of *my* beliefs into a reflection of *our* evolving identity.

Moreover, a Wealth Constitution can be both philosophical and practical. It can include guiding principles for investment (e.g. ESG alignment, community investment, impact funding), educational support (e.g. what qualifies as developmentally valuable vs. indulgent), and intergenerational expectations (e.g. age milestones for access, prerequisites for family stewardship roles). These details should not read like a compliance manual. They should flow from and be coherent with the deeper values the family holds.

It is also important to distinguish ethos from control. The document is not a posthumous attempt to engineer outcomes. It is not a covert trust clause. It is a mirror, not a leash. *The ethos invites interpretation; it does not enforce conformity.* It assumes future generations will evolve and adapt—but it offers them a framework that fosters clarity, reflection, and intergenerational coherence.

Examples from prominent families underscore this. The Rockefeller family, for instance, has long been known not just for its philanthropic infrastructure, but for its intentional family governance models—embedding values of service, engagement, and learning into generational continuity. Some enterprising families host regular "ethos forums" where younger members engage with elder stories and values through structured dialogue, rather than lectures. Others invite professional facilitators or financial therapists to help surface hidden tensions and integrate diverse perspectives. These are not rituals for the wealthy alone—they are accessible to any family willing to treat money as a vector for meaning, not just transaction.

One underestimated benefit of codifying a financial ethos is emotional resilience. In moments of crisis—be it a family rift, a market crash, or an untimely death—a clear set of shared values acts as ballast. It enables families to make decisions not from fear or urgency, but from alignment. It also helps insulate against mission drift in family enterprises or charitable initiatives. When purpose is anchored, strategy becomes a tool, not a distraction.

Equally, a Wealth Constitution can serve as an invitation. New members of the family—spouses, in-laws, or adopted children—often feel adrift in legacy systems that lack transparent values. A clearly articulated ethos can foster inclusion, understanding, and respect, allowing new participants to orient themselves not just around rules, but around shared meaning.

And for those without children, or who do not wish to establish dynastic wealth, the exercise is no less valuable. An ethos can inform how wealth is deployed in one's lifetime—through mentorship, community projects, public leadership, or institutional support. It can help distil one's highest vision for the use of capital into a coherent, intentional expression that outlives the individual not in perpetuity, but in relevance.

In the end, to write your financial ethos is to reclaim authorship. It is a refusal to let the mechanics of wealth obscure its meaning. It is a reminder that while the tools of finance are technical, the work of legacy is moral. Assets will one day change hands. The question is whether the soul of those assets will survive the transfer. With a Wealth Constitution in place, there is a far greater chance that it will not only survive—but inspire.

"When Legacy is Invisible"

Legacy is often imagined as a ledger—of bank accounts, property deeds, portfolios, and legal documents. Tangible, measurable, and easily notarised. But some of the most enduring legacies in history never passed through probate. They were not inherited in trust accounts or catalogued in financial statements. They existed in something less visible but more enduring: influence. The way someone made others feel. The courage they modelled. The ideas they shared and the beliefs they embodied. These are legacies that do not live in bank vaults—they live in memory, in habit, in culture.

The dominant narrative of legacy in Western society has long been economic. Estate planning, wealth transfer, and inheritance law have become proxies for the more complex, more human question of *what remains when we're no longer here*. But if we define legacy solely in terms of monetary transmission, we make two critical errors. First, we reduce our impact to a balance sheet. And second, we overlook the powerful, often unspoken ways in which we shape others—through generosity, mentorship, presence, values, and lived example.

It is these invisible legacies that endure in surprising ways. The teacher who awakens a sense of possibility in a struggling student. The mentor who shares their failures, not just their strategies. The grandparent whose consistent calm under pressure becomes a model for emotional resilience. These contributions do not appear in legal inventories. Yet their ripple effects can outlast fortunes.

Social science has begun to formalise what many already intuitively understand: that human beings are not only economic creatures, but narrative and relational ones. Daniel Kahneman's work on memory and the "experiencing self" versus the "remembering self" shows that the way we *remember* someone often has little to do with their status or wealth, and much more to do with how they made us feel—trusted, encouraged, seen. The implications for legacy are profound. *It is not what you give that is always remembered, but what you meant.*

This is not to dismiss financial inheritance. Capital, when aligned with values and vision, can be a force multiplier. But when legacy planning ignores the emotional and social dimensions of wealth, it risks becoming brittle. Consider the well-documented phenomenon of inherited wealth dissolution: over 70% of affluent families lose their wealth by the second generation, and 90% by the third. While often attributed to financial mismanagement, deeper research suggests the real culprit is a lack of shared meaning, preparedness, and communication. Families inherit assets, but not identity. They receive resources without receiving the *relational scaffolding* to carry them forward.

Invisible legacy, by contrast, strengthens that scaffolding. It establishes a pattern of engagement and example that money alone cannot replace. Think of a parent who models disciplined generosity—not just through donations, but in how they give attention, time, and dignity. Or a community leader who mentors young people not for status, but for continuity. Their impact cannot be monetised, yet it often proves more durable than any fund or endowment.

There is also a spiritual dimension to invisible legacy. Across cultural traditions—from African Ubuntu to Indigenous wisdom systems to Confucian ancestral rites—there is a persistent belief that we are responsible not only for our descendants, but for the moral and social condition we leave behind. Wealth, in these frameworks, is not defined by private accumulation but by public resonance. To "die rich," in the most meaningful sense, is not to die with unspent capital, but to die with nothing of value left unshared.

Modern examples of this abound. Consider Viktor Frankl, whose logotherapy was born out of profound suffering in Nazi concentration camps. He left behind no dynasty of material wealth, yet his insights into meaning, suffering, and human agency have shaped countless lives. Or Maya Angelou, whose poetry, courage, and presence influenced generations beyond her family. Their legacies are visible only through the behaviour, insight, and courage they inspired in others.

Invisible legacy also invites us to think beyond lineage. Not everyone has children. Not everyone wants to. But everyone influences someone. The colleague you mentored, the friend you challenged with love, the student who internalised your discipline—these are acts of transmission. Legacy, in its truest sense, is not about lineage; it is about leverage. How far does your example travel? How deeply does your presence affect the fabric of others' lives?

This orientation shifts the conversation from ego to ecology. It asks not "What am I leaving *behind*?" but "What am I embedding *within* others?" The former is focused on possessions; the latter on participation. And participation, unlike possession, is active until the end.

Yet this form of legacy demands a different kind of preparation. You don't need a lawyer to write it—but you do need intention. Invisible legacy is not what happens by default. It's the result of deliberate presence, consistent values, and the willingness to invest in people without guarantee of return.

It may take the form of a recurring lunch with a mentee. Or an annual family gathering where shared stories are treated as sacred, not sentimental. It may mean taking the time to explain your failures—why you left that job, how you rebuilt trust, why you chose not to pursue more when you already had enough. These moments are small in appearance, but vast in significance. *Legacy is not taught by lecture. It is taught by lived example and quiet repetition.*

Invisible legacy also calls us to consider what *we* inherited. Not just from our parents or guardians, but from friends, teachers, adversaries. What assumptions about money, fairness, generosity, or work did we absorb without questioning? What scripts are we passing on—intentionally or not? These inherited narratives often operate below our awareness, yet they shape our behaviour and expectations. The act of making invisible legacy conscious—of naming it, reshaping it, and transmitting it with intention—is itself a form of transformation.

There is, finally, an ethical imperative here. If our impact extends beyond our lifespan, then our responsibility does too. The values we normalise, the structures we support, the boundaries we respect—all contribute to the cultural soil others must grow in. Even those without material resources can influence the social DNA of their communities. A cleaner who treats their work with honour, a neighbour who shows up with food during illness, a manager who protects psychological safety on their team—all of these leave a trace. Not in headlines, but in human wellbeing.

Legacy, then, becomes less about what is remembered and more about what is *repeated.* Not everyone will remember your name, but they may repeat your habits. Your phrasing. Your courage. Your restraint. These things do not need to be written in legal documents to matter. They matter because they become part of someone else's reference point. And in that transmission, they outlive the physical and enter the moral and cultural bloodstream of the future.

To shape your invisible legacy, you do not need wealth. You need clarity. Who are you becoming, through how you behave? Who are you affirming, through what you encourage? What are you reinforcing, in how you respond to pressure or praise? These are the deep, quiet questions of legacy—and they are answered daily, whether or not we intend to.

Invisible legacy is not lesser than its material counterpart. It is *prerequisite* to it. For wealth to endure, it must be nested inside a culture of meaning. And for meaning to persist, it must be enacted, not just named.

This is not a call for perfection. It is a call for *consciousness*. To live and give as though others are watching—not to perform, but to prepare. Because they are watching. And one day, they will not only remember what you did. They will reflect it. Or not. That is the silent, powerful test of every life: not the assets accumulated, but the values *absorbed.*

Chapter 6
Money and the Mind

For most, money has never been merely a matter of maths. Scratch beneath the surface and you'll find a tangled web of control, identity, belonging, fear, pride—more psychology than arithmetic. Still, curiously, much of the financial conversation remains cordoned off from the mind. We're handed charts and checklists, told how to budget and invest, yet rarely prompted to ask why we overspend when anxious or what, exactly, we're chasing when we aim for "financial independence." The truth is a little uncomfortable: without understanding our psychological relationship with money, we're not really managing it—we're merely rearranging the symptoms.

This chapter takes up what is often overlooked in the canon of financial literacy: that our behaviour with money is not simply about habit, but about biography. Every Excel sheet tells a story—some barely conscious, others inherited like old furniture. Whether it's the echo of a childhood spent wanting, or the quiet pressure of keeping up with a curated feed, our money moves are rarely coldly rational. More often, they are emotional reflexes wrapped in familiar narratives, hardwired well before our first job or bank card.

And the price of ignoring this is not abstract. It plays out as self-sabotage disguised as discipline. It looks like promotions followed by purchases that offer diminishing returns. It sounds like shame, softly spoken in the language of debt and doubt. And, perhaps most insidiously, it feels like losing touch with who we are when we're not acquiring something new.

Take the Scarcity Script. You'll recognise it in the voice that whispers, "It could all disappear tomorrow." It often takes root in early life, in households marked by instability or silence around money. Over time, that script hardens into an operating system—one that continues to run even when the conditions have changed. You might know someone who earns well, yet hoards, resists generosity, or panics over minor fluctuations in the market. This isn't greed—it's trauma masquerading as prudence.

To rewrite such scripts is not a matter of repeating affirmations in the mirror. It's slow, deliberate work. It begins by tracing the origin story—asking where the beliefs came from and why they linger. Neuroscience confirms what many of us have felt: core money beliefs, especially those etched in childhood, are hardwired into our sense of self and emotional safety. They don't shift without effort. But they can shift—if we're willing to examine them with curiosity rather than judgement.

There's another pattern worth naming here: emotional inflation. Before the luxury car is leased or the designer bag acquired, the inner thermostat has already been adjusted. What once felt indulgent now feels standard. What was once enough no longer is. This creep isn't just financial—it's emotional. And crucially, it's contagious. We calibrate our sense of "normal" against our surroundings. Eventually, gratitude thins, replaced by the quiet hum of perpetual upgrading.

This is why fulfilment doesn't scale automatically with income. In fact, unchecked emotional inflation can lead to the absurd paradox of earning more while feeling less secure. The outward upgrades mask an internal erosion. We begin living in more expensive versions of the same discontent.

And then there's comparison—the great accelerant. Of course, comparison has always existed. But never has it been this persistent, this visual, or this engineered. Social media doesn't just show us others' lives—it showcases aspirational avatars, fine-tuned for admiration and envy. Our brains, evolutionarily tuned to seek status, read these displays not as suggestion but as instruction. This isn't about information; it's about identity. We see, we compare, we feel behind.

It's rarely the money itself that stings. It's what we believe it means in someone else's hands and what we fear its absence says about us. Quietly, the comparison game shifts our sense of agency. We begin measuring success not by whether our lives align with our values, but by how closely they mimic someone else's highlight reel.

And so our spending morphs into a kind of theatre. We purchase not just objects, but identities. The minimalist decor, the artisanal coffee gear, the eco-conscious wardrobe—they're not just things; they're signals. Aspirations in physical form. Again, this isn't inherently wrong. We are symbolic beings. But it becomes problematic when the identity being projected isn't genuinely ours. When the spending is in service to someone else's gaze, not our own clarity.

The point here is not to guilt anyone out of buying things. Nor is it a call to austerity. Rather, what's needed is discernment. The capacity to ask, honestly: is this aligned with what I care about? Or is it a costume, stitched together from someone else's aesthetic? Identity-based spending only becomes dangerous when it's reactive—when it arises from unconscious imitation rather than authentic expression.

And how do we cultivate that discernment? Through intentional practices. Not hacks, not restrictive budgets, but rituals that slow us down long enough to see. Spending fasts, for instance, act as temporary mirrors: you notice what tugs at you, what cravings surface, what voids you try to fill. Intention audits prompt a different kind of review—one less concerned with where the money went and more curious about why. These aren't about perfection. They're about presence.

Because here's the quiet truth in a world designed to keep you consuming without pause: awareness is an act of rebellion. When we pay attention—really pay attention—we begin to reclaim choice. We shift from reacting to reflecting. From unconscious repetition to conscious design. From someone else's idea of "enough" to our own.

This chapter doesn't argue for an artificial separation of money and emotion. Quite the opposite. Integration is the path to sanity. When our financial lives reflect self-awareness rather than self-deception, we stop treating money as a constant stressor and begin using it as a mirror. A means of understanding ourselves more honestly.

Because, in the end, this is what money demands of us—not mastery, but maturity. It doesn't want to be chased, nor hoarded. It wants to be understood. And if we're willing, it can teach us more than spreadsheets ever could. The areas where we overspend? They might point to emotional gaps. The accounts we ignore? They may echo past fears. Every pattern holds a lesson—if we're ready to learn.

So this chapter is less a manual than an invitation. A chance to peer into the architecture of your inner economy—the fears and beliefs and inherited scripts that quietly govern how you engage with wealth. No formula is offered here. No easy recipe for financial serenity. But a lens is. A lens through which to see money not only as currency, but as character. Not only as a tool, but as text. And perhaps, in that re-seeing, something deeper shifts.

Because until we understand the mind behind the money, no income will ever feel sufficient. And no portfolio will buy the peace we haven't yet made within ourselves.

"The Scarcity Script"

Ask someone to describe their relationship with money, and they might cite their income, spending habits, or financial goals. But ask them how they *feel* about money—instinctively, physiologically—and the answers grow complex. Often, the discomfort is not in the maths, but in the meaning. Beneath many of our adult financial decisions lies a hidden architecture of early experiences, quietly scripting our sense of worth, fear, control, and enoughness. These subconscious codes rarely speak in dollars or spreadsheets. They speak in tensions—tightness around spending, guilt around earning, anxiety around saving, shame around debt. This is the Scarcity Script, and it runs deeper than budgeting can reach.

The Scarcity Script is not a financial strategy; it is a psychological survival response. It forms in environments where resources—tangible or emotional—feel unreliable. A child growing up watching a parent juggle overdue bills may learn that money is never safe. Another, who sees wealth used as control or withheld as punishment, might internalise that money equals power and vulnerability. Still another, whose family avoids any open conversation about finances, may absorb the idea that money is shameful, mysterious, or taboo. These impressions, absorbed before critical thinking matures, crystallise into what psychologists call *core beliefs*. Unlike surface-level thoughts, core beliefs are not easily dislodged by logic. They shape identity. They define what we perceive as possible.

Crucially, these beliefs do not expire when circumstances improve. An individual who escaped financial instability in their youth may still feel constant pressure to earn, hoard, or control—even when well-off. The threat is no longer external but internalised. Similarly, those raised in abundance are not immune. If money was equated with conditional love, competition, or perfectionism, they too may grow into adulthood with distorted scripts—ones that equate self-worth with achievement or spending. *Scarcity*, then, is not about the absence of money. It's about the presence of fear—fear that there will never be enough, or that when it does arrive, it will disappear.

This internal script becomes especially insidious because it often operates beneath awareness. Someone may label themselves "frugal" when they are actually afraid. Another may overwork chronically, claiming ambition, when the driver is a fear of ever feeling poor again. Because modern economies reward productivity and accumulation, these patterns are socially sanctioned. But psychologically, they are taxing. Scarcity-based beliefs can lead to burnout, relational friction, compulsive saving or overspending, and an inability to enjoy wealth even when earned. They shrink our imagination of what is allowed.

One of the defining features of the Scarcity Script is its rigidity. It resists evidence. You might double your income, but the underlying belief—"I am not safe"—persists. This is because the belief is not updated by data; it is reinforced by emotion. Our nervous systems become attuned to chronic vigilance. We interpret financial setbacks as confirmation of danger. Even abundance is met with suspicion. This is why personal finance advice that ignores emotion so often fails to change behaviour. It speaks to the mind, but the script lives in the body.

To dismantle a scarcity script, we must do more than think differently—we must *feel* differently. This begins with awareness. What did money mean in your family? What emotions accompanied it? Who was allowed to talk about it, and who was not? Did abundance feel empowering, or did it come with pressure? Was financial hardship a shared struggle or a source of isolation? Answering these questions is not about blame—it is about clarity. Until we understand the emotional logic of our financial past, we risk repeating it unconsciously.

Rewriting the script requires practices that bridge insight and embodiment. Here are three such exercises, designed not as quick fixes but as sustained inquiries:

1. **The Origin Reflection**: Set aside thirty minutes to write your earliest memory involving money. Describe the setting, the people involved, the emotional tone. What did you learn—explicitly or implicitly—from that event? Now trace forward. Identify two or three other formative experiences that reinforced this early narrative. What beliefs did they teach you about money's role, availability, or morality?
2. **The Belief Audit**: Create two columns. On the left, write down statements you *instinctively* believe about money (e.g. "You have to work hard for every penny," "Money changes people," "We're not the kind of family that gets rich"). Don't filter. On the right, interrogate each one: *Is it universally true? Where did I learn this? Does it serve me now?* For each outdated belief, write a more expansive alternative—not a forced affirmation, but a believable upgrade (e.g. "Some wealth can come from leverage, creativity, or rest").
3. **The Enough List**: Each day for one week, write down five things—financial or otherwise—that made you feel supported, resourced, or sufficient. These might include a paid invoice, a shared meal, an unexpected act of kindness. This trains your attention to notice abundance, interrupting the brain's habitual orientation toward deficit. Over time, you begin to internalise that enough is not just a concept—it is a state that can be cultivated.

This inner work is not separate from "real" financial progress—it is foundational to it. Without addressing these scripts, even the most competent earners find themselves trapped in familiar loops: growing income but never feeling secure; building wealth but fearing loss; creating budgets but breaking them in moments of emotional overload. Money becomes a mirror—not of value, but of unresolved fears.

The irony of the Scarcity Script is that it often masquerades as financial diligence. Caution is praised. Savings are applauded. Hustle is admired. But beneath these traits may live a dysregulated nervous system, unable to relax or receive. Rewiring that system does not mean discarding prudence. It means allowing *capacity*—the capacity to pause, to trust, to breathe inside financial decisions rather than flee from or grasp at them.

There is also a cultural dimension to scarcity. For communities historically excluded from wealth access—due to systemic racism, colonialism, class stratification—the Scarcity Script is not just personal but inherited. Generational trauma around resource insecurity often calcifies into family-wide narratives: "People like us don't…" "We have to…" "You can't trust…" These are protective in origin, but limiting in practice. Financial healing, in these cases, is both individual and intergenerational. It asks not only what story you carry, but whether you will continue to carry it forward—or choose to write a new one.

Importantly, the goal is not to swing from scarcity to delusion. Uncritical abundance mantras can be just as psychologically hollow. A mature financial script is *integrated.* It honours past hardship without clinging to it. It allows you to prepare responsibly while refusing to catastrophise. It balances prudence with permission. And above all, it aligns your financial behaviour with your actual life—not your inherited fear.

The reward for this work is not merely emotional calm; it is strategic clarity. When you operate from a foundation of sufficiency, you make better decisions. You take risks not to escape fear but to honour vision. You spend in alignment with values, not to soothe anxiety. You save not out of dread, but out of stewardship. Your money ceases to be a battleground—and becomes a tool.

No financial education is complete without addressing the psychological roots of our behaviours. We cannot spreadsheet our way out of subconscious patterns. We cannot budget our way into self-worth. But we can turn toward our scripts with curiosity and courage. We can revise. We can reframe. We can, through intention and insight, author a financial narrative that honours where we come from *without being governed by it.*

And that is the essential pivot—from money as a trauma response to money as a conscious expression of freedom. Not freedom as escape, but freedom as presence. The presence to choose, to respond, to build something that is not simply reactionary, but rooted, relational, and real. That is the work of rewriting the Scarcity Script. It is not easy. But it is profound. And it is possible.

"Emotional Inflation"

You don't need to own a yacht or lease a sports car to experience lifestyle creep. Often, it begins invisibly—long before your bank balance changes—through subtle shifts in emotional expectations. Long before your expenses climb, your internal bar for what counts as *normal* rises. It's rarely about greed or ambition. It's about emotional calibration. This is *emotional inflation*—the process by which our sense of what we deserve, require, or need for contentment slowly escalates, not in line with reason, but in response to pressure, habit, and perception. The numbers may change, but the core experience—of not quite having enough—remains eerily constant.

Traditional personal finance frameworks tend to define lifestyle creep as a budgeting problem. They describe how discretionary spending increases as income rises: you trade the café for the restaurant, the budget hotel for the boutique resort, the compact car for the SUV. Yet beneath these outward upgrades lies a more complex transformation. Before the actual purchases occur, a psychological shift has already taken place: *your emotional tolerance for less has diminished.* What once felt like a luxury now feels like a baseline. That's not mathematics. That's mindset.

Understanding emotional inflation requires us to decouple consumption from capacity. You can be earning significantly more and still feel chronically under-resourced. This isn't a paradox—it's a pattern. In behavioural economics, it's observed that people's subjective satisfaction with their financial situation does not rise linearly with income. Instead, it plateaus—often far earlier than we imagine. And yet, spending continues. Why? Because satisfaction is not driven solely by what we possess, but by how we feel about what we possess. And that feeling is shaped not by absolute wealth, but by *relative expectations*.

Expectations don't arise in a vacuum. They are socially manufactured, culturally encoded, and emotionally reinforced. When a friend upgrades to a designer handbag, or a colleague moves into a newer home, or your algorithm serves you a steady stream of aspirational content, your baseline quietly adjusts. It's not just that you want more—it's that you subtly feel you *should* have more. This is the internal engine of lifestyle creep: it doesn't merely respond to what you can afford; it responds to what you can emotionally justify. That's what makes it so insidious. It feels like progress, but often it's simply re-calibrated dissatisfaction dressed as sophistication.

The psychology behind this phenomenon has deep evolutionary roots. Human beings are remarkably sensitive to status cues because, for much of history, survival depended on group belonging. To fall behind the group—economically or socially—was to become vulnerable. That legacy persists. Today, when others in our cohort elevate their lifestyle, we register it not just as difference, but as potential threat: *am I falling behind?* This comparative cognition operates beneath awareness and fuels much of modern spending. It's less about pleasure and more about reassurance. That's why luxury often loses its joy. Once normalised, it offers no emotional return—just a new standard to maintain.

To break the cycle, we must intervene not at the level of expenditure, but at the level of identity. Ask not "Can I afford this?" but "Why do I believe I *need* this now?" What internal pressure is this purchase soothing? What imagined self is being maintained or manufactured? What am I afraid it would *mean* if I opted for less?

In this context, *emotional inflation* becomes not just a financial issue, but a philosophical one. It invites questions of meaning, sufficiency, and aspiration. How do we define progress without tethering it to consumption? How do we honour growth without commodifying it? How do we sustain ambition without sacrificing equanimity?

One of the most effective antidotes to emotional inflation is cultivating *awareness rituals*—practices that create distance between impulse and action. Consider a simple but profound exercise: the *24-hour delay*. Before making a discretionary purchase over a threshold amount—say, £100—wait a full day. During that window, observe what arises: urgency, justification, rationalisation. Is the desire growing clearer or fading? Emotional inflation thrives on immediacy. Delaying reintroduces discernment.

Another strategy is the *reverse upgrade audit*. Periodically, review recent lifestyle shifts and ask: which of these actually improved my quality of life? Which merely increased my dependency on a higher threshold of stimulation, convenience, or validation? For instance, did moving from ride-share to owning a car free up time, or increase stress? Did switching to premium brands improve performance, or simply elevate expectation? This exercise fosters intentionality. It disentangles what truly serves you from what simply *signals* success.

Then there is the practice of *voluntary simplicity*, not as austerity, but as experimentation. Choose a domain—clothing, dining, travel—and intentionally reduce your spend for a set period. Not to punish, but to recalibrate. What emotions arise when you opt for less? Embarrassment? Relief? Empowerment? These moments reveal how tightly consumption is linked to identity. The aim is not to eliminate spending, but to restore agency. To spend not by default, but by design.

Philosophically, emotional inflation exposes a deeper tension: the modern confusion between *value* and *values*. Many of us have been conditioned to conflate price with worth—both of objects and of self. When something costs more, we assume it must be better.

When we can afford more, we believe we must be doing better. But this logic, while commercially convenient, is psychologically corrosive. It disconnects us from intrinsic satisfaction. It makes joy conditional on novelty. Over time, it hollows out gratitude and replaces it with habituation.

Economist Tibor Scitovsky argued in *The Joyless Economy* that affluent societies often fail to produce sustained happiness because they overvalue comfort and undervalue complexity. Easy pleasures—purchased upgrades, automated conveniences—provide momentary relief, but rarely deep engagement. In contrast, activities that require skill, attention, or creativity—gardening, music, craft—yield richer, longer-lasting satisfaction. Yet these do not scale easily. They do not signal affluence. So they are neglected in favour of easier, louder wins. Emotional inflation thrives in this environment because it replaces depth with quantity.

Social media accelerates this effect. Platforms curate idealised slices of other people's financial lives—home renovations, luxury travel, designer fashion—without context or consequence. We rarely see the debt, burnout, or ambivalence behind the feed. But our nervous system reacts as if we are falling behind. The result is a constant sense of dissonance: our lived experience versus the curated expectations. To resist this pressure is not merely a matter of willpower—it is an act of psychological resistance.

To that end, consider a final practice: *gratitude indexing*. Unlike general gratitude journaling, this involves actively noticing and recording moments when you *rejected* an upgrade—and felt whole anyway. Skipping the coffee subscription and savouring a home brew. Wearing old clothes to a new event—and receiving a compliment. Declining a premium feature—and discovering it didn't matter. Each instance reinforces your internal locus of satisfaction. Over time, it builds resilience against emotional inflation, not through denial, but through conscious reinforcement of sufficiency.

Ultimately, emotional inflation is a story—not about money, but about meaning. It reveals where our attention goes, what we believe matters, and how we measure self-worth. When left unchecked, it turns abundance into anxiety. But when brought into awareness, it becomes an invitation: to slow down, to choose consciously, to reclaim joy from the escalating curve of expectation. In a world that constantly nudges us toward more, the quiet power is in *enough*—not as resignation, but as reclamation.

This is not minimalism for its own sake. It is clarity. It is reasserting the difference between lifestyle and life. Between having more and *being more*. Between the emotion of status and the state of contentment. Those who master this distinction do not merely protect their finances. They protect their peace. And that, in the end, is the most enduring wealth of all.

"The Cost of Comparison"

At no point in history have so many people had so much access to the financial lives of others—and so little context to interpret what they see. In the analogue past, we measured our financial progress against a handful of peers: neighbours, colleagues, perhaps family members. Today, comparison operates on a global scale, algorithmically curated and infinitely scrolling. Every promotion, every house purchase, every designer handbag, every passive income post, every "I retired at 33" headline—each is a data point we absorb without context, each subtly reshaping how we perceive our own sufficiency. This constant calibration of our financial lives against the edited narratives of others is not benign. It has real, measurable effects—neurological, emotional, and behavioural. It affects not only what we spend, but how we *feel* about what we have.

To understand the cost of comparison, we must begin with the brain. Neuroscientific research confirms what philosophy has intuited for millennia: humans are profoundly social creatures, wired to detect status and hierarchy. The same regions of the brain activated by physical pain—such as the anterior cingulate cortex—are also activated by social exclusion and status threats. In other words, perceiving oneself as "less than" in a social or financial context can trigger a neurological stress response. And unlike physical threats, which are bounded in time, status threats persist as long as we remain connected to the comparative stimulus—which, in the age of social media, is essentially always.

One study published in *Nature Human Behaviour* found that social comparison on platforms like Instagram leads not only to reduced subjective wellbeing, but to increased materialistic aspirations. Even when individuals know that curated posts are selectively presented, their emotional systems still respond as if they reflect reality. This is because the human brain did not evolve to handle asynchronous, contextless, high-resolution displays of others' curated success. Our social cognition was designed for small groups and shared experience, not for digesting thousands of polished life summaries in a single afternoon.

The psychological effects are not limited to envy. Comparison subtly rewrites our internal narratives about what is enough, what is fair, and what is possible. A person may feel content with their income until they encounter someone younger with greater apparent wealth. They may feel confident in their progress until reminded of someone who has seemingly "made it" faster. This constant erosion of satisfaction undermines not just joy, but *agency*. It creates a perpetual sense of lagging behind, which in turn drives reactive financial decisions—overspending to keep up, undersaving out of demoralisation, or pivoting career strategies without internal alignment.

Importantly, the comparison effect is not confined to digital life. It shows up in boardrooms and breakrooms, at dinner parties and school drop-offs. The brand of car, the zip code of the home, the mention of a private school or a luxury holiday—all become proxies for financial identity. These moments are often unintentionally performative. Few people boast openly, but subtle cues are dropped—a casual reference to a remodel, a new investment property, an early equity exit. And for the listener, these cues register less as information and more as evaluation: *Am I behind? Did I miss something? Should I be doing more?*

Culturally, this is amplified by what sociologists have called "reference group inflation." As people rise economically, they tend not to compare themselves to their past selves, but to their new peers. A person earning £100,000 may feel comfortable until they are regularly interacting with those earning double. This psychological re-benchmarking happens quietly, but decisively. It explains why income satisfaction does not scale proportionally with earnings. It also explains the phenomenon of "rich and unhappy"—a condition increasingly documented among high earners who, despite material abundance, experience chronic financial insecurity because they are embedded in high-expectation environments.

There is also an ethical dimension to consider. Comparison culture does not just distort individual behaviour; it distorts societal narratives about success. When financial achievement is broadcast without disclosure—of inherited wealth, of unpaid internships, of spousal support, of luck—it creates aspirational myths that are structurally misleading. This is particularly damaging for young people, who internalise these distorted scripts early. When wealth is presented as a product of hustle and manifestation rather than privilege and systemic advantage, it perpetuates both personal shame and collective delusion. The cost of comparison, then, is not only emotional—it is ideological.

But what is the alternative? The antidote is not abstinence from observation. We cannot—and arguably should not—retreat entirely from social contexts. Instead, the solution lies in *disciplined discernment*: learning to interpret, rather than absorb, the signals around us. One approach is the intentional cultivation of what psychologist Carl Rogers called "internal locus of evaluation." This involves developing the habit of measuring success not by external metrics, but by personal alignment—progress toward goals that are *self-authored*, not socially borrowed.

A practical exercise: whenever you feel the sting of financial comparison, pause and ask three questions. First, *Do I want what they have, or do I want to feel how I think they feel?* Often, envy is less about the object and more about the imagined emotional state it represents. Second, *What am I not seeing?* Remember that most financial stories are heavily edited. Third, *What would success look like if I weren't watching anyone else?* This question, answered honestly, is among the most radical tools of financial clarity.

Another practice is *narrative reclamation*. This involves rewriting your financial story with conscious emphasis on values, effort, and uniqueness. Instead of framing your life in deficit terms—what you lack relative to others—focus on coherence: is your financial behaviour consistent with your values? Are your investments—of time, energy, and money—moving you toward your self-defined vision of sufficiency? This shift is not semantic. It is structural. It reorganises attention from surveillance to sovereignty.

Still, this is not easy work. Social comparison is not a modern glitch—it is an ancient feature of human cognition. But it becomes pathological when decoupled from shared context and anchored to unrealistic ideals. In pre-industrial societies, wealth was visible but bounded—limited by geography and social structure. Today, we are exposed to the lifestyles of billionaires and influencers, yet expected to feel grounded and content. This is not merely unfair—it is neurologically unsustainable.

To reclaim financial agency, we must practise *media hygiene*. Curate your inputs. Reduce exposure to accounts, influencers, or peers who provoke chronic comparison without offering value. Follow people who disclose complexity, not just results. Engage with content that encourages reflection, not reaction. The algorithm is not neutral; it rewards spectacle, not substance. If you do not curate your financial inputs, your nervous system will do it for you—often through anxiety, resentment, or shame.

Finally, remember that the ultimate cost of comparison is not just emotional turbulence. It is misalignment. When you build a financial life to match someone else's surface, you compromise your own depth. You defer decisions, delay contentment, and dilute purpose. The reward for resisting this pull is not merely peace of mind—it is strategic clarity. A person who knows what matters to them financially is immunised, not from envy, but from its dominion. They can observe others without forfeiting themselves. They can succeed on terms that are both private and profound.

This, ultimately, is the measure that matters. Not whether you are richer than your peers. But whether your money expresses your values more clearly than your fears. Whether your financial decisions reflect your internal compass, not your external scoreboard. And whether your sense of sufficiency has roots deeper than comparison can reach. That is the quiet, invisible dividend of financial maturity.

It is not about having more. It is about *needing less surveillance to know you're on course.*

"Identity-Based Spending"

At a glance, every purchase looks like a choice. But look closer, and many are not. They are performances—scripts inherited from culture, curated for status, shaped by insecurity, or driven by stories we've never paused to question. We tell ourselves we need the better car, the bigger flat, the expensive handbag, the fine bottle of wine—not always because we want them, but because we want what they signal. Financially, this is unsustainable. Psychologically, it's hollowing. Identity-based spending is not inherently problematic—on the contrary, it can be a source of deep alignment—but only when that identity is *authentic.* The real problem is not spending to express who we are. It's spending to disguise who we fear we aren't.

The phenomenon is subtle but pervasive. Consider the graduate who buys designer clothes not out of aesthetic preference, but to feel professionally valid among wealthier peers. Or the freelancer who leases a luxury car not out of love for driving, but to project credibility to clients. Or the parent who sends their child to a private school at the expense of retirement savings, driven less by educational philosophy and more by fear of social exclusion. These choices are not irrational—but they are *reactive.* They arise not from values, but from external signals that have been internalised without interrogation.

Psychology offers a compelling framework here. According to self-determination theory, humans have three fundamental needs: autonomy, competence, and relatedness. When these needs are unmet, we often compensate through symbolic consumption. Autonomy might be expressed through rebellious fashion. Competence through the display of luxury. Relatedness through shared brand affinities. Advertisers understand this instinctively, even if consumers don't. When a brand promises "confidence," "power," or "belonging," it is not selling fabric or metal—it is selling identity scaffolding to people unsure whether they belong without it.

Neuroscience reinforces this dynamic. Research using functional MRI has shown that buying products associated with social prestige activates the brain's reward centres—particularly the ventral striatum—more intensely than neutral purchases. In other words, we are neurologically primed to *enjoy* identity-reinforcing spending. The risk, of course, is when that pleasure masks debt, regret, or disconnection from genuine values. Many people do not overspend because they are reckless; they overspend because for a moment, spending offers identity reassurance. It tells them, *You're OK. You fit in. You measure up.*

But what does it mean to spend in a way that reflects who we are rather than who we're trying to impress? The answer begins with honesty. It requires the discipline to ask, *Is this purchase aligned with my values, or is it a performance for someone else's attention or approval?* The distinction is not always clear. For example, buying artisanal coffee daily may seem indulgent—but for a writer who values sensory experience and local craftsmanship, it could be perfectly aligned. Meanwhile, someone else might own a minimal wardrobe and drive an old car—not out of frugality, but to signal moral superiority. Simplicity, too, can be performative.

This is why clarity, not austerity, is the goal. Identity-based spending becomes harmful only when it is unconscious—when we outsource our financial choices to social pressure, unresolved wounds, or aspirational fictions. To reclaim agency, we must trace spending back to *meaning*. Every major expense—home, education, travel, fashion—should be examined with two questions: *Does this reflect who I am?* And: *Does it reflect who I want to become—on my terms, not society's timeline?*

The sociologist Pierre Bourdieu argued that taste is largely shaped by "habitus"—our ingrained habits, dispositions, and cultural conditioning. In other words, what we consider "normal" or "necessary" spending is rarely neutral. It reflects our upbringing, our class background, and the social circles we inhabit. A person raised in a working-class environment may see a £60 meal as wasteful; someone from a more affluent context might see it as modest. Neither is objectively correct. But recognising that your sense of "enough" is inherited—not inherent—is a critical first step in escaping reflexive spending.

Social media exacerbates this problem by collapsing context. A single scroll exposes us to hundreds of curated financial displays—from soft-launch investments to luxury staycations—all edited to maximise aesthetic impact and social desirability. Rarely do we see the trade-offs: the debt behind the travel, the anxiety behind the aesthetic, the loneliness behind the wealth. This distorts not only our expectations, but our emotional benchmarks. A purchase that once felt extravagant now feels necessary—not because our values changed, but because our point of comparison did.

The result is what behavioural economists call "relative deprivation"—the sense that one has less than one deserves, even when absolute resources are sufficient. This creates a dangerous feedback loop. Identity insecurity fuels aspirational spending. Aspirational spending leads to financial strain. Financial strain reinforces identity insecurity. The cycle continues until interrupted by crisis—or introspection.

The latter is preferable. And it is possible. Start by conducting a *spending audit through a values lens.* For one month, track every expense—not just in pounds, but in purpose. For each item, ask: What need did this serve? Whose approval was I seeking? Was this a vote for the person I am, or the persona I curate? Patterns will emerge. You may find that you consistently overspend in domains tied to self-worth—appearance, status, validation—while underspending on areas that actually nurture your well-being.

Next, write a *financial identity statement.* This is not a budget or a spreadsheet. It is a brief document that articulates your core values, your long-term aspirations, and the emotional tone you want your financial life to embody. It might include statements like: *I want my spending to reflect creativity, generosity, and calm.* Or: *I choose purchases that deepen relationships, not just decorate them.* This becomes your compass—a filter for future decisions that might otherwise be swayed by ambient social noise.

Finally, build micro-habits that anchor spending to authenticity. For example, before any non-essential purchase over £50, wait 48 hours and revisit your financial identity statement. Ask: Will this item add coherence to my life—or complexity? This simple pause creates space for reflection, which is the antidote to impulsive, image-driven decisions. Over time, you will find that fewer purchases feel performative, and more feel aligned.

Identity-based spending, when misdirected, erodes both wealth and integrity. But when anchored to genuine values, it can be a powerful expression of self-authorship. It is not wrong to want beautiful things, or to invest in status signals. The error lies in assuming they will solve a self-perception problem that must be addressed at the source.

The ultimate goal is not to eliminate identity from spending, but to harmonise it. To ensure that the financial story you're telling yourself—and the world—is both accurate and affirming. That you're not buying a lifestyle to feel like someone else, but funding a life that feels like *you*. The more aligned your spending becomes with your internal truth, the less susceptible you are to the tides of trend, the pressures of perception, or the costs of comparison.

And perhaps this is the most radical act in a hyper-curated world: to spend without signalling. To let your money reflect your meaning, not your marketing. To craft a financial life that is not just visible, but *authentic*—even if no one else sees it.

"Building a Financial Mindfulness Practice":

We tend to think of money as a system of numbers. But its real power lies not in arithmetic, but in attention. Financial lives are rarely derailed by a lack of information. They unravel in the spaces where attention lapses, emotion takes the wheel, and unconscious habits quietly consolidate. In this sense, the most impactful financial tool is not an app, a spreadsheet, or an investment vehicle—it is awareness. And awareness, like wealth, must be cultivated deliberately. To build a financial life that is both stable and self-authored, one must learn to see money not only as currency, but as a mirror. This is the central promise of financial mindfulness: to turn transactions into teachers, spending into self-study, and choice into alignment.

Unlike budgeting, which is often reactive and externally imposed, financial mindfulness is proactive and internally driven. It doesn't ask, "Where did my money go?" It asks, "What was I feeling when I spent it?" It invites inquiry before behaviour—not just after damage. The objective is not to suppress desire, nor to moralise consumption, but to insert space between impulse and action. In that space, freedom lives. Practised consistently, this can change the emotional texture of money from something that provokes stress or denial into something that reflects intentionality and self-respect.

One of the simplest yet most revealing practices is the **intention audit**. Once a week—ideally at the same time and in the same place—set aside ten minutes to review recent expenses. But rather than classifying purchases by category or size, examine them through motive. For each transaction, ask: *What was I hoping this would give me? Was I seeking comfort, control, status, escape, or joy?* This exercise surfaces patterns that financial statements alone never reveal. A £4 coffee might be less about caffeine and more about a ritual of reward after stress. A £200 gadget may reflect not utility, but a craving for novelty. The point is not to judge these motives—it is to make them conscious.

Financial mindfulness also involves subtractive practices—rituals that create temporary constraints to sharpen awareness. A well-known method is the **spending fast**: a set period, often 7 to 30 days, in which all non-essential spending is paused. But the purpose is not austerity—it is calibration. By pressing pause, we reset the emotional baseline that modern consumer culture continuously inflates. We discover that many purchases are not needs, but habits. And in their absence, we begin to differentiate between what truly adds value and what merely fills space.

To enhance this, some practitioners adopt a *single-category fast*—choosing one discretionary domain, such as dining out or online shopping, and eliminating it temporarily. This adds specificity and reduces the psychological resistance that full abstinence can provoke. More importantly, it invites reflection on the emotional ecosystem surrounding that category. Dining out, for instance, might be less about food and more about a sense of connection. When the act is paused, the need must be met differently—perhaps through home-cooked meals with others, or intentional social planning. In this way, money becomes a map—not just of spending, but of underlying values.

Another core mindfulness ritual is the **purchase pause**. Before buying anything non-essential over a self-imposed threshold—say, £50—commit to waiting 48 hours. During this window, observe the urge: Does it intensify, fade, or evolve? Ask: *What story am I telling myself about this item? What identity does it promise? What emotion is it soothing or stimulating?* This small act of delay is disproportionately powerful. It disrupts the dopamine-driven cycle of stimulus and response, creating room for self-inquiry. Over time, the mere practice of pausing rewires consumption from reflex to reflection.

Importantly, mindfulness does not mean minimalism—though the two often intersect. A financially mindful person may spend lavishly on what they love and nothing on what they don't. What separates them from impulsive spenders is not frugality, but *alignment.* Every purchase is an expression of values, not a sedative for anxiety or a bid for status. This intentionality has practical benefits—less debt, more savings, clearer goals—but the deeper value lies in coherence. The internal story and the external behaviour begin to match.

To embed this more deeply, some individuals maintain a **financial gratitude log**. Once a week, they write down a few purchases—however small—that brought genuine joy, ease, or meaning. The practice cultivates appreciation not only for what money can buy, but for the ability to choose. It shifts the focus from scarcity to sufficiency, from what is lacking to what is enough. Over time, this reframes money not as a battleground of guilt or stress, but as a canvas for conscious living.

Equally powerful is the practice of **pre-spending visualisation**. Before making a planned expense—particularly a large one—pause and imagine not the item itself, but the days and weeks after its acquisition. Does it still feel exciting once it's part of your normal? Does it simplify your life or complicate it? Would your future self thank you for it—or feel burdened by it? This anticipatory reflection can inoculate against emotional inflation—the phenomenon where imagined satisfaction outpaces lived experience. Neuroscience supports this: the anticipation of reward often generates more dopamine than the reward itself. Recognising this helps reduce the compulsion to chase highs that rarely last.

On a systemic level, financial mindfulness challenges the cultural narratives that bind money to worth. In societies where consumption is performative, and financial success is synonymous with moral success, mindful spending is a quiet act of rebellion. It says: *I will not confuse visibility with value. I will not conflate cost with meaning. I will not let external optics hijack internal truth.* This is not just a financial stance—it is an existential one.

The philosophical roots of such thinking run deep. In Stoicism, wealth is neither inherently good nor bad; what matters is how it is used. Seneca wrote, "Wealth is the slave of a wise man. The master of a fool." In Buddhism, right livelihood includes the awareness of cause and effect in economic behaviour—not just for oneself, but for others. And in modern psychology, the practice of *self-authoring* emphasises coherence between beliefs, actions, and aspirations. In this light, financial mindfulness is not a luxury—it is a moral discipline. It is how you honour your own autonomy in a system designed to monetise your attention and manipulate your desires.

Over time, these micro-practices add up to macro-transformation. You begin to sense financial tension before it builds. You become less reactive to advertising, less susceptible to trend cycles, and more attuned to what truly matters. You spend less time cleaning up after impulsive decisions and more time investing in choices that create spaciousness and satisfaction. And most critically, your relationship with money shifts from adversarial to advisory. Money is no longer something you "deal with" under stress—it becomes a language you speak with fluency and care.

This does not mean perfection. Financial mindfulness, like any form of awareness, is a practice—not a destination. You will overspend. You will rationalise. You will sometimes forget to pause. But the measure of progress is not elimination of error—it is the speed and compassion with which you return to attention. Each lapse becomes a lesson. Each choice becomes a chance to realign. The practice never ends, and that is precisely the point. Because awareness, like wealth, is not something you own. It is something you steward. Something you show up for. Every day. Quietly. Intentionally. Relentlessly.

Chapter 7
Cultural Myths, Money, and Meaning:

We seldom spend without signalling. Every swipe of a card, every deposit or indulgence, carries a freight of meaning—about who we are, what we believe we're owed, and how we imagine others perceive us. Yet the scripts that guide our financial decisions are often hand-me-downs: culturally inherited, subtly absorbed, rarely interrogated. They trail behind us like invisible scaffolding, shaping not only the way we handle money but the architecture of our identities, our relationships, and our personal definitions of what it means to succeed. This chapter holds these unspoken stories to the light—not with the aim of discarding them outright, but to examine them carefully, even tenderly. Because when left unexamined, cultural myths around money do not simply decorate our lives—they direct them.

We are taught, either explicitly or by omission, to treat money as a subject best handled with calculators and compound interest tables—an arena for accountants and analysts. But this technical framing misses the forest for the spreadsheets. Money is not merely a transactional tool; it's a cultural mirror. Throughout history, societies have layered symbolic meaning onto wealth—meanings that stretch far beyond mere subsistence. In medieval Europe, wealth connoted divine approval; in Puritan New England, thrift was treated as proof of moral fibre. In the capitalist West today, affluence often masquerades as intelligence or virtue. These linkages are so deeply embedded in our thinking that we rarely stop to question them—yet they shape our sense of worth as subtly and powerfully as any bank balance.

One of the more enduring—and frankly, exhausting—myths of our time is the celebration of the lone financial warrior: the self-made person who pulls themselves up by some imaginary bootstraps. It's a myth drenched in nostalgia and marketed as empowerment. But look closely, and it begins to fray. True financial autonomy is never achieved in a vacuum. It relies on social structures, economic legacies, and access—often invisible—to education, opportunity, and stability. The gospel of independence tends to obscure these undercurrents. Worse, it isolates people from the communal support that makes real financial resilience possible. What this chapter offers, instead, is a reframing: prosperity as a shared ecosystem, not a solitary conquest.

Status, of course, has always been part of the story. But the way we signal wealth today has grown both more refined and more pervasive. That designer bag? It isn't merely an accessory—it's an argument. An assertion of taste, discernment, even belonging. And paradoxically, the performance of rejection—the artfully frugal, the conspicuously minimalist—has become its own kind of spectacle. In this theatre of appearances, money doesn't just enable; it performs. And often, that performance comes at a cost. Many find themselves spending not out of desire, but out of a quiet panic—to stay visible, to feel enough, to chase a vision that may never have been theirs to begin with. This chapter offers a different possibility: spending not as spectacle, but as alignment—with values, with purpose, with truth.

There is another silence around money—one not of show, but of omission. In many homes, financial talk is the final taboo. We dance around it, reserve it for emergencies, or suppress it altogether. This silence breeds distortion. It hands down myths from parent to child, partner to partner, generation to generation, without ever inviting conscious choice. Sometimes, it's the legacy of trauma; other times, of cultural scripts that have long outlived their usefulness. The boy who watched arguments erupt over bills becomes the man who sidesteps every financial conversation. Not from secrecy—but from the unspoken belief that talking about money is dangerous. This chapter introduces a different language: one rooted in safety, openness, and co-authorship. Because the only way to shift the narrative is to speak it aloud.

Of course, these conversations do not happen on a blank canvas. They're framed by broader systems—some visible, others less so. Financial experiences are not evenly distributed, nor are they neutrally shaped. Gender, class, race—these are not incidental factors; they're formative. A man and a woman might earn the same salary, yet the cultural coding around what they "deserve" to do with that money can be starkly divergent. Likewise, those from historically marginalised communities are often handed not just economic disadvantage but the psychological weight of expectation—to prove, to outperform, to overcompensate. Any conversation about money that excludes identity is, at best, partial. This chapter advocates for a clearer lens—not to induce guilt, but to cultivate literacy. Because only when we see the scaffolding can we begin to redesign it.

And then there's generosity—often relegated to the end of financial planning, as though giving were something you do after everything else is in order. But generosity is not a footnote. It's not a tax strategy or a reputation builder. At its core, it is a worldview: the recognition that we are embedded in webs of care, mutuality, and shared resource. To give is not simply to part with funds—it is to reinforce the truth that value grows in circulation, not in hoarding. When approached with intent, generosity doesn't diminish—it expands. It deepens our social capital, our trust networks, our emotional wealth. Here, generosity is reframed not as charity, but as strategic design. As a choice about the kind of economic culture we wish to sustain.

What emerges from these reflections is not a tidy moral of the story, but a textured, complicated portrait of how money and meaning entwine. This chapter is not a critique of wealth in itself, nor a lamentation of ambition. It is an invitation—a provocation, even. It asks us to consider which stories about money we've internalised, which we've outgrown, and which remain unspoken. Who profits from the myths we maintain? Which truths do we sidestep, and why? And most pressingly: what becomes possible when we dare to choose our stories anew?

By the end, the aim is not enlightenment in the abstract—but something more grounded: a form of cultural literacy that sharpens your financial fluency and restores your agency. Not just to understand your numbers, but to understand what your numbers are saying. And then, perhaps, to write a different kind of financial narrative—not inherited, not improvised, but authored. Deliberate. Conscious. Yours.

"The Independence Illusion":

At the heart of modern economic mythology lies a deeply seductive fiction: the myth of the self-made individual. It is an idea so embedded in Western cultural consciousness that it rarely invites scrutiny. We applaud the founder who "started from nothing," the investor who "trusted only their instincts," the entrepreneur who "built an empire in their garage." These stories animate TED Talks, startup manifestos, and political speeches. They shape everything from career goals to philanthropic philosophies. And yet, for all their appeal, *they are almost always incomplete.* No one builds durable wealth alone. And those who try often pay for their isolation in invisible costs.

The notion of radical financial independence appeals because it promises control. It flatters the ego, suggesting that success can be secured by intelligence, grit, or hustle alone. But this narrative collapses under even minimal scrutiny. Every person who has achieved meaningful financial stability did so within a lattice of relationships, infrastructures, and inheritances—material or cultural. Access to education, family stability, geographic location, legal protections, market conditions, even unconscious biases—all of these are *forms of capital* that tilt the playing field before any personal decision is made. This is not to discredit personal effort. It is to *contextualise* it, resisting the easy erasure of the collective forces that scaffold individual gain.

Consider Silicon Valley, a region mythologised for its concentration of lone geniuses disrupting industries. The reality? Its founders rely heavily on university networks, venture capital ecosystems, government-funded research, and often, generational wealth. Even the romanticised garage is usually located in a zip code with reliable infrastructure, safe streets, and access to elite mentorship. This does not invalidate the work of its entrepreneurs—but it renders simplistic the idea that their success emerged from isolation. *They thrived within a carefully constructed ecosystem—not despite it, but because of it.*

The cost of believing in the independence illusion is not only sociological—it is psychological. Individuals who internalise the idea that they must "go it alone" often develop distorted relationships with both failure and help. If success is entirely personal, then failure becomes a reflection of personal deficiency. And seeking support becomes synonymous with weakness. This logic breeds shame, suppresses collaboration, and limits resilience. Ironically, the people most likely to burn out are not the ones with the heaviest workloads, but those with the *thinnest webs of support.* The belief in total autonomy becomes a kind of emotional austerity—satisfying in theory, but devastating in practice.

Across cultures and history, the notion of collective wealth has been far more prevalent than modern individualism would suggest. In Indigenous communities, for instance, wealth was historically understood in relational terms. The health of the tribe, the strength of intergenerational bonds, and the reciprocity of shared resources were seen as the true markers of prosperity. The Māori concept of *whanaungatanga* (kinship and relational accountability) or the African philosophy of *Ubuntu* ("I am because we are") articulates a vision of wealth that centres the group—not as a limit on freedom, but as the foundation for thriving. These models challenge Western assumptions that interdependence dilutes autonomy. *What if interdependence is not the opposite of freedom, but its precondition?*

Even in capitalist societies, interdependence reveals itself in moments of crisis. During economic collapses, natural disasters, or pandemics, it becomes immediately clear that individual insulation is a fantasy. Wealthy individuals may own private bunkers or medical care, but no one escapes systemic failure alone. Air, water, food supply chains, and collective stability are fundamentally *shared dependencies.* The illusion only survives in periods of stability—and it is precisely during those periods that we must question it most rigorously.

The independence illusion also skews how we build and sustain financial ecosystems. When wealth is treated as a private possession rather than a shared resource, it often becomes fragile. The more a system relies on isolated actors maximising self-interest, the more susceptible it becomes to volatility and disintegration. In contrast, interdependent wealth ecosystems—such as worker-owned cooperatives, mutual aid networks, or multi-family investment groups—often display greater resilience. These models distribute risk, centre transparency, and embed social accountability. *They may grow more slowly, but they fracture less easily.*

This is not an argument for collectivism at the expense of autonomy. It is a call to *refine our definitions*. True independence is not the absence of reliance on others—it is the capacity to choose interdependence with discernment and dignity. When individuals understand that wealth is more robust when shared, they become more intentional in how they build partnerships, mentor others, invest in communities, and design institutions. And when interdependence is made visible—not as a weakness, but as a feature—it enables healthier financial behaviours: sustainable scaling, ethical hiring, and the creation of wealth that benefits more than its originator.

Importantly, this reframing must begin early. Children absorb financial scripts not just from what is said, but from what is modelled. If they observe that asking for help is stigmatised, collaboration is penalised, and success must be performed solo, they internalise an identity that is at odds with how real-world success is achieved. Financial literacy programmes must move beyond budgeting and investment literacy to include relational literacy—how to build financial trust, how to partner without exploitation, how to navigate shared risk. *Teaching interdependence is not a moral add-on; it is strategic preparation.*

It is also an act of resistance. In a culture that monetises attention, individualism is profitable. Platforms that encourage competition over collaboration, comparison over community, thrive precisely because they exploit the loneliness that individualism creates. By recasting success as a *shared enterprise*, we resist the commodification of isolation. We make visible the social scaffolding that makes excellence sustainable.

In sum, the independence illusion is not only intellectually dishonest—it is operationally inefficient. Wealth, in its most durable form, is relational. It is built through trust, compounded through collaboration, and preserved through community. Whether through family, partnerships, institutions, or peer networks, every serious wealth-builder must eventually confront a paradox: *You can either appear to be self-made, or you can actually build something that lasts. But rarely both.*

To dismantle the myth of going it alone is not to diminish the role of agency or ambition. It is to honour the full ecology of success. And in doing so, to build wealth ecosystems that are not only richer in numbers, but richer in meaning, continuity, and collective strength.

"Wealth as Virtue Signalling":

Wealth has always communicated more than purchasing power. It is a language—a grammar of status, a visual dialect of belonging, and, increasingly, a vehicle for moral posturing. What once functioned to secure material needs or elevate one's comfort has, in many quarters, become performative: *a stage on which character is advertised, not just lifestyle.* In the contemporary economy of perception, we do not merely spend money—we signal with it. This signalling is not confined to the affluent; it permeates middle-class aspirations, influencer culture, start-up ecosystems, philanthropy, and even frugality itself. And yet the deeper question remains underexplored: *Are we using wealth to signal values, or to substitute for them?*

The human instinct to display resources is not new. In ancient Rome, aristocrats were required to wear togas of specific colours and fabrics to denote their rank. Among the Plains tribes of North America, horses and beadwork functioned as both economic assets and symbolic capital. In Renaissance Europe, architectural patronage was as much about faith and civic duty as it was about prestige. What distinguishes the current moment is not that wealth signals status—it always has—but *how self-aware and strategically moralised that signalling has become.* In today's world, especially within elite and aspirational circles, wealth is not just a private accumulation; it is a curated narrative about who we are.

Nowhere is this more evident than in the shift from conspicuous consumption to what sociologist Elizabeth Currid-Halkett calls *"inconspicuous consumption."* The wealthy elite today are less likely to flaunt designer logos or exotic cars and more inclined to spend on education, wellness, organic food, sustainable fashion, or cultural capital. These purchases are no less expensive, but they are cloaked in moral legitimacy. An expensive Montessori school, a retreat to an eco-lodge in Bhutan, or donations to climate causes all project both affluence and values—what philosopher Thorstein Veblen might today revise as *conspicuous virtue*. In this way, money becomes *a proxy for character*. A person's net worth is no longer just a reflection of income; it is mistaken as evidence of wisdom, discipline, and ethical clarity.

This trend raises difficult questions. If wealth becomes the medium through which we signal moral worth, then those without wealth are presumed to lack the values it supposedly conveys. The result is a subtle but corrosive inversion: rather than money being earned as a consequence of virtue, virtue is inferred from the presence of money. Philanthropy, for instance, is often viewed as a final proof of success—yet it rarely interrogates the means by which wealth was acquired. Donors who fund social justice initiatives while profiting from exploitative labour markets go unquestioned if their giving is large enough. *Here, money does not clean guilt; it masks inquiry.*

Digital culture exacerbates this dilemma. Social media platforms reward the optics of virtue—artfully filtered acts of generosity, sustainability, and civic awareness—regardless of underlying complexity. A minimalist kitchen aesthetic becomes a shorthand for "conscious consumption." A post about carbon offsetting can garner social credibility, regardless of the efficacy or ethics behind the initiative. Money is not being spent to solve problems as much as to construct narratives. These narratives are not inherently false—but they are highly edited. They reward performance over introspection, signalling over substance.

Even the act of not spending has become a signal. There is now cultural cachet in frugality—provided it is framed correctly. A tech CEO who wears the same black T-shirt every day is seen as focused and humble. A wealthy family that drives a Prius is applauded for its environmental values. This form of "stealth wealth" can masquerade as modesty, but often functions as *a sophisticated rebranding of privilege*. When thrift is elective, it is perceived as discipline. When it is enforced by circumstance, it is often stigmatised.

So, what would it mean to signal values through money in a way that is not performative but principled? The key lies in *alignment*—ensuring that the function of money mirrors the values it is purported to express. A value-based financial life does not ask, "What will this purchase or gift say about me?" It asks, "Does this transaction reflect who I am and what I stand for?" This demands internal clarity, not just external calibration.

Take, for example, investment portfolios. ESG (Environmental, Social, and Governance) funds have risen in popularity, partly as a signal of ethical awareness. But simply shifting assets to a fund labelled "sustainable" does not automatically create impact. A more meaningful approach would involve evaluating how shareholder voting power is exercised, examining corporate supply chains, or directing capital to community-owned enterprises. *Value-based signalling is not shorthand—it is specificity*. It replaces brand affiliation with genuine consequence.

Or consider charitable giving. Traditional philanthropy often serves as a reputational shield—lavish galas, naming rights, glossy impact reports. A more aligned practice would mean anonymous giving, participatory grant-making, or reparative transfers to communities historically excluded from wealth creation. This kind of giving is less visible—but arguably more honest. It moves from *signalling generosity* to *operationalising justice.*

On an individual level, value-based signalling asks us to track the emotional motives behind our spending. Are we buying a house that reflects our needs, or one that reassures our peers of our success? Are we purchasing an item because it enhances our life, or because we fear being seen as less-than? These are subtle distinctions—but they matter. *Every pound spent is a vote for a world we want to belong to.* And that vote counts, even when cast in silence.

There is also a communal aspect to reclaiming wealth from performance. Families, partnerships, and communities must have space for honest money dialogue. When children learn that wealth is not a status project but a stewardship practice, they develop healthier self-worth. When friends are honest about financial boundaries, peer pressure loses its bite. When institutions reward ethical capital as much as financial capital, cultures shift.

None of this is easy. It requires unlearning decades of messaging that equates money with virtue and visibility with validation. It also requires resisting the dopamine drip of social approval—likes, nods, compliments—that accompany curated financial behaviour. But the payoff is significant: a financial life that is not only more authentic, but more resilient.

To be clear, signalling itself is not inherently bad. It is part of human communication. We signal belonging through language, attire, tone, and taste. But *the goal is to signal in a way that is transparent, not transactional.* To say, in effect, "This is what I value—not what I want you to believe I value."

Ultimately, the question is not whether our money speaks. It always does. The real question is whether it speaks truthfully—or merely performs sincerity. In a world drowning in image, the quiet integrity of value-aligned financial choices has more power than we think. And the most compelling signals may be those that never need to be signalled at all.

"Money Shame and Silence":

Money is one of the last remaining taboos among educated, emotionally literate adults. We can discuss politics at dinner parties, explore therapy on podcasts, and debate identity in classrooms—but ask someone how much they earn, owe, or spend, and the atmosphere shifts. A subtle tension creeps in. Words slow, eye contact flickers. It is not that we don't care about money; we care so much that we're paralysed by it. *Silence, when it comes to money, is not neutral—it's a form of emotional protection.* And that silence is often rooted in shame.

Shame around money is pervasive, yet rarely named. It cuts across income brackets and education levels. The high earner who feels guilty for having more than their parents. The student who hides debt out of fear they've failed before they've begun. The couple who share a bed but not a budget. The entrepreneur who projects confidence while privately managing a crumbling cash flow. Shame is not just the presence of financial struggle—it's the sense that *you are the problem.* That your financial behaviour, your spending habits, or your bank balance are not just facts, but moral failures. And shame thrives in secrecy.

Developmentally, our relationship with money begins long before we make or manage it. Family systems are the first training ground. Some children grow up in homes where money is a weapon—used to manipulate, reward, or punish. Others experience it as a ghost—an ever-present absence that dictates decisions but is never openly addressed. There are households where abundance is quietly assumed, but never explained, and those where survivalist habits persist even after financial circumstances improve. *These early scripts do not vanish with age or income—they mature with us, often in distorted form.*

Psychologically, money shame is particularly potent because it blurs the boundary between self-worth and net worth. When someone fails to meet a financial goal, they may not think, "I made a mistake." They think, "I am a mistake." This confusion leads to chronic under-sharing: couples avoid discussing money for fear of judgement; adult children don't ask ageing parents about wills or long-term care out of guilt or awkwardness; friends split restaurant bills unequally to keep appearances intact. The result is that people navigate one of life's most complex domains—personal finance—without the relational clarity they apply to nearly everything else.

What makes this silence more insidious is that it often masquerades as politeness. We are taught not to "talk about money" because it's crass, because it's personal, because it makes people uncomfortable. But discomfort is not a justification—it's a symptom. *When something is both essential and unspeakable, dysfunction follows.* And the cost is not just individual; it's systemic. Pay inequity persists in part because people don't discuss salaries. Predatory lending thrives in the absence of communal financial education. Intergenerational trauma around debt or secrecy repeats itself precisely because no one interrupts it.

To break this cycle, we must distinguish between privacy and secrecy. Privacy is the right to keep something to yourself. Secrecy is the compulsion to keep something from others out of fear or shame. The difference lies in motivation. A private person might decline to discuss their income, but they do so from autonomy. A secretive person avoids the topic entirely, often even with themselves. *Financial maturity is not about disclosure—it's about intentionality.* It means having the ability to talk about money with those who need to understand your situation—partners, children, advisors—without defensiveness or self-condemnation.

Building this capacity requires a new language. Traditional financial discourse is filled with absolutes—good debt, bad debt, saving versus splurging, spenders versus savers. But these binaries are unhelpful. Financial behaviour is rarely about logic alone. It is filtered through emotion, context, history, and identity. A more useful vocabulary would include terms like "financial intimacy," "resource anxiety," or "value dissonance." It would make room for contradictions: you can feel proud of your earnings and ashamed of your spending. You can be generous and afraid. You can be strategic and stuck. *Ambivalence is not a failure—it's the starting point for clarity.*

Practically speaking, cultivating open money dialogue involves three foundational shifts: safety, structure, and story.

Safety means creating environments where financial conversations are emotionally non-threatening. This does not mean avoiding difficult topics—it means approaching them with curiosity, not correction. Partners, for instance, can begin with open-ended prompts: "What was your earliest memory of money?" or "When did you first feel financially independent?" These questions soften the terrain, allowing deeper patterns to surface. In families, this might look like adult children asking parents not just what is in the will, but *why*. What do they hope their financial legacy communicates? What values do they want it to reflect?

Structure means establishing regular, predictable formats for discussing money, rather than waiting for crises to force the issue. This might take the form of a monthly financial review with a partner, an annual values-alignment audit for personal spending, or scheduled family meetings where financial topics are normalised—not only in emergencies. Structure depersonalises money. It turns the conversation from a reactive emotional flare-up into a shared responsibility.

Story is about reshaping the internal narratives we carry. If someone believes, "I'm bad with money," that belief will unconsciously dictate their behaviour—often more powerfully than actual numbers. Techniques drawn from cognitive behavioural therapy or narrative coaching can help identify and rewrite these scripts. One method involves mapping out one's financial timeline: major events, feelings, turning points, and inherited beliefs. Another is reframing the "money story" not as a fixed identity ("I'm irresponsible") but as a dynamic process ("I learned to avoid money talk because it created tension in my family, but I'm learning a new approach now"). *Narrative is not cosmetic—it is strategic reframing with emotional stakes.*

Breaking silence around money also means questioning the cultural norms that reward secrecy. In many professional environments, money talk is still governed by fear—fear of being judged, penalised, or seen as difficult. Yet the industries with the most opaque financial practices—finance, tech, media—are often those with the widest disparities. *Transparency is not a radical act. It is a prerequisite for equity.* Initiatives like open salary bands, community lending circles, or collective wealth funds challenge the assumption that money must be handled individually. They recognise that financial clarity is not just a private virtue—it is a public good.

There is no single formula for eliminating money shame. It emerges differently in each context—woven into personality, identity, social class, and historical memory. But the antidote is always some version of honest conversation. Not public confession. Not performative vulnerability. Just grounded, mutual engagement. A partner saying, "I want us to understand each other's financial fears." A parent telling a child, "Here's what I've learned about wealth, and what I hope to pass on." A friend asking, "Can we talk openly about what we can actually afford for this trip?"

Such conversations are rarely comfortable. But comfort is not the goal—*connection is.* And financial connection, like all connection, is built not on perfection, but on presence. On the willingness to say, "This matters. Let's talk about it." Without shame. Without performance. With the understanding that clarity, however imperfect, is always kinder than silence.

"Gender, Class, and the Wealth Conversation":

Money is not neutral. It is not simply a numerical tool or a mechanism of exchange. It is a system of power—one that reflects, reinforces, and often deepens existing inequalities. Any conversation about wealth that ignores identity does not merely omit context—it distorts the truth. Because financial outcomes are not only shaped by effort, skill, or choice. They are also shaped by gendered expectations, class structures, and inherited social positions that invisibly calibrate who is permitted to build wealth, under what terms, and at what cost. To understand money clearly, we must examine not only individual decisions but also structural design.

Begin with gender. Globally, women own less wealth, earn lower wages, and accumulate fewer assets than men. These disparities are not just artefacts of history—they are actively produced. In the United Kingdom, for instance, the gender pension gap persists at an estimated 35%, a reflection not of individual failure but of systemic design: career breaks for caregiving, occupational segregation, and investment confidence gaps all converge to reduce women's long-term financial security. Pay gaps, while often cited, are just the surface. *The deeper injustice lies in what is unpaid, unseen, and unaccounted for.* Care work—whether raising children, supporting elderly relatives, or sustaining community networks—remains chronically undervalued, despite being essential to economic stability.

Beyond the wage packet, gendered dynamics shape financial behaviour in more subtle ways. Research in behavioural economics reveals that women are more likely to prioritise security over risk in investing, yet they often outperform men in long-term returns due to their consistency and prudence. Meanwhile, financial advice and literacy programmes still disproportionately target men, framing investing as a masculine pursuit. This is not merely a branding oversight—it is a cultural signal that wealth-building is coded male. When women do succeed financially, they are frequently subject to double binds: assertiveness may be read as greed; ambition as selfishness. The financial world continues to police not only outcomes but attitudes.

Now consider class. Class is often misrepresented as a function of income. In reality, it is more enduring than a payslip. Class is an inheritance of access—access to networks, education, language fluency, geographic proximity to opportunity, and the unwritten codes of belonging. A high-income individual raised in poverty may still carry the internalised vigilance of scarcity. Conversely, someone with average earnings but intergenerational support—help with a deposit, emergency buffers, tuition subsidies—may enjoy upward mobility without the visible markers of wealth. *Class shapes how risk is experienced.* To invest, to negotiate, to move cities for work—all these decisions are easier when failure is buffered.

Financial systems often reward those who can afford to wait. This is especially true in property markets, pensions, and business ownership. Time, not just money, becomes the lever of advantage. Those from working-class backgrounds, especially if they are first-generation professionals, may find themselves navigating environments where money is not only a resource but a social code. The discomfort of not knowing how to speak about investments at a networking event, or how to interpret "family office" in a conversation, is not trivial—it reveals the invisible curriculum of class. Financial inclusion is not merely about opening accounts; it is about decoding systems.

The intersections between gender and class compound these dynamics. A woman from a low-income background faces compounded barriers: lower initial capital, weaker networks, and greater scrutiny when she attempts to assert financial agency. For Black, Brown, immigrant, and LGBTQ+ individuals, these intersections multiply further, introducing race, migration, and identity into the equation. Asset ownership in the UK, for example, is sharply racialised. According to the Resolution Foundation, Black African households are less than one-third as likely as White British households to own their home—a disparity with cascading effects on intergenerational security, housing costs, and community wealth.

Crucially, identity-based disparities are often disguised under the banner of meritocracy. Financial success is publicly framed as evidence of character—thrift, discipline, intelligence—while structural exclusions are rendered invisible. This narrative serves the status quo. It allows systems to present themselves as fair while continuing to favour the already favoured. *Meritocracy, in this context, is less a reality than a performance—one that obscures how race, class, and gender are embedded in the scaffolding of economic life.*

To challenge these systems, individuals must first learn to see them. That means cultivating financial discernment that includes structural literacy. For example: when evaluating investment advice, ask who the audience is. When considering property as a wealth strategy, ask who is displaced. When reading headlines about inflation, interest rates, or inheritance tax, ask who benefits—and who is burdened. Financial decisions do not occur in a vacuum. They occur in an ecosystem shaped by policy, history, and ideology.

Consider also the narratives we accept about success. The archetype of the self-made entrepreneur is often celebrated without acknowledging the quiet scaffolds beneath their ascent: early loans from family, access to elite education, second chances denied to others. Conversely, those who struggle financially are often portrayed as irresponsible or short-sighted, ignoring the precarity baked into their context. It is intellectually dishonest—and ethically corrosive—to isolate outcomes from the conditions that make them possible. *If we do not challenge these frames, we participate in their reinforcement.*

Practically, this means expanding financial education beyond budgeting and investing. It requires cultural education—teaching people how to recognise inequity, how to advocate for fairer systems, and how to design inclusive economic models. In workplaces, that may involve publishing salary bands, rethinking parental leave policies, and auditing performance reviews for bias. In schools, it may mean embedding class consciousness into economics curricula. In families, it might look like naming privilege without guilt—acknowledging that advantage is not a sin, but silence about it often is.

Importantly, equity is not the same as charity. Structural fairness is not achieved through generosity alone. It demands redesign. That includes policy shifts—such as wealth taxes, universal basic services, childcare subsidies—but it also includes narrative shifts. Who is allowed to be a financial expert? Whose stories are told as aspirational? Whose mistakes are forgiven?

Reshaping the wealth conversation begins with an act of intellectual humility. It means acknowledging that systems are not neutral, and that any attempt to manage money wisely must include an analysis of power. The goal is not to induce shame among the privileged or resentment among the excluded. It is to cultivate financial agency that is both personally empowering and socially responsible. To build wealth that does not depend on other people's exclusion. To craft a financial future in which success is measured not only by what you accumulate, but by how many people your success makes space for.

This requires a new kind of financial fluency—one that includes history, systems, and ethics alongside numbers. One that teaches not only how to save or invest, but also how to see. Because without structural vision, financial advice becomes a mask—well-meaning, perhaps, but fundamentally misdirected. *Clarity is not only about knowing your net worth; it is about understanding the world in which that worth is calculated.*

That is the work of conscious wealth: not perfection, not purity, but precision. The capacity to act wisely with money in full awareness of the privileges and penalties that shape our financial landscapes. The ability to pursue prosperity that uplifts rather than excludes. And the willingness to participate in a conversation that is as political as it is personal—because money, like identity, is never just about you.

"The Philosophy of Generosity":

Modern wealth culture tends to define generosity in narrow terms: charitable donations, volunteer hours, corporate giving campaigns. The underlying assumption is that generosity is a gesture—a benevolent act performed by those with "enough" to spare. It is optional, additive, and ideally tax-deductible. But this framing diminishes generosity to a form of moral accounting. It detaches giving from the very systems that produce and concentrate wealth. Worse, it implies a hierarchy: the giver is elevated, the recipient grateful, and the exchange asymmetric. This is not generosity. It is performance.

True generosity is not a transaction. It is a philosophy of reciprocity, a way of participating in a shared ecosystem of value. To be generous, in the most generative sense, is not to give from surplus but to act from interdependence. It is to recognise that the wealth we hold—whether material, social, or emotional—only becomes meaningful when it circulates. *Generosity is not what you offer after you've succeeded; it is how you succeed.*

Anthropologists have long observed that reciprocal giving, rather than accumulation, is what sustains human communities. In the classic ethnographic study of the Trobriand Islanders, for instance, wealth took the form of shell necklaces and armbands passed from one island to another. The point was not possession but circulation. The status of the object, and of the giver, increased the more often it changed hands. In many Indigenous cultures across the globe, from the potlatch ceremonies of the Pacific Northwest to the ubuntu ethos of southern Africa, wealth is defined by how well it flows, not how tightly it is held.

Contrast this with contemporary capitalist models, which frame wealth as private, measurable, and inert. In such systems, generosity becomes a tool of image management. Corporations donate to soften public scrutiny. High-net-worth individuals endow foundations bearing their names. Social media users document acts of kindness for algorithmic reward. None of this is inherently wrong. But when generosity is instrumentalised, its ethical dimension is compromised. *What is intended as contribution becomes a performance of virtue.*

To reclaim generosity as philosophy, we must decouple it from charity and re-anchor it in reciprocity. This shift has profound implications. Where charity often preserves hierarchy—the powerful aiding the powerless—reciprocal generosity insists on mutual dignity. It does not ask, "What can I spare?" but rather, "What can I share that will strengthen the whole?" This reframing challenges the dominant logic of scarcity, in which one person's gain is another's loss. Generosity, by contrast, rests on an abundance mindset: *the idea that value grows when it is exchanged, not hoarded.*

This is not merely ideological. Neuroscience offers a parallel insight. Generous acts activate the brain's reward systems. Functional MRI studies show that giving—whether of money, time, or support—stimulates the mesolimbic pathway, releasing dopamine and oxytocin. These are the same neurochemicals associated with pleasure, trust, and bonding. In other words, generosity is not only ethically sound; it is physiologically rewarding. The impulse to give is not a defect to overcome with rational budgeting; it is part of what makes us wired for connection.

Crucially, generosity also enhances resilience. Individuals who give regularly—whether through mentorship, hospitality, or service—tend to report higher levels of wellbeing, purpose, and social support. Communities that embed reciprocal exchange in their economic practices—through mutual aid networks, cooperative enterprises, or time banking—demonstrate greater capacity to withstand shocks. In volatile environments, generosity is not naive. It is strategic. *It builds the social capital that wealth alone cannot buy.*

And yet, the modern financial paradigm often severs generosity from economic practice. Generosity is relegated to the "impact" section of a portfolio or the year-end giving drive. It is considered a personal virtue rather than a systemic imperative. This is a profound error. If we take seriously the idea that money is a social construct—a proxy for trust, value, and shared commitment—then *the most meaningful use of money is to reinforce the very relationships it represents.* Generosity is not a soft add-on to a hard system. It is the foundation that gives economic systems coherence and legitimacy.

Consider how this plays out in family wealth. When generosity is reduced to handouts—birthday cheques, emergency bailouts, or conditional gifts—it often produces resentment or dependency. But when families articulate a philosophy of shared wealth—where resources are mobilised to support each other's growth, security, and contributions—the financial ecosystem becomes cohesive. Adult siblings who co-invest in education or home ownership, parents who support start-ups in lieu of inheritance, or multigenerational families who fund sabbaticals and caregiving: these are not acts of charity. They are acts of solidarity. *And they build a relational infrastructure stronger than any trust fund.*

This principle extends to business. Companies that integrate generosity into their operational models—through employee ownership, transparent profit-sharing, or community reinvestment—tend to cultivate stronger cultures, lower turnover, and more loyal customers. These outcomes are not incidental. They emerge from the alignment between values and systems. When generosity is embedded into the design, not just the branding, it becomes an engine of resilience and a source of competitive advantage. *Stakeholder capitalism may sound abstract, but at its core is a basic truth: people invest more fully in systems that invest in them.*

To practice generosity at scale, however, requires intention. It means setting parameters. What percentage of your income is earmarked not for expenses, savings, or investment—but for contribution? What time in your calendar is protected for mentoring, volunteering, or supporting others' projects? What privileges—professional introductions, insider knowledge, access to capital—can be shared without depletion? These are not theoretical questions. They are architectural ones. *To live generously is to design your life around flow, not containment.*

Of course, generosity must also be sustainable. Giving that depletes the giver, erodes boundaries, or distorts power dynamics is not generosity—it is martyrdom. That is why generosity must be tied to discernment. The most effective givers are not those who give indiscriminately but those who give with clarity. They know the difference between enabling and empowering, between rescuing and supporting. They understand that true generosity is not about fixing other people's problems—it is about strengthening their capacity to solve them.

This understanding is particularly urgent in the context of global inequality. Generosity cannot be a substitute for justice.

Philanthropy, however well-intentioned, cannot repair the damage done by extractive economies, racialised capital flows, and environmental degradation. But it can serve as a bridge—*a way of redirecting energy and resources toward repair, not perpetuation.* When generosity moves beyond sentiment and becomes structurally aligned with equity, it becomes part of a regenerative wealth model. One that restores rather than exploits. One that expands rather than concentrates. One that distributes not only capital, but also power and possibility.

Ultimately, the philosophy of generosity invites a reorientation of financial life. It challenges the myth that success is solitary, that wealth is a personal reward, and that giving is ancillary. It asks us to see our assets not as endpoints but as instruments—to understand money not as the measure of worth, but as a medium of connection. In this frame, generosity is not a virtue signal. It is a *vital sign*—a measure of aliveness within a wealth ecosystem. When we give well, we do not lose. We circulate. We amplify. We belong.

Chapter 8
The Financial Design Audit:

Wealth, for all its numerical trappings, is never just arithmetic. It's architecture—deliberate or accidental. Most of us assume we're making reasoned financial decisions. In reality, we're moving through half-built frameworks: fragments of inherited wisdom, cultural scripts we never quite agreed to, ad hoc habits dressed up as strategies. It's not necessarily ruinous. But it does introduce drag. You might be earning, investing, even building—yet the experience often resembles living in a house cobbled together without plans: some rooms work, others sag, and the whole thing lacks a sense of integrated design. This chapter is a prompt to pause, take stock, and begin that design afresh.

Now, the term "financial audit" may conjure visions of columns, calculators, and cold scrutiny. But that's not where we're headed. Think of this less as bookkeeping and more as architecture school for your economic life. The purpose here isn't to catalogue transactions but to surface meaning. Not just *what* you've done with money—but *why*, and whether the whole scaffolding supports the life you're genuinely trying to lead. Wealth, after all, isn't built from assets alone. It requires shape, narrative, and a form that reflects purpose. That's the work before us: to craft that form with both mind and intention.

At the centre of it all is a quietly radical idea: your current financial reality is no accident. It's the downstream expression of a system—one that you've either inherited or unconsciously constructed. That system reaches beyond salaries and savings accounts. It includes the invisible circuitry of how money moves in and out of your life, the instincts you've developed around scarcity and risk, the silent deals you've struck in relationships, and the unspoken beliefs you hold about legacy. This chapter isn't going to offer a budget. What it will offer is a reframe—a new way of seeing how your money infrastructure either fortifies or erodes your vision of a well-lived life.

We start with your Current Wealth Blueprint. Not for compliance. For clarity. This is not a spreadsheet exercise, though it may include one. It's an exploration: What stories are embedded in your spending? Where do patterns repeat or fray? Which parts feel sturdy? Which reveal contradiction? True design begins with what is—not what should be. No system can be reimagined until it's truly seen.

From there, we confront a common culprit: complexity that masquerades as sophistication. For many, financial chaos doesn't stem from carelessness. It arises from an overgrown ecosystem—accounts scattered across platforms, apps clamouring for attention, financial hacks and habits layered without integration. Lattes are not the problem. Fragmented attention is. This chapter's segment on *Cash Flow, Chaos, and Clarity* isn't about austerity; it's about identifying the small leaks—of money, of focus—that signal deeper design flaws.

Then comes the structural scan. We examine your four primary layers of wealth: emergency, income, investment, and legacy. These aren't merely categories—they are the load-bearing beams of financial resilience. Your emergency fund speaks to your shock absorption. Income, to your independence and mobility. Investments, to your relationship with time and growth. And legacy—to your ability to transmit not just money, but meaning, across generations. Most people overbuild in one area and neglect another entirely. This chapter helps you surface where that imbalance lies—and how to begin correcting it through practical, design-based shifts.

Yet even the best-laid systems falter when they're animated by misplaced goals. Which brings us to the core distinction between *Design Goals* and *Ego Goals*. The latter are outward-facing—milestones chosen for status, optics, or borrowed expectations. A certain net worth because others have reached it. A house, because it's "what success looks like." These goals are not evil, merely empty when decoupled from the inner architecture of your values. *Design Goals*, on the other hand, are inwardly tethered. They emerge from how you define beauty, safety, usefulness, or freedom. This chapter doesn't reject ambition—it refines it, ensuring it is driven by alignment, not applause.

This all builds toward a culminating invitation: craft your *Wealth Thesis*. Just as institutional investors articulate guiding beliefs to anchor decision-making, so too can individuals. Your Wealth Thesis is a personal statement—a one-page declaration of the principles, priorities, and definitions that will govern your financial life. It's a compass. A defence against drift. A benchmark for consistency in future decisions around spending, investing, giving, or risk-taking. Without it, financial life remains reactive. With it, you begin to live by design.

The aim of this chapter isn't to prescribe a singular path. It's to offer the tools to build *your* path with rigour. It doesn't champion frugality over generosity, nor simplicity over scale. It champions coherence—where your use of resources reflects your beliefs rather than betrays them. Whether you earn a modest income or wield substantial capital, you already have a financial system in place. The real question is whether it's serving you—or simply carrying you along.

What follows is a rhythm of reflection and reengineering: diagnosing your present setup, identifying friction points, and reshaping the system so that your financial decisions aren't just efficient, but meaningful. This isn't about paring down to the bare essentials, nor ballooning into financial excess. It's about harmony—when your money, actions, and ethics move in sync.

You won't walk away with tidy perfection. But you'll gain something far more durable: an architecture that responds, evolves, and holds you steady. Money will still ebb and flow. Plans will shift. But if the structure is sound, you won't unravel. You'll adapt, iterate, continue. Because in the end, true wealth isn't what you accumulate—it's what your system allows you to become.

"Your Current Wealth Blueprint"

Few people know the full structure of their financial life, not because they are reckless or uninformed, but because that structure was never formally designed. Instead, it was assembled gradually—shaped by necessity, influenced by culture, and altered by events. Most wealth systems are the result of drift: job changes, windfalls, emergencies, tax seasons, milestones. The result is a set of disconnected components—savings accounts, retirement plans, insurance policies, scattered investments—without a central philosophy to bind them. Like a house that's been extended room by room without a master plan, it may be livable, but it is rarely elegant or resilient. The purpose of this subchapter is not to prescribe the right structure—it is to help you discover the one you already have, understand how it functions, and identify where it supports or undermines your goals.

Every individual operates within a financial architecture composed of four foundational layers: emergency, income, investing, and legacy. These are not technical categories; they are functional ecosystems. Each plays a distinct role in your life's stability, adaptability, and long-term value creation. What follows is not a checklist, but a set of lenses—through which to examine how your money moves, accumulates, and influences. You are not here to tidy your finances. You are here to trace design principles—some conscious, some inherited—and to question whether they still serve you.

Begin with the **emergency layer**, which could more accurately be described as the *resilience layer.* It represents your capacity to withstand economic shocks without destabilisation. This includes traditional savings buffers—three to six months of expenses—but also liquidity mechanisms: accessible credit, insurance coverage, flexible income streams. What matters is not the amount alone, but its usability and responsiveness. For example, a £30,000 savings account is of little use if it's psychologically untouchable or functionally distant in a crisis. Conversely, a modest emergency fund, coupled with robust family networks or flexible work arrangements, may confer more real-world resilience. Ask yourself: *When uncertainty strikes, how does your system absorb it? How quickly can it adapt without cascading stress?* Most people's emergency layer is either overbuilt (excess cash hoarded out of fear) or neglected (deferred indefinitely under the illusion that emergencies are rare). The goal is not maximalism, but proportionality: *enough resilience to move calmly, not enough to stagnate.*

Next, examine your **income layer**—the primary engine of financial motion. Income is not just salary. It is any recurring stream that sustains your cost of living: business profits, dividends, royalties, pension payments, rent. What matters is both *diversity* and *durability*. Is your income reliant on one client, one employer, one industry? How would a disruption in that source affect the rest of your system? Many professionals operate on a single-source dependency while overestimating its permanence. Others pursue multiple income streams prematurely, creating cognitive overload and reducing effectiveness in their core field. Income design is about *sovereignty, not scale*. A £70,000 income with high stability, low stress, and time autonomy may be far more powerful—structurally and psychologically—than a £200,000 income with volatility, overwork, and existential insecurity. The audit here involves asking: *Is my income structured to protect my attention, my optionality, and my future self?*

The **investment layer** is where time and capital intersect. Most view investing as a technical game—asset allocation, market timing, tax strategy. While these mechanics matter, the deeper issue is alignment: *What are you actually building?* Too often, people outsource their portfolios to advisors or apps without interrogating their end goals. Is your investment strategy designed for compounding security, early freedom, generational transfer, or philanthropic leverage? Are you building wealth that serves a function, or are you accumulating by default? Equally, what is your risk philosophy? Not in theoretical terms, but in lived terms. Would a 20% market drop unsettle you into bad decisions? Are you holding assets you understand, or merely mimicking peers and pundits? The investment layer is where clarity and confidence compound—or where confusion quietly erodes potential. *An audit here involves naming your timeline, your tolerance, your intentions—and checking whether your portfolio reflects them.*

Finally, the **legacy layer**, which is often neglected or mischaracterised. Legacy is not merely estate planning or inheritance. It is the intentional design of what you leave *in* people, not just what you leave *to* them. This includes intergenerational values, philanthropic structures, knowledge systems, mentorship pathways, and social capital. It is the most narrative-driven and least technical layer—yet it holds disproportionate power. Consider a business owner who passes on assets but not leadership philosophy, or a parent who bequeaths property but not clarity around its purpose. Without narrative, legacy becomes either burdensome or squandered. This layer asks you to articulate: *What do I want others to experience because I lived? What structures am I building to carry that experience forward?* The audit here is both logistical and emotional. It involves looking at trusts and wills, but also family dynamics, cultural continuity, and narrative clarity.

What makes this blueprint powerful is not its precision, but its *pattern recognition*. Financial lives are dynamic. Your blueprint will evolve. But unless you see it clearly today, you cannot shape it for tomorrow. This is why a written audit—however imperfect—is indispensable. It moves your design from abstract to concrete, from unconscious to explicit.

One effective method is to sketch your four layers visually, with each quadrant representing one domain: emergency (resilience), income (recurrence), investment (growth), and legacy (transmission). Populate each with current structures, tools, behaviours, and assumptions. Then annotate with questions: *Is this serving me? Is this future-proof? Is this coherent with my values?* This exercise often reveals not just gaps, but redundancies: duplicated insurances, overlapping accounts, contradictory goals. The audit becomes a mirror—not just of your finances, but of your thinking.

Beyond diagnosis, this blueprint invites critical reflection. What philosophies underpin your system? Do you operate from scarcity or stewardship? Are you optimising for autonomy, impact, status, or safety? These are not binary choices, but your structure should reflect a conscious weighting. For example, someone optimising for autonomy might choose lower fixed expenses and greater cash reserves. Someone prioritising impact might channel excess capital into high-risk, high-reward social ventures. *The integrity of your system lies not in its complexity, but in how well it reflects your inner architecture.*

Importantly, this process also helps dismantle inherited scripts. Many financial structures are legacies themselves—passed down from parents, mentors, culture. Some serve. Others constrain. The blueprint you inherited is not the one you are required to sustain.

But you cannot redesign what you have not first made visible. This chapter is that reckoning—a confrontation with the implicit structures shaping your life.

At its core, your wealth blueprint is not a spreadsheet or a software dashboard. It is a reflection of your design orientation: are you living reactively or architecturally? Are you waiting for stability to appear, or engineering it deliberately? The answers are not found in products or plans. They are found in coherence—when each layer of your financial life reinforces the others, aligned by a centre that is personal, intentional, and evolving.

What begins as a technical exercise ends as a philosophical one. Because wealth is not about having more—it is about designing better. And every design starts with understanding what already exists, how it behaves, and what it could become if guided with care.

"Cash Flow, Chaos, and Clarity"

For all the complexity that modern finance presents—global markets, digital assets, algorithmic trading—most individual wealth is not built or lost on esoteric instruments. It is shaped, silently and persistently, by how money flows in and out of one's life each month. Cash flow is not the glamorous frontier of financial strategy, but it is the most immediate and revealing one. If the investment layer of your wealth is where your future is growing, then cash flow is where your present either supports or sabotages that future. And yet, remarkably few people truly understand their own.

The most common assumption is that cash flow is self-evident. People often believe that because they know their salary, pay their bills, and track major expenses, they must already have clarity. In practice, what they often have is *functional awareness*, not *systemic understanding*. They know the shape of their spending, but not its tendencies. They understand their obligations, but not their automatisms. They can quote their rent, but not their leakages. And herein lies the problem: *money does not vanish by accident; it vanishes by repetition.* Unconscious spending is not a momentary lapse but a patterned erosion, and the first step to clarity is learning to see the erosion while it is still small.

Cash flow complexity rarely stems from scale. A six-figure earner can have messier financial dynamics than someone on half the income. Why? Because complexity emerges from fragmentation—multiple accounts, poorly coordinated subscriptions, erratic spending categories, automatic deductions no longer tracked. Many households operate with five to ten different payment platforms, three or more active credit cards, legacy insurance products, dormant investment accounts, and overlapping app-based tools. This diffusion doesn't just dilute attention—it breeds opacity. And opacity is the enemy of stewardship.

Psychologically, we are wired to prioritise the immediate and visible. Behavioural economists call this *present bias*: the tendency to overvalue near-term gratification at the expense of long-term well-being. Add to that *mental accounting*—our habit of treating money differently depending on its source or form—and it becomes easier to understand why someone might splurge on dining out while delaying a dental check-up or underfunding a pension. These aren't rational inconsistencies. They are neurological patterns, reinforced by design. Most financial systems—apps, banks, marketplaces—are optimised to *facilitate spending*, not to illuminate it.

To restore clarity, we must reframe the purpose of cash flow analysis. It is not merely to budget. It is to *diagnose how your values translate into practice*. A values-driven audit begins not with the numbers but with the question: *what is this money supposed to be doing for me?* If your answer is stability, but your outflows are dominated by volatility (impulsive purchases, variable fees, reactive lending), there is a structural mismatch. If your answer is freedom, but you are locked into lifestyle commitments that depend on continual income growth, your cash flow is not a facilitator—it is a leash.

Let us take a more granular example. Consider a high-earning professional who earns £10,000 a month post-tax. On paper, they are affluent. But if £6,000 goes to mortgage, school fees, and fixed household costs, £2,000 to discretionary spending, and £1,500 to minimum payments on past debts, they are operating with less flexibility than someone earning £4,000 with a leaner structure. Liquidity—your buffer and flexibility—is not a function of income. It is a function of structure. *Cash flow clarity is not about what you earn. It is about what your structure permits you to experience.*

Much of what we call financial stress is actually *cognitive overload*—the fatigue of managing multiple moving parts without a coherent view. Simplification is not a reductionist gesture. It is a strategic one. This does not mean austerity; it means integration. The fewer places your money hides, the easier it is to manage without constant vigilance. Consolidating accounts, automating transfers to priorities (savings, pensions, investments), and building friction into non-essential spending are not dull housekeeping moves. They are interventions in behavioural design.

Of particular concern are what we can call *drain points*: regular, small outflows that accumulate into significant erosion over time. These include subscription creep (unused digital services, duplicate media accounts), lifestyle inflation (micro-upgrades that become permanent), and inefficient utilities (unnegotiated rates, outdated plans). Each seems harmless in isolation. Collectively, they siphon off capital that could have been compounding toward goals, reducing stress, or expanding optionality. The audit here is not puritanical. It is philosophical. Ask yourself: *Does this outflow represent alignment or autopilot? Is it a contribution to my future or a residue of my past preferences?*

The emotional dimension of cash flow must not be underestimated. Many spending patterns are not logistical but compensatory. They signal identity, soothe anxiety, or sustain belonging. A person who spends heavily on social dining may not be indulging in hedonism—they may be buying proximity, affirmation, or a sense of significance. These motivations are not irrational; they are simply unexamined. And when financial audits ignore this emotional substrate, they fail to produce durable change. *You cannot redesign behaviour unless you understand what that behaviour is solving for.*

Clarity does not require micromanagement. It requires *conscious calibration.* One of the most effective tools is a simple cash flow review ritual: once per month, sit with your actual spending—no apps, no filters, just raw statements—and annotate. Mark what was necessary, what was joyful, what was regrettable, and what was surprising. Over time, patterns will emerge. You will see not just where the money goes, but what it means. Does joy cluster in a particular category? Do regrets stem from a particular trigger—late-night browsing, social pressure, fatigue? Financial clarity is emotional literacy in numeric form.

For those ready to advance the practice, an annual *spending stratification* exercise can be revelatory. Take your year's total outflows and categorise them by alignment: essential (non-negotiables), growth-oriented (investments, education, health), joy (pleasure with no guilt), and leakage (unnecessary or misaligned). Most are surprised by the ratio of leakage to joy. They are not the same. *Leakage is not how much you spend—it's how much you didn't mean to.*

Another layer of complexity worth surfacing is *financial delegation.* Many households, especially couples, develop an implicit division of financial responsibilities. One partner may handle bills, the other investments; one may focus on earnings, the other on budgeting. These arrangements are functional until they are not—when life events, illness, or separation disrupt the pattern. Cash flow clarity must be collective when finances are shared. Each party should be able to articulate the flow architecture, even if they are not executing every transaction. Financial asymmetry creates not just risk but resentment, often silently.

Ultimately, cash flow is the bloodstream of your financial life. If it is opaque, the entire system is compromised. If it is erratic, long-term goals become harder to sustain. If it is clear and aligned, even modest incomes can produce extraordinary resilience and freedom. The aim is not perfection but precision: not to eliminate every mistake, but to *reduce the cost of unconsciousness.* When you know what is flowing, you regain authorship over what it funds, what it fuels, and what it reflects.

The greatest myth in modern personal finance is that wealth begins with income or investment. It does not. It begins with *awareness.* Until you understand how your money behaves, no tool, product, or strategy can serve you well. Cash flow clarity is the gateway—not to wealth accumulation, but to financial integrity. And once you have it, you never again confuse activity with progress.

"Mapping the Weak Links"

In the architecture of a resilient financial life, strength is not found in what is most advanced, but in what is most complete. A person with a sophisticated investment portfolio but no emergency fund is not financially secure. A high-income earner without legacy planning is not financially whole. The illusion of financial health often arises from partial strength—a well-developed area masking a critical deficiency elsewhere. But unlike physical structures, where weak foundations visibly crack under pressure, financial weaknesses often remain dormant until a stressor—job loss, illness, market volatility, death—makes them undeniably evident. *By then, the cost of reinforcement is exponentially higher.*

Financial success is not the sum of isolated wins. It is the product of integration. Most people engage with their finances in silos—treating income, savings, debt, investments, and estate planning as discrete topics to be managed separately. But these are not parallel lines; they are interdependent load-bearing systems. A failure in one compromises the integrity of the whole. This is why *diagnosing your weakest financial layer is more valuable than refining your strongest one.* Just as a chain's reliability depends not on its average strength but its weakest link, so too does a person's financial life hinge on what is least examined, least supported, and most vulnerable.

To assess this properly, we must think in terms of four interlocking layers: Emergency, Income, Investing, and Legacy. Each corresponds to a specific dimension of resilience and time. Emergency planning ensures you can survive shocks. Income is your present engine. Investing secures your future autonomy. Legacy ensures continuity and stewardship beyond your lifespan. They are not phases; they are coexisting responsibilities that evolve in depth, not in sequence. The goal is not to achieve perfection in each simultaneously, but to *identify where disproportionate attention is hiding systemic fragility.*

Begin with Emergency. This is the foundation—the capacity to withstand sudden disruption without destabilising your entire financial life. The classic guidance—a 3-to-6-month buffer—is not arbitrary. It reflects behavioural research that shows the psychological threshold for feeling "safe" in uncertainty. But this is not a static number. If your income is volatile, your dependents many, or your health precarious, your buffer should be greater. Equally, if your access to credit is unreliable or your obligations inflexible, liquidity becomes not just a comfort but a form of moral protection. Without this base, even a temporary income gap can cascade into debt, liquidation of long-term investments, or emotional burnout.

Now consider Income. Many people confuse high income with income strength. They are not the same. Strength lies not in the quantum but in the stability, diversification, and alignment of income. Are you overly dependent on one employer? One industry? One market? If your income were paused for 90 days, what would activate—insurance, side revenue, partnership support, contractual fallback? And does your income align with your actual time and values, or merely with financial pressure? *Sustainable income is not just earned—it is designed.* The most overlooked weakness here is neglecting to audit income reliability. Job prestige can mask precarity; self-employment can mask volatility. The litmus test is simple: does your income allow you to plan with confidence or only react under pressure?

Investing is often where ambition thrives and illusion festers. People may have active portfolios, multiple accounts, and a sense of momentum—but no coherent strategy. The real question is not whether you are investing, but whether your investing structure matches your financial objectives, risk capacity, and time horizon. Many over-allocate to equities without a corresponding liquidity cushion. Others hoard cash while inflation silently erodes their real value. Still others invest by imitation—mirroring friends, influencers, or trends—without interrogating fit. *An investment strategy without clarity is just market exposure.* A critical weak link here is fragmentation: overlapping funds, redundant platforms, no rebalancing discipline. If you cannot articulate your investment thesis in a paragraph, you do not have one. You have motion without architecture.

Then there is Legacy, often deferred or avoided entirely. Yet it is the only layer that truly integrates money with meaning. It is not about being wealthy—it is about being *intentional with continuity*. Who will inherit your financial choices, your assets, your liabilities, your unfinished intentions? Legacy planning includes wills, power of attorney, trusts, beneficiary designations, and—perhaps most overlooked—*communication*. Many families unravel not due to lack of assets but due to lack of clarity. A silent legacy is a chaotic inheritance. The weakness here is emotional avoidance masquerading as irrelevance. Young professionals say, "It's too soon." Parents say, "It's too complicated." Partners say, "We'll do it later." Later is rarely when it should have been done.

So how do you identify your weakest link with precision? Begin with a diagnostic question set, one that confronts each layer not with surface metrics but with *functional truth*.

For Emergency: Could you cover three unexpected months of living expenses, without selling assets or incurring debt?

For Income: If your main income stream stopped tomorrow, how long could you sustain your commitments? Do you have built-in diversification or backup?

For Investing: Can you clearly define your investment strategy, its time horizon, and how it integrates with your other priorities?

For Legacy: If something happened to you today, would your dependents know what exists, where it is, and what to do?

Whichever question you hesitate on—that is your weak link.

It is critical to resist the temptation to compensate for weakness with overdevelopment elsewhere. No amount of investing offsets the absence of an emergency fund. No legacy planning corrects for present income fragility. A robust wealth structure *flows across timeframes*. Think of it as four interlinked circuits: if any one short-circuits, the rest are affected. The strongest financial ecosystems are not the ones with the most capital—but the ones where *each layer is at minimum threshold viability*, and none is dangerously neglected.

Behaviourally, people tend to reinforce what they already understand. An investment-savvy person pours more time into markets. A high earner obsessively optimises tax strategy. A planner updates their spreadsheets quarterly. But these are strengths—default modes of control. Growth often requires turning toward the area you resist most. That is where the next inflection point lies.

And reinforcing weak links does not always require radical restructuring. It begins with visibility. Naming the deficiency. Assigning it priority. Seeking expertise without shame. Most people avoid their weak link because it makes them feel unsophisticated. But sophistication is not knowing everything—it is *knowing where your blind spots are and building around them thoughtfully.*

For example, a 45-year-old entrepreneur with high income but minimal investing knowledge may choose to automate contributions to a diversified passive fund while learning the fundamentals. A young couple with little legacy structure might begin by documenting accounts, assets, and passwords in a shared folder, then book a session with an estate solicitor. A freelancer with variable income may choose to maintain a 6-month liquidity buffer and integrate revenue smoothing tools. These are not grand gestures. They are *architectural reinforcements.*

Financial wholeness is not a final state—it is an ongoing calibration. Life evolves, and with it, each layer must be reassessed. A new child alters emergency needs. A career pivot reshapes income. Market cycles test investments. Aging parents or expanding families change the legacy terrain. The diagnostic tool is not a one-time map—it is a compass. Revisit it yearly. Ask the same questions, expecting different answers. Then act accordingly.

When the weakest link is known, you no longer operate under false security. You operate with clarity. And when that link is fortified, the entire system strengthens—not linearly, but exponentially. Because resilience compounds. Integration multiplies. And when all four layers stand, not perfectly but coherently, *you become not just financially stable—but structurally sovereign.*

Design Goals vs. Ego Goals

A remarkable paradox of modern finance is that people often work harder for a life they don't actually want. They strive, save, and sacrifice—not in service of authentic desires—but in response to inherited templates, social mirroring, and unconscious scripts. The result is a peculiar form of economic restlessness: individuals achieving numerical success while feeling misaligned, burned out, or vaguely dissatisfied. The deeper cause is not a budgeting error or investment misstep. It is the failure to distinguish between *design goals*—internally coherent financial objectives—and *ego goals*—those tethered to status, validation, or identity performance. Until this distinction becomes explicit, effort is misdirected, clarity remains elusive, and the architecture of wealth becomes structurally unsatisfying.

A design goal is functional, values-driven, and context-specific. It arises from an understanding of one's unique priorities, constraints, and definition of enough. An ego goal, by contrast, is comparative, symbolic, and often unexamined. It is rarely about the goal itself, but about what that goal is presumed to signal—success, intelligence, sophistication, desirability. *The key diagnostic is this*: would you still pursue this goal if no one else ever knew about it? If stripped of performance, does it still feel purposeful?

Consider two individuals aiming to buy a house. One does so to stabilise their family life, anchor their community involvement, and create generational continuity. The other does so to emulate peers, meet cultural expectations, and avoid the appearance of financial inadequacy. Both may end up with similar assets—but only one will have achieved alignment. The other may find themselves trapped in a mortgage they resent, a neighbourhood that disconnects them from their values, or a lifestyle that strains their finances for the sake of optics. This is *ego architecture*: financially costly, emotionally hollow, and often defended with remarkable tenacity.

Financial ego goals are not always obvious. They often masquerade as prudence, ambition, or good planning. A person may aim for a seven-figure net worth not because they need it, but because it's become a social shorthand for having "made it." Another might chase early retirement not out of real disillusionment with work, but from internalised narratives that equate freedom with escape. Others still seek high-profile investments, advanced tax strategies, or luxury purchases not for utility, but because *complexity itself becomes a proxy for sophistication.* This is the trap: ego goals often feel smart, even while they erode clarity and reduce authenticity.

Modern technology amplifies this confusion. Social media, with its curated displays of wealth and success, saturates individuals with a continuous stream of someone else's design goals. What was once a private benchmark—say, a retirement age or annual income—is now publicly relativised. This turns financial vision into competition, not calibration. People begin optimising for the optics of wealth rather than the experience of it. They pursue lives that look better than they feel.

To resist this drift, financial introspection must become a structured discipline. Begin by interrogating your existing goals. For each major financial objective—be it saving for a home, reaching a specific net worth, retiring early, or launching a business—ask: Where did this idea come from? What personal values does it serve? What would happen emotionally if I didn't achieve it? If the answer includes shame, embarrassment, or loss of identity, there is a high likelihood that *ego, not design, is driving the goal.*

Design goals, in contrast, withstand quiet reflection. They are often less grandiose, but more stable. They may include working four days a week to protect mental health, maintaining a modest emergency fund to support risk-taking, or saving to support an ageing parent without derailing one's own life plan. These goals often don't photograph well. They aren't headline-grabbing. But they generate genuine satisfaction because they are structurally honest. *They reflect the life being lived, not the life being displayed.*

There is also an architectural difference in how these goals interact with risk. Ego goals tend to distort one's perception of acceptable risk. They often push people into over-leveraging, over-scheduling, or over-investing—because the goal must be achieved not just for itself, but to preserve a certain identity. Design goals, however, are more conservative in spirit, not because they lack ambition, but because they are rooted in sustainability. They favour *resilience over performance*, coherence over comparison.

The financial services industry, ironically, often incentivises ego goals. Advisors, content creators, and platforms know that status-based messaging sells. Phrases like "build generational wealth," "be your own boss," or "retire at 40" appeal to identity aspirations more than strategic design. These aren't inherently bad ideas, but when they become generic prescriptions rather than tailored designs, they can mislead even the most thoughtful individuals. *Sophisticated financial literacy must include the ability to decode the messaging of the market itself.*

Historically, different cultures have offered contrasting views on wealth and its meaning. In some traditions, wealth has been a private matter—more tool than trophy. In others, wealth is performative, designed to demonstrate dominance, piety, or lineage. Today's hypercapitalist model—especially in Western contexts—tends to blur these lines, incentivising outward display while pretending to value humility. This cultural incoherence is part of what makes financial design so psychologically fraught. Individuals must construct clarity in the face of contradictory cues.

One useful framework for recalibrating priorities is the concept of *financial congruence*: the alignment between values, use of resources, and life experience. To apply this, choose three personal values—say, autonomy, contribution, and learning. Then examine how your current financial goals support or contradict these. Does your pursuit of a larger house enhance autonomy or bind you to a rigid income stream? Does your investment strategy allow for contribution to causes you care about, or is it optimised solely for return? Do your professional choices support continuous learning, or only financial maximisation?

This exercise reframes money not as an end, but as an instrument. It removes the default setting of "more is better" and replaces it with *"more aligned is better."* This shift is subtle but transformative. It allows for downsizing without failure, pivoting without shame, and strategic generosity without self-sacrifice. It also protects against the trap of infinite scaling—pursuing ever-higher numbers without revisiting the why behind them.

Of course, ego is not inherently problematic. It is part of human motivation. The danger lies not in having ego, but in *allowing it to silently drive decision-making.* When ego goals are acknowledged and managed, they can even serve a useful role—driving performance, sparking innovation, or providing temporary motivation. But when they are mistaken for core life design, they distort priorities, increase anxiety, and produce brittle forms of success.

Ultimately, the question is not whether your goals are big enough. It is whether they are *yours.* In a world that rewards display and penalises deviation, maintaining financial authenticity is an act of quiet courage. It requires stepping back from the noise, turning down the volume on comparison, and building a system that reflects your actual life—not the one you've been taught to aspire to.

This is not easy work. It requires intellectual honesty, emotional maturity, and periodic recalibration. But the reward is clarity. Not just in your financial plan, but in your time, your energy, and your relationships. You begin to spend, save, earn, and invest in ways that feel coherent rather than performative. And when that alignment is felt—not just understood—it creates a form of wealth no market can manufacture: *a life designed from the inside out.*

Crafting Your Wealth Thesis

If money decisions are the architecture of a life, then most people are building without blueprints. They make choices under pressure, influenced by urgency, fashion, fear, or imitation. They optimise for isolated metrics—return on investment, income growth, or retirement age—without ever defining what the structure is meant to hold. The result is not just inefficiency but incoherence. A strong investment portfolio paired with a chronically overstretched calendar. High income, but no clarity on what it's for. Generosity that feels compulsive rather than joyful. *The antidote to this fragmentation is a personal wealth thesis*: a concise, considered articulation of what you believe about money, what you are designing toward, and how you will make decisions when clarity is most needed. It is not a budget, nor a plan, nor a list of goals. It is a philosophical foundation that supports everything else.

A well-crafted wealth thesis sits upstream of strategy. It reduces noise and narrows choices. More importantly, it protects you from importing the assumptions of others—your parents, your peers, your culture—without analysis. Without a thesis, you are vulnerable to the dominant narratives of the moment. When the prevailing story is that freedom means early retirement, you may find yourself building a life of escape rather than engagement. When the trend is passive income at all costs, you may neglect the value of meaningful work. When financial independence is sold as a moral achievement, you may quietly judge interdependence or generosity as weakness. A thesis gives you a filter. It allows you to say not only *what* you are doing, but *why you're doing it in that particular way.*

Think of the wealth thesis as your personal constitution. It doesn't predict the future. It doesn't pretend certainty. But it does give you a stable framework for navigating ambiguity. It holds when markets change, when your career evolves, or when life offers you difficult trade-offs. When written well, it does not just inform what you save, invest, or spend—it influences how you think, how you interpret the financial behaviour of others, and how you evaluate opportunity and risk. *Its value is not in its length but in its clarity.*

Begin by observing your current decision-making patterns. What do your existing financial choices reveal about your assumptions? Do you believe more is always better? That debt is dangerous? That generosity must be earned? That risk-taking is admirable only when it pays off? These ideas may have never been explicitly chosen, but they shape your financial landscape like gravity. The first task in writing your thesis is to surface them—to interrogate not just the choices but the logics behind them. Not all assumptions are flawed, but many are inherited. Your job is to examine which ones belong to you.

Next, identify your design anchors. These are the core ideas that your wealth thesis will revolve around. They might include autonomy, contribution, creativity, family legacy, intellectual growth, or environmental responsibility. Anchors are not the same as goals. A goal might be "save £500,000 by age 50." An anchor is "financial flexibility matters more to me than owning real estate." Goals are measurable and time-bound. Anchors are directional—they guide, rather than prescribe. Once articulated, these anchors will become the lens through which you evaluate all other financial priorities.

Then comes the articulation. A strong thesis is one page or less. It reads like something between a manifesto and a user manual. It avoids jargon, yet it is precise. It is not aspirational—it is descriptive of how you want to relate to money now. It might include lines like:

"Wealth is a tool to create time-rich, obligation-light living."

"My financial system prioritises resilience over efficiency."

"I do not outsource decisions that shape my character, even if they reduce profit."

"I design for optionality, not optimisation."

"Success includes the capacity to support others without resentment."

There is no universal template. The point is not to adopt impressive language, but to craft something that feels unmistakably yours—something that would make no sense printed on someone else's fridge.

Importantly, a wealth thesis is not static. It evolves. Major life events—children, illness, career shifts, economic shocks—may force recalibration. That is not a failure of planning; it is a feature of self-awareness. A sound thesis will not collapse under change; it will update, refine, and deepen. What begins as a tool for clarity can become a record of maturity—a trail of your evolving financial consciousness.

The writing of a wealth thesis is also a diagnostic process. It reveals tensions between what we say we value and what we fund. A person might claim that environmental sustainability matters deeply to them, while investing heavily in extractive industries. Another may insist that time with family is their top priority, yet maintain a work schedule that leaves them emotionally unavailable. These are not failures of morality—they are mismatches between declared and demonstrated priorities. The wealth thesis makes those misalignments visible, and once visible, they become addressable.

There is a deeper reason this work matters. Without a clear wealth philosophy, money becomes a proxy for unresolved identity questions. We begin to use it not just to meet needs, but to soothe anxieties, signal belonging, or defend against perceived inadequacy. The person who constantly upgrades their lifestyle might not be materialistic, but insecure. The one who refuses to spend, even when they can afford to, may not be frugal, but ashamed. A personal wealth thesis interrupts this drift. It invites the question: *What is this money for, and how do I want to feel in its presence?*

Institutions, too, are governed by their implicit wealth theses. Corporations, governments, and philanthropic foundations all behave in ways that suggest a core belief about the purpose of capital. Yet most never make it explicit. The consequences are visible: misaligned programmes, reactive strategies, and missed opportunities for coherence. What is true at scale is true for the individual. Without a stated philosophy, financial systems grow by accident, not by intention. The cost is not just financial. It is existential.

There are no perfect wealth theses. There are only coherent ones. A thesis does not protect against failure, uncertainty, or discomfort. But it does reduce confusion. It provides a fixed point in a volatile landscape. When you are offered a new opportunity—an investment, a job, a windfall—you no longer ask only "Is this good?" but "Is this mine?" You stop trying to win someone else's game and instead become deeply fluent in your own.

If crafted honestly, your wealth thesis becomes one of the most powerful pages you will ever write. It transforms financial planning from a compliance exercise into an act of authorship. It doesn't just direct your resources; it reflects your ethics, your imagination, and your intention. It becomes a quiet compass, one that you can return to not just when things go wrong, but when they go well—and you need to remember what success was supposed to mean.

This is the work of financial adulthood. Not simply earning more, saving better, or diversifying smarter—but building a life that makes sense on your own terms, with money as servant, not master. The wealth thesis is not the end of that work. But it is the beginning of doing it with rigour, clarity, and care.

Chapter 9
Crisis, Change, and Financial Anti-Fragility

There is no such thing as a life untouched by crisis. No matter how carefully composed your portfolio, how steady your income, or how meticulous your planning, the unpredictable knocks of life will, at some point, shake the foundations. Illness, redundancy, geopolitical turmoil, economic shifts, death—these aren't outliers, they're eventualities. So the question isn't how to avoid disruption (you can't), but whether your system is built to weather it—and ideally, to emerge more robust in the aftermath. This chapter isn't about merely surviving shocks; it's about shaping a financial architecture that can actually gain from them.

Now, that may sound counterintuitive. We've all heard the language of "resilience"—that comforting notion of bouncing back, of recovering to a prior state. But let's be honest: resilience is a start, not a strategy. To be fragile is to break under pressure; to be anti-fragile, as Nassim Nicholas Taleb has memorably argued, is something else entirely. It's the capacity not just to endure volatility, but to be transformed by it—strengthened, refined, made sharper. In the context of wealth, this doesn't mean seeking calamity or glorifying hardship. It means building financial systems—and lives—that flex rather than fracture. Because when pressure mounts, it's not the size of your holdings that determines the outcome. It's the behaviour of the system itself.

Much of conventional financial advice focuses on what you might call peacetime tactics: trimming fat from the budget, nudging up returns, hitting performance benchmarks. All useful, of course—but somewhat theoretical when the storm rolls in. The real test isn't in the spreadsheets; it's in how your system responds when reality turns hostile. What gives first? Where does the strain collect? Which elements adapt—and which collapse? At such moments, the design reveals itself. Those who've put in place layered systems—emergency liquidity, alternative income pathways, flexible investment horizons, durable legacies—aren't spared the disruption.

But they don't spiral. They adjust the right layer without tearing the whole structure down.

The notion of crisis, mind you, isn't hypothetical. It has visited us repeatedly, and often violently: the global financial implosion of 2008, the economic tremors of the COVID-19 era, political unrest, currency devaluations, market corrections. Each of these served as a kind of audit, distinguishing between those who clung to brittle strategies and those who reoriented in real time. Think of the businesses that pivoted to digital models amid lockdowns. Or the investors who stayed the course not out of blind faith, but because their portfolios were already set to endure the turbulence. These weren't happy accidents. They were signs of preparation—the kind that goes deeper than number-crunching.

But let's not pretend this is purely mechanical. There's an emotional dimension to financial disruption that too often gets overlooked. When savings vanish, salaries evaporate, or the medical bills start climbing, it's not just the balance sheet that buckles. The mind narrows. Panic sets in. Perspective shrinks. And in the grip of stress, rationality takes a back seat. If these episodes aren't processed properly, the trauma lingers. It embeds itself into future choices—manifesting as hoarding, chronic anxiety, or compulsive control. So while this chapter is grounded in strategy, it also reaches into the emotional terrain. You'll learn how to apply a kind of psychological first aid: to soothe the nervous system, regain clarity, and anchor yourself in agency before the damage compounds.

Still, we're not waiting for disaster to show up unannounced. This chapter asks you to practise crisis—not masochistically, but diagnostically. Fire drills exist for a reason. Likewise, financial rehearsals—consciously simulating destabilising events—can be remarkably revealing. What happens if your primary income dries up for half a year? If markets lock up? If you're suddenly unable to work or decide to relocate unexpectedly? These are uncomfortable scenarios, no doubt. But better to confront them in controlled conditions than during an actual emergency.

There's another myth we must dismantle: the idea that simply surviving a crisis is enough. Survival is entry-level. The real opportunity, post-disruption, is to rebuild better—to use the rupture as a reckoning. Crises don't just break things. They illuminate. They expose what was already fragile, already flawed. That overdrafted account? That dependency on one client, one skillset, one assumption? The pressure didn't cause the weakness—it revealed it. But just as often, crises unearth hidden strengths: a support network you hadn't fully valued, a longstanding habit of frugality that now proves invaluable, or a sudden realignment with what truly matters. Recovery isn't about reconstruction alone—it's about intelligent revision.

Unfortunately, one of the most common post-crisis reactions is overcorrection. People jettison their financial systems wholesale, mistaking pain for failure. Investments are dumped, generosity withdrawn, budgets become rigid fortresses. Some recalibration may indeed be necessary, but let's be clear: throwing everything out is almost always a mistake. Wise design doesn't mean rigidity—it means discernment. An anti-fragile structure knows how to isolate the stress point, address it, and preserve what still serves. Not everything has to change when everything changes.

That brings us to the tender, often neglected matter of financial identity. Many people don't realise how tightly their self-worth is bound up in their bank statements. When losses strike, the shame kicks in: I failed. I should have predicted this. I've lost control. These internal scripts can be more damaging than the external blows. What's needed isn't denial, but reframing. You are not your income, nor your net worth. The mature path isn't about stoicism or perfection—it's about resilience without shame, accountability without self-flagellation.

There's a broader lens here, too. History, if you care to examine it, is a brilliant tutor in anti-fragility. Economies themselves are dynamic creatures. They evolve in response to stress—through policy reform, grassroots innovation, or in some cases, outright collapse and rebirth. Look at post-war Europe's reconstruction, or the agile resistance of informal economies under oppressive regimes. What patterns emerge? The most adaptive systems are diverse, decentralised, and capable of pivot. At the individual level, the same holds true. Those anchored to a single income, industry, or idea tend to flounder in volatile environments. Those who diversify—whether in skillsets, asset classes, social capital, or purpose—are the ones who find their footing when the terrain shifts.

We're entering a time where volatility is less an exception and more a feature of the landscape. Climate, politics, demographics, AI—all are reshaping the ground beneath us. What's required isn't just financial literacy (though that's essential), but something deeper: design fluency. The ability to discard what no longer works, adopt what does, and remain centred amidst all the motion. It's about being principled, not doctrinaire; flexible, not flaky.

This chapter isn't going to hand you a to-do list. You won't find tidy formulas or guaranteed outcomes. What you will find is a shift in orientation. A way to think more clearly, plan more wisely, and react less destructively. You'll learn how each of your wealth layers—emergency, income, investing, and legacy—responds under strain. And you'll learn how to reinforce the weakest links without setting fire to the rest.

To build an anti-fragile financial life is to accept that no system is fail-safe. But it is also to believe that with preparation, perspective, and practice, you can meet disruption without losing direction. The goal isn't to outrun instability—it's to navigate it with intelligence and integrity. The anti-fragile person doesn't avoid the fall. They learn how to land. And when they do, they often stand up stronger than before.

If you've ever wanted to stop living at the mercy of what might go wrong, if you've ever wondered how to turn adversity into refinement, this chapter is your invitation. Not to control the chaos—but to meet it with design.

When the Ledger Gets Shaken

Financial stability is often framed as a matter of numbers: income exceeds expenses, liabilities are managed, assets accumulate. But that framing omits a crucial truth—financial stability is *not a state*. It is a condition that holds only until it doesn't. A diagnosis, a redundancy notice, a market crash, a divorce, a family emergency—none arrive on a calendar. Yet each has the potential to destabilise not just cash flow, but confidence, clarity, and cohesion. The ledger, once neat and logical, becomes volatile. And the real test of a financial system is not how it performs during equilibrium, but how it *responds when the equilibrium breaks.*

The modern economy has normalised fragility. Many people live one shock away from a breakdown—not because they are reckless, but because the systems around them are brittle. A society that glorifies hustle, outsources care, and monetises every waking hour rarely builds in slack. Even among high earners, the safety net is often illusory: tightly coupled expenses, no liquidity buffer, and little structural redundancy. Financial stress, in this context, is not a surprise—it's a certainty deferred. The challenge is not just avoiding the fall; it's *designing for impact absorption.*

Every wealth system rests on four layers: emergency, income, investing, and legacy. Each serves a distinct purpose under stress. But under normal conditions, their roles are often misunderstood or neglected. When crisis hits, the interactions among these layers determine whether a household will bend or break. To prepare for volatility is not to predict every possible threat. It is to ensure that no single failure can cascade uncontrollably across the entire system.

The first layer—*emergency*—is often reduced to a simplistic recommendation: three to six months of living expenses in cash. But this misses the point. Emergency liquidity is not about a fixed formula; it is about *proximity and speed.* In a crisis, time is the scarce resource. The question is not "how much is saved" but "how quickly can funds be accessed without penalty or panic?" A job loss or health crisis may not last three months. It may last twelve. The point is not to cover every possibility, but to create *breathing room*—space to think clearly, recalibrate, and act intentionally rather than reactively. This layer is not the fortress. It is the airlock.

The second layer—*income*—is where fragility often hides in plain sight. For many, income is concentrated in a single source: a salaried job, a business contract, or a primary client. This concentration is efficient in peacetime, but exposes critical risk under duress. When disruption occurs, the velocity of income interruption is immediate; its recovery is often slow and nonlinear. Income anti-fragility requires two qualities: *diversification and elasticity*. Diversification can take the form of multiple revenue streams—earned, passive, or collaborative. Elasticity means having a plan for income replacement that does not require starting from zero. This might be a freelance skillset, a rentable asset, or a partnership that can activate when primary channels go dark. In disruption, the difference between delay and desperation is often measured in *days, not months*.

The third layer—*investing*—is the one most visibly affected by external forces. Market volatility, interest rate shifts, political instability—all echo through portfolios. During a crash, this is often the site of emotional turbulence: panic selling, withdrawal regret, or cognitive paralysis. But a sound investing layer is not designed for daily comfort. It is designed for *strategic endurance*. To be useful in crisis, investments must be structured with purpose and timeline in mind. Long-term assets should not be forced into short-term roles. If retirement accounts are raided to cover present emergencies, the long-term plan is cannibalised. This is not merely a financial error; it's a structural design flaw. Liquidity must come from liquidity layers. Growth must be insulated from shock absorption. Investing under pressure teaches a core design principle: *use each layer for its intended job, especially when it's tempting to break the rules*.

The fourth layer—*legacy*—may seem irrelevant during crisis, but it is more consequential than it appears. Legacy is not limited to inheritance or estate planning; it includes *systems of continuity, resilience, and clarity*. Who knows where the passwords are? Who can access shared accounts? What happens if decision-making is impaired? Families that have never discussed these issues find themselves paralysed when crisis strikes. The legacy layer holds the operating manual of the financial system. Under stress, clarity of intention becomes a stabiliser. If a household knows what must be preserved—children's education, elder care, a business continuity plan—then trade-offs can be made with *confidence, not confusion*. A well-articulated legacy plan reduces ambiguity. And in crisis, ambiguity is expensive.

But even a layered system cannot prevent disruption. What it can prevent is *collapse*. The goal is not invincibility, but modularity: when one layer falters, others can adapt without snapping. This is the core of anti-fragile design. But for that to work, the system must be periodically stress-tested. Most people discover their weaknesses during the crisis. The more effective approach is to diagnose fragility before the storm. Ask: If my income halved tomorrow, which expenses could I eliminate in 72 hours? If my partner fell ill, what documentation would I need access to immediately? If the market dropped 40%, how would I behave differently—and why? These are not theoretical exercises. They are *calibration tools*.

It's also essential to distinguish between *shock response* and *overreaction*. Crisis often triggers a desire for control—sometimes expressed as obsessive budgeting, irrational frugality, or unnecessary asset liquidation. These are understandable reflexes, but they can do long-term damage. The key is *responsive modulation*: making specific, proportional adjustments rather than wholesale system abandonment. For example, reducing discretionary spending for 90 days to preserve liquidity is rational. Selling a well-structured investment portfolio out of fear is not. Knowing the difference requires preparation, perspective, and—in many cases—external counsel. When the ledger gets shaken, *clarity must replace chaos*.

There is also an emotional layer to this entire architecture. Financial trauma is real, and it often outlives the crisis itself. People who lose income, homes, or savings in a downturn may carry invisible scars into every future financial decision. They overcompensate, avoid planning, or distrust even healthy risk. Addressing these patterns requires not just financial repair but *psychological integration*. Processing the story of the crisis—what failed, what held, what was learned—becomes part of the redesign. Without this work, future strategies may be subconsciously shaped by fear rather than foresight.

Ultimately, a financial system should not only grow during good times; it must *reveal its intelligence during bad times*. The measure of a financial architecture is its capacity to adapt *without loss of coherence*. That doesn't mean avoiding all pain. It means knowing which pain is signal, and which is noise. It means recognising which parts are temporary, and which require structural overhaul. It means staying tethered to values even when numbers drop.

When the ledger gets shaken, the question that matters is not just "how much did you lose?" but "how well was your system designed to absorb, adapt, and emerge wiser?" The answer to that question does not arrive in the crisis. It is embedded in *what was built before it.* And now—before the next shake—is the time to begin.

"Lessons from Collapse"

Collapse is not a metaphor—it is a recurring pattern in economic history. The fragility of financial systems is rarely visible in prosperity, but always revealed in stress. The study of financial collapse is not just about numbers, markets, or headlines; it is a study of human psychology under duress, institutional design under pressure, and systemic weakness brought into daylight. The question is not whether another collapse will happen. It is *what we learn when it does*—and how well that learning is integrated into the structures we rebuild.

The mythology of economic collapse often begins with spectacle: the Wall Street trader packing boxes in 2008, the long ATM queues during Argentina's default, or the haunting silence of bank runs in Cyprus or Lebanon. But collapse rarely starts with a bang. It begins with denial, accelerates through overconfidence, and is fuelled by complexity people believe they understand—but don't. In every case, collapse strips systems of their illusions. It forces a reckoning. And paradoxically, *this is where resilience is born.*

To understand what makes a system resilient, we must first examine what causes one to fail. The Global Financial Crisis of 2008 is often framed as a banking failure, but at its core, it was a *failure of abstraction.* Derivatives, credit default swaps, and collateralised debt obligations became so complex, so layered, and so far removed from the real assets they referenced that risk became invisible. When liquidity vanished, the underlying structures collapsed under their own informational opacity. The most dangerous phrase in finance—"It's too complicated to fail"—was exposed as intellectual hubris. What followed was not just economic contraction, but mass disillusionment. The institutions that had been trusted were revealed to be vulnerable, misaligned, or actively exploitative.

Resilient systems, by contrast, are characterised by *transparency, modularity, and redundancy*. After 2008, the financial sector began to rebuild around these principles—stress testing became mandatory, liquidity ratios were recalibrated, and capital reserves rethought. But even as regulatory frameworks tightened, many individuals and households continued operating fragile systems at the personal level: single points of failure in income, overleveraged lifestyles, no savings buffer, no decentralised support network. The lesson that institutions began to heed—design for failure before it happens—was less widely adopted in personal finance.

History offers earlier examples, each with distinct lessons. The Weimar hyperinflation in 1920s Germany taught that *currency stability is not merely an economic variable but a social contract.* When money ceases to hold meaning, chaos is not only financial—it is moral and existential. People bartered with bread, bought houses with wheelbarrows of notes, and saw life savings obliterated overnight. The collapse of value is also the collapse of trust. Systems recovered only when a credible anchor—first the Rentenmark, then institutional reform—restored confidence. The insight here is clear: *resilience is not merely fiscal; it is emotional and cultural.*

Fast-forward to 1997's Asian Financial Crisis. What began with Thailand's devaluation triggered a chain reaction across East and Southeast Asia. But countries that had local consumption buffers, diversified trade partnerships, and less foreign-denominated debt recovered more swiftly. South Korea, for instance, launched an aggressive set of structural reforms, including fiscal transparency, corporate governance overhauls, and public savings campaigns. Citizens even donated gold jewellery to reduce the country's debt. Recovery wasn't just institutional—it was participatory. The key insight: *shared sacrifice accelerates recovery when trust and transparency align.*

Collapse is rarely even-handed. It disproportionately affects those least equipped to respond. The COVID-19 pandemic offered the most recent global stress test. Within weeks, entire sectors—

hospitality, transport, education—were shuttered. Governments scrambled to inject liquidity, provide income relief, and prevent mass insolvency. Yet the impact was asymmetrical. Those with secure employment, home offices, and existing assets saw inconvenience. Those in precarious work or informal economies saw devastation. What emerged was not just an economic crisis, but a *design test* of financial systems across layers: emergency funds, passive income streams, redundancy in supply chains, psychological resilience.

What distinguished the households and businesses that adapted from those that unravelled? It wasn't merely luck. Three characteristics consistently appeared: *adaptive structure, decentralised support, and clarity of values*. Adaptive structure meant not being rigidly reliant on one income source or cost structure. Decentralised support referred not only to financial assets, but to social capital—networks that could offer time, skills, or short-term aid. Clarity of values allowed for *quick, values-aligned decisions*: What is non-negotiable? What can be paused? Where do we allocate scarce energy?

From these observations, we extract an essential principle: *collapse is not purely destructive—it is revelatory*. It reveals what was hidden, what was fragile, and what was already broken but temporarily held together by circumstance. In personal finance, these revelations often come too late. But viewed correctly, past collapses become diagnostic tools. They show us what questions we must ask *before* disruption: Where are my income dependencies? What is the psychological trigger that would cause me to liquidate investments prematurely? Who in my household understands the system if I become incapacitated?

There's a temptation after a collapse—whether institutional or personal—to *seek permanent insulation*. But resilience is not about invulnerability. It is about *recoverability*. Japan's recovery after its 1990s asset bubble collapse took decades, and yet it cultivated one of the most stable savings cultures in the world. Iceland's 2008 banking collapse led to a total rethink of national scale relative to institutional ambition. Rather than bail out oversized banks, it chose to protect citizens first, prosecute fraudulent executives, and rebuild a downsized financial system. Recovery was not linear, but it was *intentionally redesigned.*

These examples offer a framework: resilient systems recover not by returning to the status quo, but by *emerging changed, clearer, and structurally upgraded.* This demands an attitude of learning, not denial; an ethic of design, not drift.

The same applies to personal systems. A job loss should lead to a rebalancing of income diversification strategy. A failed business should inform clearer liquidity buffers and contingency partnerships. A divorce that reveals financial opacity should result in *financial transparency protocols* in future relationships. The mistake is not in the fall. It's in rebuilding the same structure that collapsed, assuming it will behave differently next time.

And this leads to the final insight: *collapse creates opportunity—but only if we choose to redesign rather than reassemble.* Many people, eager to "get back to normal," miss the moment for transformation. They seek stability by restoring what was, rather than questioning whether what was built served them well in the first place. The most resilient individuals and institutions treat collapse as *an audit.* What do we want to preserve? What must we retire? What truths did the crisis expose that we were too comfortable to confront?

Wealth that endures is not built solely on growth; it is built on recovery. And recovery is not about bouncing back—it is about *building forward, informed by what broke.* Collapse is painful. But it is also precise. It tells you, if you are willing to listen, exactly what must change. And those who treat collapse not as the end, but as a demanding teacher, build systems that are not only more stable—but more intelligent, more human, and more durable than what came before.

"Pivoting Layers, Not Abandoning Them"

A financial plan is only as useful as it is *adaptable.* This truth is often overlooked until the moment of stress—when a job loss hits, a housing market swings, a family emergency arises, or inflation eats into spending power with quiet, unrelenting force. In those moments, individuals face a critical decision: whether to dismantle their existing financial architecture in panic, or to *pivot within it* with intelligence and calm. The distinction between these two responses marks the boundary between fragility and resilience. Strategic agility is not the abandonment of structure; it is the art of reconfiguring it without losing its integrity.

Every robust wealth design rests on four foundational layers: emergency, income, investing, and legacy. These layers are not fixed compartments but *living, interdependent systems*. When one is stressed, the others must adjust—not disintegrate. The problem is, under financial pressure, people are rarely trained to think in terms of pivots. The dominant instinct is binary: either preserve the plan in rigid denial, or scrap it in fear. Both responses create unnecessary damage. The discipline we require is a third path—adaptive realignment based on principles, not panic.

To grasp what pivoting truly means, consider the role of *cash flow* within the broader design. Suppose a household's income stream becomes temporarily unstable—say, due to freelance contracts drying up or a primary earner going on medical leave. The knee-jerk reaction might be to raid long-term investments, halt retirement contributions, or accrue debt. But an agile response would begin by examining which layers can absorb short-term pressure without long-term distortion. Can discretionary expenses be compressed temporarily to relieve cash flow tension? Can short-term liquidity be sourced from a non-retirement investment account rather than triggering tax penalties? Can a time-bound withdrawal from the emergency fund be paired with a timeline and plan to replenish it? *Adaptation within the existing structure is almost always preferable to improvisation outside it.*

Historically, societies that have withstood economic shocks effectively do not discard their financial infrastructures at the first sign of instability. Instead, they re-prioritise. During the post-WWII rebuilding period in the UK, for example, the government didn't abandon the welfare state model under fiscal stress; it reoriented expenditures to protect healthcare and housing while scaling down military commitments and deferring certain capital projects. That strategic pivot preserved the system's core values. Individuals can do the same. A parent funding a child's education during a recession may pause investment growth targets or scale back charitable giving—but should not abandon insurance coverage or sell long-term equity positions out of fear. *Preserving the architecture while adjusting the load is the core discipline.*

Psychologically, the difficulty lies in the false perception that a plan that needs to be changed was somehow wrong from the outset. This belief leads to shame and avoidance rather than clarity and recalibration. But all intelligent systems—whether biological, ecological, or financial—are designed to *respond*, not remain static. The body increases cortisol to manage acute stress and lowers it when the threat passes. Financial systems must be allowed similar flexibility: temporary tension is not a flaw, but an *expected condition to be managed with intelligence.*

One of the most powerful tools for adaptive thinking is *scenario mapping*. This practice—borrowed from military and organisational strategy—asks the individual to imagine and rehearse a range of stress events, from minor income disruptions to multi-year economic downturns. The aim is not fear-mongering, but to build *cognitive agility*. In doing so, individuals begin to see the relationship between layers. If a rental property's vacancy rate spikes, what is the timeline before it affects monthly cash flow? If an investment portfolio drops 30%, which expenses (if any) need to be reviewed? What non-financial resources—skills, relationships, alternate income options—could be deployed temporarily to reduce strain? This practice strengthens the mental habit of pivoting rather than reacting.

A key element in this is *knowing which layers are flexible and which are sacred*. Emergency funds are designed to be used, not idolised. Selling long-term equities in a bear market should be a last resort, not a reflex. Insurance policies, once compromised, may be difficult or impossible to reinstate under the same terms. Clarity around the role of each financial layer allows for confident pivoting without compromising core structural integrity. It becomes possible to say, "We will pause investing contributions for six months, but we will not touch the long-term portfolio." That distinction matters enormously—not just mathematically, but *psychologically*.

Agility is not just a design principle; it is an *emotional competency*. Many financial decisions made under duress are not truly financial—they are attempts to relieve anxiety. People seek certainty where none exists, or attempt to control outcomes by overcorrecting in the wrong domain. Panic-selling, insurance lapses, or debt spirals are not strategic decisions—they are *emotional flinches*. Training the mind to interpret discomfort as a signal—not a command—enables better outcomes. And this is not abstract theory. In the early days of the COVID-19 pandemic, the most effective individual financial responses were not acts of brilliance, but acts of *restraint*. People who preserved their asset allocation plans, rebalanced according to schedule, and reduced discretionary outflows without uprooting their entire system fared far better than those who tried to "time" markets or made drastic withdrawals. *Discipline, not drama, is the hallmark of agility*.

It's worth noting that pivoting is also about opportunity, not just survival. In moments of disruption, there may be chances to reposition certain assets, renegotiate contracts, or learn new income-producing skills. The assumption that financial strategy is only about defence during hard times ignores the creative potential of adaptation. During the 2022 inflation spike, some households took the opportunity to reassess car ownership costs, relocate to lower cost-of-living cities enabled by remote work, or launch side businesses to monetise dormant skills. These were not acts of desperation, but of strategic pivoting—a willingness to evolve without abandoning long-term goals.

This requires a subtle but essential mindset: *tactical flexibility with strategic fidelity*. The plan may change in its surface expression—its cash flow forecasts, its savings rates, even its sequencing—but its *intent* remains intact. Wealth, when built intelligently, is not a brittle castle. It is more like a suspension bridge: capable of swaying in the wind without collapsing. The materials matter, yes—but so does the design, the joints, and the willingness to reinforce one area while another is under strain.

We should also be cautious of overcorrection after the crisis passes. A common post-crisis error is *overbuilding* the layer that failed while neglecting the system as a whole. Someone who lost a job may become obsessively income-focused to the exclusion of investing or estate planning. Another who experienced a medical bill shock may hoard excessive cash at the expense of growth. These are understandable reactions—but they are *trauma responses*, not strategic adjustments. True pivoting requires *whole-system awareness*—reinforcing the weak point, yes, but not at the cost of creating new blind spots elsewhere.

Ultimately, what this subchapter argues is deceptively simple: *agility outperforms perfection.* The best financial plans are not the ones that never need to change. They are the ones that know *how to change, when to change, and—critically—when not to.* The sophistication of a financial strategy lies not in its rigidity, but in its responsiveness. Agility is not the absence of structure. It is structure designed to bend, intelligently and purposefully, when the winds of life inevitably shift.

"Emotional First Aid for Financial Trauma"

The psychological impact of financial loss is often underestimated—both by those experiencing it and by the professionals tasked with helping them recover. A sudden job loss, a foreclosure, a divorce that shatters economic stability, or even an unexpected medical expense can create levels of psychological distress comparable to bereavement or trauma. And yet, while we accept the importance of emotional first aid in the context of physical injury or psychological crises, we rarely extend the same logic to financial upheaval. We speak in terms of "tightening the belt" or "bouncing back," as if resourcefulness were simply a matter of spreadsheets. It is not. Financial trauma embeds itself in the nervous system, warps perception, impairs decision-making, and, if left untreated, can calcify into shame, paralysis, or self-sabotage. Recovery, therefore, must begin not just with a strategy, but with *soothing the system that will execute it.*

The first principle of financial first aid is deceptively simple: *safety precedes clarity.* In the immediate aftermath of a financial shock, the nervous system often enters fight, flight, or freeze mode. Decisions made in this state are reactive, not reflective. This is not weakness; it is biology. The amygdala, our brain's threat detection centre, overrides the prefrontal cortex—responsible for logic and planning—when it perceives danger. This means that even the most financially literate individual can find themselves unable to process information, access solutions, or ask for help. The first priority, therefore, is not to "figure things out," but to *calm the system.* This may involve deep breathing techniques, somatic grounding (such as placing feet flat on the floor and naming tangible sensations), or simply acknowledging the emotional reality: *this feels terrifying, and it's okay to pause.* Only once physiological safety is restored can clarity begin to re-emerge.

Language plays a powerful role here. The way people narrate financial loss to themselves and others either supports recovery or entrenches distress. The phrase "I failed financially" is a categoric identity statement—it equates the outcome with the self. "I experienced a financial failure" is something else entirely; it names the event as external, specific, and bounded in time. This linguistic distinction is not academic—it's therapeutic. The former reinforces shame; the latter creates space for change. *Shame is the enemy of financial recovery because it isolates and silences precisely when connection and reflection are most needed.*

This is where relational repair becomes essential. One of the most damaging effects of financial trauma is that it often remains hidden. People talk about breakups and health scares; they don't talk about defaulting on a credit card or secretly draining their savings. This silence creates a false sense of isolation—everyone else appears stable, competent, and intact. But research consistently shows the opposite: financial insecurity is widespread, and vulnerability is more common than people let on. Breaking this silence requires courage, but it also requires *curated contexts*—spaces where financial struggle is not pathologised or moralised. A financial therapist, trusted peer, or structured group setting can offer the relational containment necessary for true processing. Vulnerability in this context is not indulgent; it is *repair in action.*

Once the emotional landscape has been acknowledged, the task shifts toward *meaning reconstruction.* People often assume that financial healing is purely behavioural—create a budget, pay off debt, rebuild savings. And while those steps are vital, they are insufficient. Without a shift in the narrative, behavioural change remains brittle. A person may pay off their debt but still carry a belief that they are irresponsible or doomed to repeat the pattern. Financial trauma embeds not just a loss of money, but a loss of trust—in oneself, in systems, in the future. Rebuilding that trust requires internal narrative work. What did this experience reveal? What was within my control, and what wasn't? What new commitments or values might emerge from this rupture? *These are not rhetorical questions—they are cognitive scaffolding for a post-trauma identity.*

At this stage, practical tools can begin to re-enter the conversation—not as punishment or correction, but as supports for coherence. One highly effective intervention is the "financial grounding plan." Unlike a standard budget or forecast, this tool begins with emotional checkpoints: How do I want to feel this month around money? Where do I feel tension in my financial life? What's one micro-action I can take this week to restore a sense of agency? From there, the plan moves into numbers—but with emotional context in tow. This approach respects the psychological recovery arc. It recognises that re-engaging with numbers too soon, without emotional readiness, can trigger further avoidance or dysregulation.

Importantly, emotional first aid also involves *boundaries*—not just with money, but with information. In the age of financial media overload, people recovering from trauma often compound their distress by immersing themselves in dire economic forecasts, social media comparison loops, or productivity hacks that ignore the reality of their emotional state. Part of recovery involves *curating input.* This may mean limiting financial news to once per week, muting comparison triggers on social media, or unsubscribing from newsletters that promote urgency rather than stability. The mind, like the body, needs a calm environment to heal.

It is also worth naming that financial trauma is not evenly distributed. Marginalised groups—due to race, gender, disability, or immigration status—often experience chronic economic stressors that make financial recovery more complex. The trauma is not only from an acute event, but from cumulative disadvantage. This reality demands that any discussion of healing must include *systems awareness*. People do not recover into neutral systems; they recover into environments that may still be structurally hostile. For this reason, emotional first aid must be paired with *structural clarity*—understanding not just what went wrong personally, but what is wrong structurally. This clarity is not disempowering—it is *liberating*, because it prevents self-blame and opens the door to collective solutions.

Reclaiming agency is the final arc of the recovery process. This does not mean returning to "business as usual." It means building a new baseline from which strategic decisions can be made with clarity and care. This often includes re-evaluating old financial rules. Perhaps the rigid belief that "debt is always bad" needs softening. Perhaps the pressure to max out investments at the cost of basic wellbeing needs to be rebalanced. Financial healing invites a new kind of alignment—one in which money serves the person, not the other way around. It is a reassertion of self-authorship.

The work of emotional financial repair is not linear. Grief resurfaces. Shame returns. Progress feels slow. But what distinguishes recovery from re-enactment is *reflection with support*. There is no single roadmap—but there are well-trodden paths of resilience. What matters most is not perfection, but the willingness to pause, to examine, to reconnect, and to move forward with compassion for both past and present selves.

Emotional first aid is not a soft skill—it is a strategic necessity. Without it, financial strategies become brittle; with it, even modest plans become sustainable. The nervous system is the operating system of all behaviour. Tending to it after financial trauma is not optional. It is the most intelligent investment one can make in the restoration of long-term economic wellbeing.

"Resilience Rehearsals"

The human imagination is a formidable instrument—capable of conjuring dread from shadows and resilience from preparation. In financial life, however, imagination is often stunted. People plan for prosperity but not for disruption. They fine-tune investment portfolios while ignoring what might happen if income dries up, a partner becomes incapacitated, or the economy enters a prolonged downturn. This is not simply optimism; it is a cultural blind spot. *We are taught to visualise goals, not to rehearse breakdowns.* And yet, every robust system—be it a military, an airline, or a hospital—undergoes simulations not only of success but of failure. Fire drills, black swan scenarios, and pressure tests exist because *the capacity to respond depends less on courage in the moment than on calm built in advance.* The same logic applies to personal finance.

Resilience rehearsals are simulated financial stress-tests designed to probe the durability of your system *before* reality demands it. They are not abstract visualisations or doomsday fantasies. They are deliberate exercises grounded in your actual numbers, obligations, and decision-making frameworks. Their purpose is not to induce fear but to *inoculate against panic*—to reveal friction points while stakes are still low. A well-designed rehearsal reveals more than vulnerability; it teaches agility. Just as athletes train under resistance so that real performance feels lighter, financial rehearsals build the reflexes necessary for composure in actual disruption.

Begin by asking: what kind of shocks are most relevant to your financial life? Not all crises are global. A job loss may be more destabilising to a freelancer than a salaried professional. A health event may ripple through a family differently depending on caregiving responsibilities, insurance access, or immigration status. Rather than focusing on hypotheticals that don't match your context, focus on *plausible stressors.* What if your primary source of income disappeared for six months? What if interest rates spiked 3%? What if your co-founder quit? These are not abstract prompts—they are diagnostic instruments for identifying pressure points within your current financial infrastructure.

One powerful exercise is to simulate a "zero-income month." This does not mean voluntarily ceasing work, but it does mean documenting, in full, how you would respond if no money came in for thirty days. Which bills are automated? Which subscriptions could be paused? How quickly could you reduce discretionary spending without harm? Could you make partial payments on fixed costs, and if so, with whom would you negotiate? This simulation immediately surfaces both technical and emotional friction. Perhaps you realise your emergency fund is underfunded. Perhaps you notice a fear of asking for flexibility. Perhaps you find relief in discovering just how lean you could go. The value lies not in perfection but in exposure—to *how your system, and your psyche, behave under strain.*

Another rehearsal worth running is the "sudden expense audit." Imagine a £10,000 unexpected expense—medical, legal, or familial—arrives tomorrow. Could you absorb it without derailing your long-term goals? What sequence of actions would you take? Would you liquidate an asset? Take on short-term debt? Tap into community support? More importantly, *how quickly could you make that decision*—and on what criteria would it rest? This is where rehearsals become diagnostic. People often overestimate their preparedness because they conflate the *existence* of resources with *clarity around access.* The rehearsal separates the two. It makes visible the lag between theory and execution.

Critically, resilience rehearsals must also test psychological variables. Financial crises do not unfold in spreadsheets. They unfold in kitchens, hospital rooms, and sleepless nights. A robust rehearsal therefore includes *an emotional readiness protocol.* Who are your emotional first responders? Who has access to your financial information if you are incapacitated? Have you documented critical passwords or points of contact? These questions may feel excessive—but they are not about paranoia. They are about *relational continuity.* When people are in crisis, they do not rise to the occasion—they fall to their level of training, of delegation, of preparation. A resilient financial system is not just liquid and diversified; it is *legible to others.*

To make rehearsals practical rather than overwhelming, set a cadence. Quarterly is often sufficient. Treat it as you would a fire drill: non-negotiable, brief, and taken seriously. Rotate scenarios so that each layer of your financial architecture is tested over time. One quarter might focus on income disruption, another on market volatility, a third on legal risk or caregiver transitions. Over time, patterns will emerge. Perhaps you realise that all your weak points stem from over-concentration in a single income source. Or that your lifestyle has crept upward in ways that compromise adaptability. These are not small insights—they are strategic pivots earned in advance.

A critical benefit of resilience rehearsals is that they neutralise shame. Often, when people encounter a real financial shock, their first reaction is self-judgment: *I should have been more prepared. I should have known this could happen.* This retrospective blame not only delays response—it corrodes confidence. But if a person has *already rehearsed* the event, they meet it not as a personal failure, but as a known variable. There is no shame in a rehearsed fire; only protocols, steps, options. The practice transforms crisis from a moral referendum into a logistical challenge.

This concept finds precedent in other high-stakes domains. Pilots use simulators not to avoid failure but to normalise it. Elite athletes practise not just winning plays but failure recovery. Even cybersecurity professionals regularly stage breaches to test system defences. In every one of these domains, the logic is the same: *when risk is inevitable, rehearsal is non-negotiable.* Personal finance deserves the same rigour. It is not only about wealth accumulation; it is about *resilience under interruption.*

Importantly, resilience rehearsals are not about adopting a scarcity mindset. Their goal is not to shrink your life but to *expand your range.* A person who knows they can adapt with composure is *freer*, not more fearful. They can take informed risks, because they know the edge of their capacity. They can speak more honestly with partners, clients, or collaborators, because they are grounded in reality rather than bravado. The psychological dividend of rehearsal is confidence—not the brittle confidence of assumption, but the earned confidence of exposure and response.

There is also a moral dimension. People who have rehearsed crisis are more likely to respond wisely when others are in need. They do not project their fear, avoid difficult conversations, or hoard resources impulsively. They know what is required under stress, and they can model steadiness. In this sense, *resilience is not just an individual trait—it is a civic capacity.* It radiates outward. Rehearsal is, in this light, an act of collective responsibility.

To dismiss these exercises as unnecessary is to misread the age we live in. Volatility is not an anomaly; it is the substrate. Whether geopolitical instability, ecological disruption, or market dislocation, the forces shaping our lives are increasingly non-linear. Traditional financial planning models, built on assumptions of stable income and gradual progress, are no longer sufficient. What is required is *adaptive literacy*—the ability to read conditions, reframe assumptions, and reallocate resources in real-time. Rehearsals develop this literacy not by teaching answers but by training *responsiveness.*

Ultimately, resilience rehearsals are not about predicting the next crisis. They are about becoming someone who does not fracture under stress—someone who knows their weak points, trusts their protocols, and adapts with clarity instead of chaos. That transformation cannot be willed into existence in the heat of a breakdown. It must be cultivated through quiet, consistent practice. *Not because crisis is coming—but because integrity demands readiness regardless.* And in that readiness, real peace of mind begins.

Chapter 10
The Sovereignty Blueprint

Sovereignty is so often misread—as though it were some kind of stoic self-exile, the lone figure on a mountaintop, beholden to no one, answering to nothing. But that's a distortion. The true essence of sovereignty, especially in the realms of wealth and life design, isn't about detachment or isolation. It's about discernment. It's the deliberate, hard-earned ability to act in accordance with one's truest convictions—to choose without being steered by pressure or panic, to respond with inner clarity rather than external conditioning. Autonomy may suggest self-sufficiency; sovereignty, by contrast, demands self-authorship. It's not only about meeting one's needs—it's about the depth of wisdom required to define those needs in the first place, and to resist the ever-churning machinery of cultural suggestion trying to redefine them on your behalf.

There are no shortcuts on this road. This chapter assumes you've already weathered some complexity—perhaps walked through the intricacies of financial planning, wrestled with the emotional terrain of money, survived a few crises. If you've made it this far, competence is no longer enough. It's time for philosophy. Sovereignty cannot be bought, delegated, or inherited. It must be shaped, deliberately. And its design? It should be both dynamic and grounded—not ornamental, but structural. Not theoretical, but alive. What follows, then, is less a how-to list and more a living framework—one that redefines success not as a static metric of wealth, but as the daily expression of alignment: how you decide, how you adapt, how you teach, and how you live.

A key early distinction: freedom isn't sovereignty. Many individuals who appear "free" on the surface—high income, impressive portfolios—are, in fact, dangerously overleveraged. Not simply in their finances, but in emotion, time, and energy. They know their asset allocations to the decimal, yet can't say what compromises those numbers represent. They're rich in holdings but impoverished in coherence. The Sovereignty Blueprint calls for a different sort of ledger. What if peace of mind were measured? Or the capacity to say "no" treated as a financial resource? What if goals were built around alignment rather than ambition?

To ground that idea, we propose a reimagined wealth dashboard—still tracking the classics: income security, liquidity, asset spread—but layered with subtler, and arguably more critical, dimensions: time freedom, alignment with values, decision-making lag, resilience of legacy. These aren't lofty abstractions—they are pressing design imperatives. Ask yourself: could you walk away for a month without the scaffolding collapsing? Does your calendar honour your principles or someone else's urgency? Are your financial decisions reinforcing your integrity—or quietly chipping away at it? And whose well-being does your system ultimately serve—just your own, or that of others, too?

This is where the concept of financial ritual becomes more than just a tidy notion. Money, for many, exists in extremes—either pursued feverishly or avoided altogether. In a sovereign design, however, money isn't a crisis or a conquest. It's a rhythm. Daily practices—such as brief check-ins on cash flow or mindful spending pauses—build awareness. Monthly reviews give space for interpretation: not only what was done, but how it felt. Annual rituals become the scaffolding for redesign—be it tax strategy, philanthropy, or broader recalibration. These routines are not bureaucratic burdens—they're acts of stewardship. They anchor your intent and ward off the entropy of default living.

Sovereignty, it must be said, is not a solitary end. A system that is truly sovereign ought to be transmissible. Not through inheritance of capital alone, but through the inheritance of understanding. Teaching someone to navigate a ledger isn't about arithmetic—it's about insight. What's the story in these numbers? What's absent from this picture? What values do our choices silently encode? When we translate financial knowledge into shared capability, we shift wealth from being a private defence to becoming a public contribution.

That said, translation is rarely clean. To move towards sovereignty often means unlearning what we never chose to believe—scarcity scripts, hollow definitions of worth, the performance of affluence.

So much of our financial identity is absorbed, not authored. And that's precisely where sovereignty begins: in the act of reclamation. In choosing to construct a financial life that reflects who you are now, rather than who you were told to become. The legacy, then, becomes less about numbers on a will, and more about narrative. True inheritance is behavioural. It lives in how your children interact with money, how your partner navigates adversity, how your community endures after your presence has faded. It's in rituals, policies, shared language, and expectation. It's not what you leave—it's what they carry forward.

Designing for lasting relevance requires more than resilience—it needs resonance. Systems endure when they make emotional, ethical, and practical sense. A legacy isn't just sustained—it must be inhabited. And that demands a feedback loop. Is your system working—for whom, and under what strain? Sovereignty, if it's to survive the test of time, must remain fluid. It must be responsive. It must be asked, again and again: is this still true? Does this still serve? What worked at one stage of life, in one cultural or economic context, may not work in another. A sovereign structure breathes with its steward.

Throughout this chapter, you'll encounter tools and prompts designed not to instruct but to illuminate. We will probe familiar assumptions—about independence, about success, about how much control is really possible. We'll look at how systems can be shaped to affirm your values rather than dilute them. We'll examine how small rituals protect big intentions. And above all, we'll pose one essential question, often left unspoken at the moment of decision: what is this choice making me more of?

This is not a chapter of tidy conclusions. It's one of reckoning. It asks for depth, for the courage to be uncomfortable. It asks for a kind of coherence—the willingness to align money with meaning, structure with soul. Because in the end, a financial life well designed is not the one that hoards the most, nor even the one that plays the game best—but the one that, even under pressure, reflects you—truthfully, unflinchingly, and without compromise.

That is the promise of the Sovereignty Blueprint. Not a fixed map, but a dynamic architecture. Not a one-size doctrine, but a practice to inhabit. What you build with it—well, that becomes the real legacy. Not merely how much you have, but how free you are to live it.

Autonomy vs. Freedom

The language of modern self-empowerment is saturated with the word "freedom"—financial freedom, time freedom, location freedom. It's a seductive ideal, often framed in numbers or visualised in exotic lifestyles: the entrepreneur on a beach with passive income, the early retiree unmoored from the daily grind, the minimalist whose costs are so low they needn't answer to anyone. But when pressed for definition, these freedoms frequently collapse into their simpler cousin: autonomy. That is, the ability to do things on one's own, to opt out of dependency, to operate without interference. Yet autonomy is not the same as freedom. *Autonomy is tactical. Freedom is strategic.* One is a tool. The other is a state of being. And conflating the two leads not only to superficial financial planning but to lives built around misidentified priorities.

Autonomy is self-sufficiency—the ability to meet one's own needs. It's undeniably valuable, particularly in financial systems designed to trap dependency through consumer credit, inflated housing markets, and opaque asset classes. Learning how to earn, manage, and protect your own money is foundational. But *autonomy can also harden into isolation.* It can disguise itself as freedom while quietly reinforcing the same patterns it intends to escape. Consider the self-employed consultant who left corporate life in search of independence, only to discover that her schedule, income, and emotional bandwidth are now at the mercy of client demands. Or the FIRE (Financial Independence, Retire Early) adherent who achieved a low-expense lifestyle but lives in quiet anxiety, avoiding new experiences for fear of disrupting the spreadsheet. Autonomy has been achieved—but freedom? That remains elusive.

Freedom, in contrast, is not merely about optionality. It is about *alignment*—the ability to act in ways consistent with one's values, without being coerced by scarcity, social pressure, or unresolved fear. It encompasses emotional and ethical dimensions as much as financial ones. To be truly free is not only to have choices, but to know what matters deeply enough to choose *well.* It is the difference between being unshackled and being *sovereign.*

That distinction is more than philosophical; it has practical consequences. Autonomy tends to privilege control and optimisation. Freedom privileges clarity and trust. Autonomy might push you to own every piece of the puzzle—generate all your income, manage all your investments, eliminate all liabilities. Freedom asks a more nuanced question: *What dependencies do I choose, and under what terms?* It acknowledges that complete self-sufficiency is neither possible nor desirable in a complex world. Instead of seeking to sever all ties, it seeks to design *healthy, intentional interdependencies.* The financially sovereign individual does not fear collaboration, delegation, or mutual support. They build systems that reflect both competence and coherence.

This is where emotional sovereignty becomes central. A person who is financially autonomous but emotionally reactive is not free. They may make all their own decisions but still do so from a place of unresolved trauma, scarcity conditioning, or ego-driven comparison. Their ledger may be robust, but their internal compass is compromised. They are not free *from fear*, and thus not free *to choose.* Psychological research has long demonstrated how scarcity—whether real or perceived—narrows cognitive bandwidth. It makes us more impulsive, more risk-averse, more susceptible to short-termism. Emotional sovereignty means cultivating the self-awareness and regulation needed to withstand this distortion. It is not stoicism; it is maturity. The kind of maturity that can say: *I am safe. I am enough. And I do not need to prove it through consumption, accumulation, or avoidance.*

Ethical sovereignty, too, is frequently overlooked in personal finance discourse. Autonomy allows one to succeed within a given system. Freedom interrogates that system. Is my wealth creation aligned with my values? Does it reinforce systems I critique? Am I designing my life in a way that is extractive—or regenerative? These are uncomfortable questions because they blur the line between personal responsibility and collective impact. Yet they are essential for any reader seeking to move beyond survival or status toward meaning. Financial freedom that ignores ethical coherence is not freedom. It is moral evasion disguised as success.

This brings us to the architecture of financial systems. Autonomy is often expressed through tactics: budgets, income streams, investment strategies, debt payoff schedules. These are essential, but they are *instruments*, not foundations. Freedom demands architecture: the intentional structuring of systems that hold integrity under stress. For example, an autonomous earner may have five clients and a six-month runway. A sovereign builder asks: *What happens when two clients walk? What principles govern which opportunities I accept? What emotional infrastructure supports me through volatility?* Freedom designs not just for capacity, but for *resilience.* It is anti-fragile by nature—built not only to function, but to evolve.

There is a reason why many of the wealthiest people in the world are neither free nor sovereign. Their choices are constrained by reputation, by corporate structures, by family obligations, or by the inertia of maintaining an image. They have autonomy in spades—the ability to buy, travel, hire—but they lack sovereignty. And so they suffer the quiet imprisonment of lives built around external validation. True freedom cannot be engineered by scale alone. It must be *authored*—from within.

Consider how this distinction plays out in everyday financial decision-making. The autonomous path might lead someone to optimise for early retirement through maximal savings and aggressive frugality. The sovereign path asks a different set of questions: *What is the purpose of my time? What is enough? What rhythms of work and rest are most life-giving?* Similarly, someone might pursue property ownership as a badge of independence. But a sovereign view interrogates the assumptions: *Is ownership the best expression of stability and value for me, or am I inheriting someone else's dream?* Autonomy performs. Sovereignty discerns.

Sovereignty also redefines power. Under the autonomy paradigm, power comes from control—over time, money, tasks, decisions. Under the freedom paradigm, power emerges from alignment—between values and actions, between needs and systems, between inner clarity and outer expression. This is not a soft idealism. It is a rigorously designed state. And it has economic consequences. A sovereign investor resists herd behaviour. A sovereign leader builds cultures that prioritise truth over optics. A sovereign household designs for stewardship, not status. These expressions of power are not loud, but they are *durable.*

To move from autonomy to freedom, then, is to shift from strategy to *philosophy.* It is to replace the question "What can I do on my own?" with "What kind of life is worth designing—and how must my financial systems reflect it?" It is to let go of optimisation as a moral imperative, and instead prioritise coherence, adaptability, and integrity. It is to stop performing independence, and instead *inhabit sovereignty.*

This shift cannot be completed through hacks or templates. It requires slow thinking, system redesign, and deep reflection. It asks the reader not only to understand their money but to understand themselves. And that understanding must include their biases, their histories, their wounds, and their aspirations. It is not enough to own the ledger. You must *interpret it*—and perhaps, at times, *rewrite it entirely.*

As we continue through this chapter, we will explore how to architect this deeper form of financial freedom. We will examine the metrics that matter—not only net worth but net *integrity.* We will introduce rituals that reinforce sovereignty, frameworks that clarify priorities, and questions that challenge inherited scripts. And we will do so not in pursuit of abstract liberation, but in the service of something more grounded and more radical: the ability to choose a life, fully and freely, that you recognise as your own.

That is the promise of sovereignty. Not the absence of limits, but the presence of authorship. Not the capacity to escape, but the capacity to *design wisely*—with your eyes open, your values intact, and your agency fully engaged. Autonomy is the starting point. Freedom is the destination. And sovereignty is the bridge between them.

The Metrics That Matter:

Ask someone how wealthy they are, and they're likely to answer with a number—net worth, annual income, perhaps a monthly surplus. Some may rattle off portfolio values, property holdings, or business revenues. These figures are tidy, quantifiable, and familiar. But the most revealing metrics of wealth rarely show up on balance sheets. A spreadsheet cannot tell you whether someone sleeps soundly, whether their money aligns with their values, or whether they could walk away from a toxic client, city, or job if they needed to. *Conventional metrics measure capacity. But sovereign wealth demands we also measure coherence.* A modern, resilient life requires a dashboard that reflects *what matters most*—peace of mind, alignment, time sovereignty, and future-proofing.

Traditional financial metrics emerged from a system designed to standardise performance. Net worth, for example, mirrors corporate valuations; return on investment mimics shareholder logic. But individuals are not corporations, and wealth is not merely a game of accumulation. When life is viewed only through the lens of growth or efficiency, financial planning becomes divorced from well-being. The result? People who look successful on paper yet feel chronically behind, anxious, or trapped. They have assets, but no traction. Options, but no freedom. Wealth, but no wisdom. *Metrics shape behaviour. When the metrics are narrow, the behaviour is often misguided.*

To design a more sovereign financial life, we need a broader evaluative lens. Not to replace the old metrics, but to *contextualise them.* Money should be assessed not only by how much there is, but by what it enables—and at what cost. This calls for a new dashboard. Not one that exists only in software, but one that lives in reflection, ritual, and regular inquiry. Each element of this updated dashboard invites a deeper question—not about money in isolation, but about money in *context.*

Peace of Mind: The Missing Line Item

Financial plans often emphasise returns, but rarely ask: *Does this plan let you sleep at night?* Peace of mind is not the same as absence of risk.

It is the sense that your systems can absorb shocks, that your obligations are aligned with your capacity, and that you are not trading your future for your present—or vice versa. In behavioural finance, it's well-documented that perceived financial scarcity activates the amygdala, narrowing our ability to make long-term decisions. This isn't just emotional discomfort; it's neurological constraint. A sovereign wealth system must include buffers—not only emergency funds, but emotional reserves: clarity about boundaries, a plan for when things go wrong, and financial rituals that regularly recalibrate internal and external expectations.

Peace of mind, therefore, is both structural and psychological. Structurally, it may mean a simplified portfolio, predictable cash flow, or lifestyle downsizing to reduce pressure. Psychologically, it may involve redefining success, addressing inherited money scripts, or creating space for honest conversation in relationships. Without peace of mind, even an enviable net worth can become a source of anxiety rather than assurance.

Alignment: Is Your Money Expressing Your Values?

Alignment refers to the degree to which your financial behaviours reflect your personal values. This is not moralistic accounting; it's about integrity between stated intentions and actual actions. Many people say they value family, creativity, freedom, or service—yet spend the majority of their resources on things that serve neither. The misalignment is often not due to hypocrisy, but to inertia. Financial plans are inherited, templated, or copied. Rarely are they *authored.*

Assessing alignment requires asking: *Where does my money go—and why? What am I prioritising without realising it? What am I delaying or denying in the name of safety or status?* One client, a high-earning executive, found that her monthly spending reflected more on her past insecurities than her present convictions. Her charitable giving was transactional, her investments impersonal, her schedule dictated by commitments she no longer respected. Realigning her finances was not about drastic cuts, but about *intentional redirection.* Money, when aligned, becomes an amplifier of purpose rather than a substitute for it.

Time Sovereignty: Wealth's Most Overlooked Currency

Time is the currency most people trade first and reclaim last. Conventional wealth planning tends to treat time as a by-product—if you save enough or retire early, then you'll have time. But this framing delays sovereignty. It treats freedom as a reward for performance, not a *design principle* in the present. Time sovereignty asks: *How much of my time is truly mine? How flexibly can I deploy it? What parts of my schedule are dictated by others, and which are chosen?*

This does not mean eschewing work or responsibility. Rather, it's about constructing systems that reflect your rhythms and allow for agency. Can you pause when needed? Do you control the pacing of your days? Is there room for creative downtime, care work, or spontaneous connection? In one study of high-income earners, those with the least control over their time reported the lowest satisfaction levels—regardless of income. Sovereign wealth recognises that time, not money, is often the binding constraint—and designs accordingly.

Time sovereignty is also a litmus test for hidden dependencies. If your financial life collapses the moment you take a sabbatical, that's a design flaw—not a personal weakness. Sustainable wealth must be structured to support different modes of being: sprinting, resting, caregiving, and innovating. These are not luxuries; they are human necessities. Any wealth plan that ignores them is incomplete.

Future-Proofing: Designing Beyond the Forecast

Forecasting is the illusion that if we optimise well enough, we can predict the future. But in reality, most financial disruptions are not forecastable—they are emergent. Illness, recession, technological change, climate volatility, or care responsibilities can all reconfigure a household overnight. Sovereign financial planning doesn't pretend to predict the future. It prepares *for volatility itself.* Future-proofing is about adaptability. It asks: *What parts of my financial life are brittle? Which assumptions would break under pressure?*

This may mean diversifying not only assets, but income sources, skills, and even social capital. It could involve redundancies, scenario rehearsals, or opting out of lifestyle inflation to keep your overheads nimble. It also means designing systems with fail-safes—like contracts that allow for renegotiation, agreements that include buffers, and habits that respond to early signs of strain. Future-proofing is less about optimisation and more about *optionality*. In the language of antifragility, it's about building systems that *gain from disorder*—not merely survive it.

This approach also challenges the assumption that wealth is static. In reality, a sovereign wealth system is dynamic. It must evolve with life stages, identity shifts, and external realities. What worked at thirty may not work at fifty. A career-centric dashboard may need to give way to one centred on contribution or legacy. Future-proofing is not about freezing a plan; it's about *training adaptability* as a skill.

Tracking What Actually Matters

The most transformative part of adopting a new wealth dashboard is that it shifts the *definition* of progress. Instead of asking "How much did I earn or save this year?", the questions become:

– *Did my financial systems reduce or increase my stress?*
– *Did I make decisions consistent with my stated values?*
– *Did I feel agency over my time and attention?*
– *Am I better prepared—emotionally, structurally, relationally—for uncertainty?*

These are not soft metrics. They are *strategic indicators of durability*. They tell you whether your life design can hold under complexity, whether your systems are built around the person you are—or the image you're performing. They force a shift from performance to presence.

For those in positions of leadership—within families, teams, or communities—this dashboard also becomes a teaching tool. Children raised in financially literate households often inherit knowledge about budgets and investing. But how many inherit a model of *financial discernment*? How many learn to evaluate whether their spending reflects their values, or whether their work respects their time? A metrics dashboard rooted in peace of mind, alignment, time sovereignty, and future-proofing is not only a tool for planning—it is a framework for cultural change.

Wealth, as currently measured, is often a reflection of what the market rewards. But sovereign wealth is a reflection of what the individual values. It reclaims the power to define success on your own terms—and to track that success through the lenses that *actually matter*. This requires more than a new budgeting app. It requires a new philosophy of measurement—one that places life, not capital, at the centre.

The numbers still matter. But they are not enough. In a world shaped by speed, noise, and extraction, the metrics that matter most are the ones that remind us not just how to live, but *why*.

The Role of Financial Rituals:

The modern mind has been conditioned to associate money with planning, strategy, and performance—but rarely with *ritual*. That word, "ritual," is more commonly reserved for religious services, spiritual practices, or community ceremonies. Yet, when we examine the role of ritual across cultures, we find it consistently serves three vital functions: it instils order, reinforces meaning, and marks transition. *Applied to finance, ritual becomes the bridge between abstract planning and embodied behaviour.* Without ritual, financial systems become mechanical and detached. With it, they become lived, relational, and sustainable.

It is not a lack of financial literacy that undermines most personal wealth structures; it is the absence of rhythm. Financial wisdom is not built in a burst of inspiration, nor preserved by intermittent panic. Like physical health or relational trust, it is maintained through *regular engagement*. This is where ritual re-enters the frame—not as superstition, but as structure. A sovereign wealth life is not merely one that knows what to do, but one that has embedded *when* and *how* to do it into the fabric of everyday life. Financial rituals, when intentionally designed, provide this scaffolding.

What makes a ritual different from a routine? A routine is a sequence of actions. A ritual is a sequence of meaning. It contains reflection, choice, and symbolic significance. Paying your bills might be a routine. Reviewing them while asking, "Does this reflect my priorities?" transforms the act into a ritual. Ritual adds depth to habit and dignity to discipline. It allows financial behaviour to become a site of personal expression—not just compliance.

The Case for Daily Rituals

Daily rituals are the pulse-check of sovereignty. They do not require complexity; in fact, the simpler they are, the more likely they are to endure. A morning glance at a budgeting app is not merely about control—it is about *relationship*. Just as daily greetings maintain intimacy in close relationships, daily financial touchpoints build intimacy with one's system. These rituals should be short enough to do without friction, but meaningful enough to provoke awareness.

One such ritual may involve reviewing planned spending at the start of each day. Another might be asking, "What am I buying today, and does it honour my values?" These practices don't exist to suppress desire; they exist to surface intent. *Unconscious spending is rarely driven by greed—it is driven by absence of reflection.* When daily financial engagement becomes a moment of presence rather than a background task, the compounding effect over time is extraordinary.

Some individuals find benefit in closing the day with a brief "ledger meditation": noting where money was spent, whether any impulses hijacked intent, and how choices felt. This is not about perfection, but about pattern. These check-ins begin to surface the emotional architecture beneath money decisions—an essential precursor to mastery.

The Function of Monthly Rituals

If daily rituals are about attunement, monthly rituals are about *alignment.* They are an opportunity to pause, recalibrate, and make small course corrections before drift becomes dysfunction. Monthly financial rituals often involve reviewing bank statements, categorising expenses, and comparing actual spending to planned goals. But in sovereign finance, this process also includes *reflective inquiry.*

Questions might include:

– "Which expenses this month felt truly nourishing, and which felt extractive?"
– "Where did I spend reactively, and where did I invest proactively?"
– "Did I honour my time and energy with how I used my money?"

Monthly rituals are also a time for strategic decisions. Is it time to adjust a savings rate? Review an investment allocation? Revisit a debt-reduction strategy? These decisions, when clustered in ritual time, prevent them from becoming scattered, reactive, or emotionally charged. They are addressed not in crisis, but in cadence.

For couples or families, monthly rituals can take the form of "money meetings"—not to interrogate or blame, but to *understand.* When ritualised, these meetings become predictable, safe spaces to collaborate and dream. They allow shared systems to be regularly re-authored rather than silently resented. In this context, ritual becomes not just financial upkeep, but relational hygiene.

Annual Rituals as Financial Pilgrimage

The annual financial ritual is the highest-order reflection point—a personal audit, a strategic horizon scan, and a symbolic threshold all in one. It asks not only, "What did I earn or save?", but "What did I learn?" It reviews not just performance, but philosophy. The annual ritual should feel like a pilgrimage—set apart, intentional, even sacred in tone.

This is the time to revisit your *wealth thesis*, assess whether your current strategies are still fit for purpose, and name any emerging tensions between your financial life and your evolving identity. It is an opportunity to reconnect with long-range vision: retirement models, legacy planning, insurance adequacy, or estate architecture. But perhaps most importantly, it is a time to *celebrate.*

Modern finance, in its obsession with accumulation, often forgets to mark achievement. The annual ritual is where milestones—no matter how modest—are named and honoured. Paid off a credit card? Celebrate. Reached a savings milestone? Mark it. Managed a difficult year without financial collapse? Recognise the resilience. *Celebration is not indulgence—it is reinforcement.* It tells the nervous system: this work matters, and it is making a difference.

Some may choose to do their annual ritual alone, others with a partner, a financial coach, or even a peer group. What matters is the intentional space, the holistic lens, and the ritualistic framing. This is not a task to check off—it is a dialogue with one's future self.

Cultural and Psychological Dimensions

Rituals also hold cultural significance. In many traditions, financial ritual is embedded into seasonal festivals, tithing practices, or rites of passage. These functions helped communities maintain shared economic rhythms and ethical boundaries. In secular modernity, those communal anchors have eroded. What's left is a vacuum often filled by consumption-driven behaviour disguised as autonomy. Reviving ritual allows us to reclaim financial practices as *cultural acts*—steeped in meaning, not marketing.

Psychologically, rituals anchor identity. They stabilise behaviour under stress and provide continuity through change. After job loss, illness, or transition, financial rituals offer familiarity and re-orientation. Research in behavioural science confirms that rituals reduce anxiety and enhance performance—even when the rituals themselves are arbitrary. In finance, they are far from arbitrary. They are containers for clarity.

From Transaction to Transformation

At the heart of this subchapter is a quiet but powerful provocation: what if your financial life could feel *sacred?* Not in a religious sense, but in the sense that it reflects care, consistency, and consciousness. What if every payment, every review, every budget meeting was not just a transaction, but a *micro-act of design?* This is the promise of ritual. It transforms what is often tedious or avoided into something grounding, rhythmic, and even meaningful.

Financial rituals are not a productivity hack. They are the embodiment of sovereignty. When designed with intent, they create a holding environment for both discipline and freedom. They reduce the likelihood of drift, increase the visibility of misalignment, and build the muscle of continuity. And in a world that glorifies extremes—radical minimalism on one end, indulgent consumerism on the other—ritual offers something far more enduring: *a life in tune.*

As we move towards the end of this book's architecture, we see that the power of wealth is not in scale, but in sovereignty. Ritual is how sovereignty becomes habit. It is the practice of remembering what matters—and responding accordingly. Daily. Monthly. Annually. Quietly. Consistently. And always, with care.

Teaching the Ledger:

One of the least discussed yet most consequential aspects of financial sovereignty is its transmissibility. Financial literacy, when hoarded, stagnates. When shared, it multiplies. It is not enough to master the ledger for oneself; wisdom becomes enduring only when it is passed on—artfully, contextually, and relationally. The idea that financial knowledge should remain siloed within the technically capable or economically advantaged is not only inequitable, it is strategically short-sighted. *The strength of any financial system is not measured by the sophistication of its architecture, but by its ability to endure beyond the original designer.*

Teaching the ledger is not a technical tutorial. It is not a matter of transferring Excel formulas or app recommendations. It is an invitation into worldview. It is about handing over a lens through which to see money—not merely as currency, but as a mirror of values, time, trade-offs, and trust. Those who grasp this are not just more competent with spreadsheets; they are more discerning with their lives. And those who teach it well don't just create better investors or savers—they cultivate *sovereign citizens* who can act with clarity in the face of complexity.

The temptation is to think of financial education as a one-time event—a workshop, a conversation, a signed cheque accompanied by advice. In truth, it is recursive, situational, and relational. It unfolds over years. Sometimes it is delivered directly, through explicit instruction. Other times it is absorbed peripherally, through observed behaviour. Either way, the ledger is always being taught. The only question is whether it is being taught with intention.

When working with children, the stakes are not in explaining compound interest by age nine, but in embedding *agency*. Children who understand that money is earned, that choices have trade-offs, that budgets reflect values—not restrictions—enter adulthood with a different orientation. They are less prone to seeing wealth as random or morally binary. They are more inclined to see it as a system to be stewarded, not feared. But teaching children well requires *developmental attunement*. The conversation about money with a seven-year-old is different from the one with a teenager. Younger children benefit from transparency about cause and effect—"We're saving for this, so we're choosing not to spend on that." Older children benefit from insight into strategy and uncertainty—"This investment carries risk, and here's how we evaluate that." The goal is not omniscience. It is literacy through exposure, inclusion, and dialogue.

Too often, money is the last topic families discuss—if it is discussed at all. Parents are willing to talk about sex, ethics, even politics before they will talk about net worth or credit card debt. This silence breeds shame. It also breeds confusion. Children sense the tension, absorb the avoidance, and inherit distorted scripts. *To teach the ledger is to unlearn the secrecy.* It is to make money speakable. Not through performative transparency or burdening them with adult stress, but by normalising financial discussion as a part of life—not apart from it.

The same holds true with partners. Couples often operate under the illusion that shared accounts equal shared understanding. But financial clarity in relationships requires *ritualised communication.* This means recurring, agenda-based conversations that go beyond logistics. "What are our goals?" "What do we value most right now?" "Are our systems matching our philosophy?" These questions help prevent asymmetries of knowledge or responsibility from calcifying into resentment. In many relationships, one person assumes the "money role"—not always by expertise, but by default. While division of labour is practical, *division of awareness is dangerous.* If one partner is making all the financial decisions, the other is not being spared stress—they are being disempowered. Teaching the ledger in this context is about equalising understanding, not equalising tasks.

It is also worth examining how financial education happens within communities—friendships, neighbourhoods, workplaces, cultural or religious circles. Here, the stakes are less about inheritance and more about *replication.* When someone models a grounded, ethical, sovereign financial life, others around them begin to recalibrate. This is the ripple effect. It rarely happens through preaching. It happens through shared decision-making, honest disclosures, and mutual accountability. A friend casually sharing how they built an emergency fund is more influential than a viral budgeting tip. A colleague being transparent about salary negotiation can shift a peer's trajectory for life.

Community-based teaching of the ledger becomes especially potent when it challenges inherited narratives. For example, in cultures where talking about money is taboo—or where prosperity is viewed either as suspect or aspirational—shared financial dialogue can recalibrate norms. Conversations that deconstruct inherited myths ("You must own property to be successful" or "We don't talk about money in this family") allow new frameworks to emerge. They move communities from inherited scripts to chosen strategies. This is not just cultural work—it is sovereignty work.

There is also a structural implication. Schools and universities, for all their academic breadth, still treat personal finance as optional knowledge. This is intellectually incoherent. You can graduate with honours in economics and remain illiterate in how to manage a credit score. This disconnect persists not because of oversight, but because of institutional inertia. Those who have learned to teach the ledger—whether parents, mentors, or self-taught practitioners—play a corrective role. They bridge the gap between theory and life. They demystify systems that are often designed to be exclusionary. They decentralise financial wisdom.

But to teach well, we must also examine our motivations. Are we teaching the ledger to control outcomes—to ensure our children never make mistakes, our partners follow our frameworks, our communities mirror our philosophies? Or are we teaching it to cultivate capacity—to allow others to think critically, make aligned decisions, and adapt to complexity? The difference is profound. The former is instruction. The latter is *transmission.* Financial wisdom transmitted well is always accompanied by humility. It includes stories of mistakes, reflections on failure, and openness to evolution. It creates an environment in which others can form their own financial identity—not replicate yours.

Finally, we must address the ethical dimension. Those who understand the ledger hold an advantage in a system that often penalises ignorance. To hoard that knowledge is to participate in inequity. To share it is not charity—it is justice. Financial knowledge, when taught well, becomes an act of social equity. It empowers individuals to navigate predatory systems, negotiate with confidence, plan with clarity, and build with intention. It is the most scalable form of empowerment available to us.

Teaching the ledger, then, is not a task to be checked off. It is a posture—a commitment to inclusion, transparency, and co-creation. It is the acknowledgement that wealth is not measured only by what is held, but by what is *shared.* Every conversation, every example, every invitation to collaborate becomes part of this pedagogy. And over time, as more people learn to teach, the ripple becomes a current. The ledger becomes not just a private tool, but a communal inheritance. Not just a record of what has been spent, but a signal of what has been stewarded. And through that, wealth ceases to be silent. It becomes wisdom in motion.

A Life Designed to Endure:

Wealth, in its most resilient form, is rarely visible. The balance in a savings account or the yield from a diversified portfolio may offer a sense of security, but neither tells us whether a person is truly well-fortified against uncertainty, nor whether their wealth is designed to outlive market cycles, emotional shocks, or generational transitions. *Endurance—true financial durability—does not begin in the bank. It begins in the behaviours, beliefs, and systems we embed into daily life, often long before the first pound is earned or invested.*

The fundamental error of many wealth strategies is that they are built for growth, not for continuity. Growth is appealing—linear, measurable, optimistic. But it is not necessarily sustainable. Endurance requires architecture, not merely acceleration. It requires that we build our financial lives with an eye toward what will still matter when growth slows, when the markets fluctuate, or when life's complexity interrupts our plans.

Resilient wealth begins with *behavioural design.* At first glance, this might seem like a matter of habits—spending less than you earn, automating savings, reviewing your investments. But those are merely tactics. Behavioural design, at its core, is about removing friction between intention and execution. It means structuring one's environment—both physical and psychological—in a way that supports wise choices when cognitive bandwidth is low or emotions are high. A person who reviews their financial dashboard every Friday morning is not just being diligent. They are creating ritualised touchpoints that anchor decision-making in clarity rather than reactivity. A household that has agreed in advance how to handle unexpected windfalls or downturns is not merely organised—they are inoculated against future volatility.

In contrast, many individuals—even high earners—rely on hope, mood, or willpower to guide financial decisions. They store knowledge but not structure. They understand risk conceptually but haven't designed mechanisms for absorbing it practically. The result is a system that performs well under ideal conditions but collapses under duress. It's not lack of intelligence—it's absence of design. *Enduring wealth is less about what you know and more about what you've pre-engineered to survive your moments of weakness.*

The second pillar is *beliefs*. Not merely the slogans we say aloud—"money doesn't buy happiness," or "it's important to save"—but the deeply embedded assumptions that drive unconscious behaviour. Do we believe wealth is finite or expandable? Do we associate money with control, with freedom, with status, with safety? Do we see generosity as abundance or depletion? These beliefs are often absorbed long before adulthood and are rarely examined directly. But they influence everything—from the partners we choose to the risks we take, from the assets we favour to the debts we tolerate. If beliefs remain unexamined, no strategy will feel satisfying for long. We will self-sabotage progress in order to confirm the worldview we have not yet confronted.

Those who cultivate enduring wealth therefore engage in *belief audits*. They ask uncomfortable questions: "What financial behaviours do I justify that contradict my values?" "Whose definitions of success am I operating under?" "What am I afraid of financially, and where did that fear come from?" These are not idle reflections. They are diagnostics for locating misalignment. And when beliefs and actions are congruent, wealth becomes more stable—not because the numbers have changed, but because the internal conflict has quieted.

The third pillar, often ignored in popular finance, is *systems*. While behaviours shape daily outcomes and beliefs shape motivation, systems shape continuity. A financial system includes everything from your spending architecture to your insurance cover, estate plans, investment frameworks, communication protocols with partners, tax strategies, and beyond. But a well-designed system is not merely complex. In fact, *the most enduring systems are often elegantly simple*. Simplicity here is not about lack of sophistication; it's about clarity of function and ease of operation. A system that can be understood and operated under stress—by you or by someone stepping in on your behalf—is exponentially more valuable than a labyrinthine strategy only decipherable by its creator.

This becomes especially relevant in the face of life transitions: illness, incapacity, relocation, or death. Who can step in and execute your systems if you're not available? Are your records coherent, your intentions documented, your mechanisms accessible? Many well-meaning individuals spend years refining their strategy without ever ensuring it can be transferred, scaled, or maintained by others. *Wealth that cannot be translated cannot endure.*

Designing for endurance also means acknowledging the role of entropy. Systems degrade. Beliefs drift. Behaviours erode under pressure. So the work is not to find the perfect system, but to design one that can adapt, self-correct, and evolve with minimal disruption. This is where rituals re-enter the conversation—not as sentiment, but as strategic scaffolding. Monthly reviews, annual recalibrations, estate planning updates, communication cadences—these rituals are not administrative chores. They are how we maintain coherence between life and ledger.

Importantly, a life designed to endure also resists the tyranny of *comparison.* The cultural script around wealth is steeped in benchmarking—against neighbours, colleagues, Instagram reels, and celebrity profiles. But true financial endurance is immune to fashion. It is not dictated by external signals. It is driven by fit: *Does your system serve your priorities, your constraints, your aspirations?* Does it hold up not just under scrutiny, but under stress?

There is also a moral and intergenerational dimension. The choices we make today—what we insure, what we save, what we disclose, what we teach—either burden or liberate those who come after us. A will left unsigned, a financial plan never shared, a system held only in one partner's head—these are not oversights. They are liabilities in waiting. *To design for endurance is to act as a future ancestor.* It is to take seriously the question: "What am I leaving behind—financially, structurally, philosophically—that will outlast me?"

And this, finally, is what distinguishes enduring wealth from performative prosperity. One can accumulate assets while remaining financially fragile. One can appear affluent while being entirely unprotected. Enduring wealth is not flashy. It is not loud. It does not seek validation. It is characterised by its calmness—by its ability to continue functioning when the world does not. Its power lies not in what it proves, but in what it preserves.

In a world increasingly obsessed with optimisation, growth hacks, and momentary wins, the decision to build for endurance is quietly radical. It means resisting the pressure to constantly recalibrate toward novelty. It means saying no to complexity that outpaces capacity. It means placing faith not in financial products, but in thoughtful architecture, enduring values, and behavioural integrity.

Ultimately, the most durable form of wealth is what persists when circumstances change. It is what remains when inheritance is distributed, when income fluctuates, when markets correct, when bodies age, when loved ones transition. *It is the architecture of sovereignty, not the accumulation of surplus.* And it is available not only to the privileged, but to the deliberate. Not only to those who inherit assets, but to those who design wisely with whatever resources they have.

The question, then, is not just "What are you building?" but "Will it last?" And more pointedly: "Will it matter when you're gone?" Designing a life that endures is not about resisting change. It is about being prepared for it—systemically, psychologically, relationally. It is about embedding continuity into the fabric of how you live. And in doing so, you ensure that your wealth is not just counted. It is carried forward.

About the Author

Luca Moreau is an independent wealth strategist, systems thinker, and advocate for designing financial lives with intention and meaning. With a background in behavioural finance and a deep curiosity for global cultural models of wealth, Luca bridges the pragmatic and the philosophical. His work draws from Eastern and Western traditions, personal financial psychology, and the enduring wisdom of stewardship. Known for his holistic and human-centred approach, Luca has helped professionals, creatives, and entrepreneurs move beyond short-term goals to craft resilient wealth systems that reflect who they are—and who they wish to become. The Unshakable Ledger is his manifesto for those seeking not just money, but sovereignty.